FROM HEBREWS TO REVELATION

A Theological Introduction

Lewis R. Donelson

Westminster John Knox Press
Louisville, Kentucky

Copyright © 2001 Lewis R. Donelson

Book design by Sharon Adams
Cover design by Night & Day Design

First edition
Published by Westminster John Knox Press
Louisville, Kentucky

This book is printed on acid-free paper that meets the American National Standards Institute Z39.48 standard.♾

PRINTED IN THE UNITED STATES OF AMERICA

01 02 03 04 05 06 07 08 09 10 — 10 9 8 7 6 5 4 3 2 1

Library of Congress Cataloging-in-Publication Data
Donelson, Lewis R., 1949–
  From Hebrews to Revelation : a theological introduction / Lewis R. Donelson.— 1st ed.
    p. cm.
  Includes bibliographical references (p.) and index.
  ISBN 0-664-22236-6 (alk. paper)
  1. Bible. N.T. Hebrews—Theology. 2. Bible. N.T. Catholic Epistles—Theology.
3. Bible. N.T. Revelation—Theology. 4. Bible. N.T. Hebrews—Criticism, interpretation,
etc. 5. Bible. N.T. Catholic Epistles—Criticism, interpretation, etc. 6. Bible. N.T.
Revelation—Criticism, interpretation, etc. I. Title.
BS2775.5 .D66 2001
227′.061—dc21
                                                                              00-34986

Contents

Preface

The introductory character of this volume obscures somewhat the deep indebtedness of the volume to previous scholarship. The six essays that follow avoid both footnotes and internal references in the text to other scholars. Even the bibliographies do not attempt to give a full accounting of the various influences on the arguments of this volume. Instead, the bibliographies are designed to introduce readers to standard works and good starting points for further reading. Nevertheless, anyone aware of the scholarship on these nine New Testament books will recognize how much these essays depend on the work of other people. This volume relies, from beginning to end, on the work and ideas of other scholars. Thus, even though I do not explain the genealogy of the arguments in the essays, I want to assure the readers that, to some extent at least, no argument in this volume is entirely my own.

Many thanks go to Carey C. Newman at Westminster John Knox Press. The original idea for this volume was his, as was the decision, for good or ill, to ask me to write it. He has shepherded me through the writing process with generous encouragement and lots of specific advice on how to improve the work. Throughout the entire process it has been an enormous pleasure to work with him. I hope the final results match his initial vision at least a little bit.

I would also like to thank the faculty and administration of Austin Presbyterian Theological Seminary for supporting me on the sabbatical during which this volume was written. Thanks go to Ernie Gardner, Shannon Crawford, and Robbie Rhodes for their excellent proofreading. Finally, as most writers of books must admit, it is our families who deserve the most credit. Thus, above all, I want to thank my wife, Lin, and my children, James and Sarah, for providing me with both the necessary time and the requisite humility for the writing of this volume.

Introduction

Part of the reason we read, perhaps even the major reason we read, is to learn something useful. This volume is written under the conviction that the books of the New Testament that run from Hebrews to Revelation, the last nine books of the Bible, have much to say that is useful to the modern reader. It is certainly true that these books have never attracted the loyal following which Paul and the Gospels have enjoyed. They have suffered from a certain amount of neglect. It is hoped that the readings of these books provided here will demonstrate that these texts deserve careful and loyal reading. These last nine, somewhat neglected, books of the New Testament are actually wonderful and powerful texts.

If we call this volume a "theological introduction," it is to signal that a certain kind of reading of these texts is offered here. There is perhaps no more persistent controversy in the church and the academy than the question of how to read the Bible properly. And no reading of a biblical text can avoid taking a stance on the question of how to read. Thus, the "theological introduction" offered here implies a series of decisions on how to read these texts.

In some ways it is nearly impossible to read any of these nine texts without thinking about theology. They are theological texts. The subject matter is theology, or at least "theology" as broadly conceived. All of these texts deal in a general way with God, Jesus, faith, ethics, and other traditional issues of theology. Thus, to read these texts without thinking about theology requires a studied avoidance of some kind. When the subject matter of a text is theology, then readings of the text will naturally become theological readings. Thus, an introduction to texts that are theological will almost inevitably become a "theological introduction."

The readings offered here are, in some ways, the most natural and normal readings one can make. We are pursuing the explicit subject matter of the texts. We are trying to understand for ourselves what these texts are saying about their subjects. When Hebrews talks about sacrifice, we shall try to understand what is really being said in the text about sacrifice. When 1 John talks about love, we want to understand what 1 John really says about love. These texts pursue issues and present proposals that are explicitly theological. Since

1

we want the texts to direct our readings, we shall follow them into their theological arguments.

However, there are problems with such a relaxed approach to the act of reading. If we let ourselves simply drift to the subject matter of the text as it seems appropriate, we tend to introduce our own voices too soon. Our own thoughts about the subject matter of the text can easily overwhelm the thinking of the text on this subject. There is something dangerous about reading in a way that simply feels natural. If it feels natural, there may be too much of the reader in the reading.

It is the danger of drowning out the voice of the text with our own voices that drives much of our attraction to the historical readings of texts. There is an ethic that should come into play in every act of reading. We the readers are not the only persons who have a claim on or a right to the text we are reading. The original author, for instance, still has a claim on the text. When we read, we become obligated to the intentions of the author who wrote the text. The historical-critical method is largely an attempt to meet this obligation to the author.

Nevertheless, there is a stunning diversity of proposals both for how much force this obligation to the original author should have and for what methods of reading might best meet this obligation. Although we cannot chase down the full diversity of such proposals in a volume like this, we can and must make certain decisions about these proposals. While the readings that follow focus upon the ideas we find in the text, the readings also assume the original embeddedness of these ideas in a certain moment in history. These ideas did not emerge today; they emerged in a time distant and somewhat alien to us. In order to hear them properly, we must attempt to hear them in their original setting. We shall proceed throughout under the assumption that one of the tasks of a "theological" reading is to understand the theological ideas of the text in their original setting.

Part of the ethics of reading includes a focus upon the moment of origin of the text. This focus upon the "archaeology" of the text is the primary task of an "historical introduction." An historical reading of a text must try to reconstruct the origin of the text. It must attempt to identify the author, the recipients, the setting, and the purpose of the text. There are seemingly endless questions one can ask about the origins of a text. Guiding these questions are two obligations that seem to me to be formidable and to some extent unavoidable. Both of these obligations have to do with the claims that certain persons other than us have on the text.

First, as mentioned above, the intentions of the original authors when they wrote these texts cannot simply be ignored or abused in our reading. It does not seem adequate to read a text and intentionally ignore what the original author wanted the text to say. Second, the original readers of the text have an ongoing claim on the text. How the text was originally heard by its intended readers must influence how we choose to read today. Scholars have devised numerous reading methods out of respect for these claims.

Although to some extent these methods resist any neat classification, we can divide them into two general types for the purposes of this volume. First, we try to collect and analyze the historical facts. All the classic questions of "who," "what," "when," and "why" emerge at this point. The historical facts also include the history of ideas and movements. We might ask where ideas came from and how the ideas in our text connect to other ideas of the same moment in history. Furthermore, in our attempt to understand this setting, we impose various forms of social analysis on the setting. Sociological, economic, ideological, and political readings are useful at this point. In all of this we try as best we can to recreate and to understand the historical framework and forces of the text. The text becomes a window to a complex history and reality behind the text. By recreating the reality behind the text we believe we can better understand the text itself. The readings in this volume do not perform this historical task; instead, these readings assume and build upon the historical readings of other scholars. We shall therefore focus on the ideas in the text and use the historical work of other scholars to help us read these ideas. We shall also show, on occasion, how different decisions about historical context change the way we perceive the theology of the text. But in all of this it will be our pursuit of the ideas in the text that will determine how and when we employ historical data.

Second, the text is read not simply as a piece of history but as a literary object. Texts have certain properties as texts that determine how they can and should be read. Enormous attention has been devoted to the rhetoric of biblical texts. Unless we understand the literary structure and style of a document it is nearly impossible to read it well. Again, in the readings in this volume we shall include the insights of these literary readings without first engaging in all the debates and possibilities. Decisions about the genre of the text, the literary structure of the text, the kind of images employed, and other rhetorical concepts will direct our readings. We shall also show from time to time how different decisions about literary structure can transform our understanding of the theology of the text. However, as with the traditional historical categories, literary insights will be employed not for their own sake but in order to assist our theological readings.

For all the strengths—and even the necessity—of these readings, they have attracted much criticism. The criticisms of the historical methods of reading a text are formidable and numerous. For our purposes, two criticisms seem most relevant. First, many people argue that the original intentions of an author cannot and perhaps should not govern our readings. We can never know what the author was thinking at the moment of inscription. All we have are the words of the text. In the name of trying to articulate what the author wanted to say, we end up writing another text to replace the real text. The intentions of an author cannot govern our readings, because the intentions of the author are absent from the text. In fact, the intentions of the author should never govern a text. Once a text is written it does not belong to the author anymore; it belongs to history, to readers, to the world of texts, but not to the author.

Second, many people point out that a recreation of the historical context of a text also cannot and perhaps should not govern our readings. Once again, we can never know for certain what really was the proper historical setting. All our reconstructions will involve some guesswork. Whatever historical context we impose on a text will always have a certain arbitrary feel to it. Furthermore, texts do not belong to their historical moments in such an absolute way. They do emerge in history, but part of the power and purpose of texts is to escape their historical moment. Texts, in their very origin, want to reach beyond their moment of inscription to new moments. Therefore, we should not, contrary to their natural force, confine them to any given moment.

The criticisms of literary readings of texts are also numerous and formidable. There are so many kinds of literary readings and so many concomitant criticisms that we cannot begin to address all the issues here. Again for the purposes of the readings that follow, two criticisms seem most relevant. The first mirrors the criticisms above. All decisions about literary structure are insecure. It is impossible, critics point out, to know for certain what the proper rhetorical forces in a text might be. While it is true that all texts must have rhetorical structures or they would not be texts, all such structures are to some extent frameworks imposed on a text from outside. Furthermore, while all texts follow rhetorical norms, every text at the same time escapes those rhetorical norms.

Second, literary critics often have a tendency to treat a text as referring only to itself. They read the text as a self-contained world. This tendency is especially awkward for someone who is reading the text for the ideas in the text. The theological readings in this volume assume that the ideas we encounter in these texts do not belong solely to the syntax of these texts. We assume that we can take these ideas and work with them outside that original syntax.

The various issues raised in all these debates have a considerable impact on the readings that follow. The view taken here is that these criticisms are formidable and irrefutable, but that the need and justification for historical and literary judgments still stand. For instance, it is true that we can never know precisely what the author was thinking at the moment of inscription. We can never know what anyone is really thinking. But this does not mean that we cannot know anything at all. And it certainly does not mean that this final ignorance gives us permission to ignore the claim of the original author.

The view of texts in what follows is that the place of a text is occupied by many faces and forces. The original author, the first readers, subsequent readers, and the person reading right now all have proper place in a text. When we read, we therefore can and should give attention to our own instincts as readers, to our sense of the author's intentions, and to the voices of other readers of this same text. The place of the text is also occupied by many historical forces, some of which belong to the original moment and some of which do not. It is the nature of texts to hunt for contexts not original to it. We should not forbid this.

One way of thinking about the multiple forces that belong to a text (a way already suggested) is a threefold division: the world behind the text, the world of the text, and the world before the text. The world behind the text is composed of the historical faces and forces that gave origin to the text. The world of the text is the text itself, the brute fact of a sequence of a certain set of words, and the capacity of these words to interact with one another. There is a world that is somehow internal to the text. The world before the text is the world the text projects upon a real reader. This world emerges from an unprogrammed interaction between the words of the text and the act of reading. This threefold distinction has proven to be helpful, even though I find it a bit too neat. Along with many others, I would argue that these three worlds are not only always proper to a text but that they must overlap. There cannot be any one of these worlds without the presence of the others. In fact, what makes a text work is how it pulls in and belongs to all these forces and faces at the same time.

In the readings that follow, not only shall we give place to all three worlds and voice to all these various faces, we shall keep the lines between these worlds rather fuzzy. My conviction is that texts have an instability about them that is necessary to their function as texts. Words, in order to work as words, drift in many directions. Words escape any single control over them. The original author cannot control the meaning of the text. The original readers cannot. No historical context can fully limit what a text can say. Modern readers cannot master a text. For instance, I cannot control these texts by naming or comprehending the ideas to which they might point. A text, because it is a text, drifts from any final control over it.

The power of texts to drift, especially the power of one text to drift into another, is sometimes known as "intertextuality." Without giving a full description or justification here, it is the conviction of many readers that texts only speak because they belong to other texts. Every text is in some sense a citation of an earlier text. And every text is in some sense a potential citation in subsequent texts. The interconnectedness of texts, of words, of thoughts, of readings, of historical moments, means that a text can only be a text as it drifts into other texts, to other moments, to other readers. The theological readings offered here assume this intertextuality of texts.

When we call this volume a theological introduction, we do not mean that we are forcing these texts to answer certain theological questions or that we are forcing the texts into predetermined categories. In the following readings we do not decide ahead of time what theology is. We do not ask what each text says about a certain set of classical theological topics: God, Christ, salvation, ethics, redemption, and so on. Instead, we wait for the text to suggest its own topics as we read it. This attempt to let the text generate its own theological categories and questions is not, of course, a pure attempt. My necessary role as reader means that some impositions will occur. However, I hope this attempt to let the text speak is not totally impure either.

In these readings we try as best we can to let the text speak in its own terms. We try to hear it in its proper historical and literary voice. After—or even as— we hear the text, we try to engage with the ideas of the text. We try to understand "what" the text is talking about. To do this requires a certain amount of play. We cannot read or understand by following a scientific program. We have to turn ourselves loose as readers. We have to pursue the drift of the text. There is a certain playfulness in all of this. We cannot program this ahead of time. The act of reading is always a step into the unknown and unforeseen.

We hope that this playfulness is also serious. As we engage, or play with, the ideas of these texts, we want to meet our many obligations. We want to be honest to the original authors, to recall faithfully the faces of the first readers, to embed the text in its original moment, and to give the text space to move to other moments. We want to be faithful to the many readers throughout the centuries who have also read these texts. We want to meet our obligations to ourselves and to the readers who are reading these texts with us today.

One of the results of trying to meet these diverse obligations is that the readings in this volume seek to address the core theological issues of each text. We hope that every reading will identify and discuss both the explicit theological topics of each text and the issues that have surrounded these texts in subsequent Christian theology. These readings have an introductory character in the sense that we want to cover all the basic theological issues of each text.

At the same time, there is an attempt to push the theological discussion of the texts in certain directions. There are better and worse ways to think about the theology of these texts. Thus we try, by way of these readings, to improve our thinking about these texts.

Finally, we hope that these readings will reveal that these somewhat neglected last nine books of the Bible are wonderful and powerful texts.

1

Hebrews

At the heart of Hebrews lies a fascinating and obscure naming of Jesus as the "great high priest." Jesus is a great high priest, the perfect and final priest, a priest according to the order of Melchizedek. In fact, the more familiar images of Jesus as "Son," or even as "pioneer" and "perfecter" of faith, ultimately interact with and depend on this notion of Jesus as "high priest." As we shall see, the author of Hebrews constructs an inviting and illuminating theology around this image. Furthermore, this notion of Jesus as high priest, and the implications drawn from it, has led many readers to declare that the author of Hebrews is one of the great theologians of the New Testament, second in creativity only to Paul.

For the modern reader notions of priesthood and sacrifice are unfamiliar, but Christians of the first century spent their lives in the shadows of temples and in the company of priests. Everyone, whether Jewish or Roman, knew the sights, sounds, smells, and perhaps even the theologies of temples. Few of us—probably none of us—have ever killed an animal in a holy place to expiate sins. Not many of us know the Old Testament texts about priests and sacrifices that feed the priest imagery in Hebrews. We typically skip over such seemingly irrelevant images. Hebrews, instead, lingers on the details of Old Testament narratives and regulations about priests and sacrifices. It constructs its theology out of those details.

Modern readers of Hebrews thus discover a curious conflict in the act of reading. On the one hand, we encounter wonderful, challenging, illuminating, and inviting passages. We find ourselves *drawn* to the image of Jesus as pioneer, to the divine promise of rest, and to the examples of faith. We also find ourselves challenged and comforted by the various imperatives that frequent the text. On the other hand, we feel a certain *alienation*, not only from Hebrews' categories of priesthood, but also from those of perfection, no second repentance, and judgment. We are in various ways both included and excluded by the text. We find ourselves at one moment quite at home in this text and in the next moment in a seemingly strange place.

It is this sense of estrangement from ancient texts which provides much of the justification for historical readings of the Bible. We cannot, it is argued, by an act of will or by the power of good intentions overcome our estrangement. These texts emerged in a world quite different from ours. Therefore, if we want to read them, we have work to do: we must do historical research and learn the world of the ancient text; we must, as best we can, hear it with first-century ears.

Our estrangement raises the question of the ethics of reading. As we noted in the introduction, part of the task of reading is to try to understand the text as the author intended it to be understood. The text does not belong just to us; the author maintains a claim upon it and upon us who read it. When we read a text we fall under some sort of obligation to the author. This sense of obligation provides much of the force in historical readings of the Bible. Not only do we want to overcome our estrangement from these ancient texts for our own sake, in order to feel more at home in the text and even to learn something from the text; we also want to overcome this estrangement out of moral obligation to the author, out of our personal respect for the intentions of the author. Thus, the first thing that strikes most readers of Hebrews is that we have work to do, historical work, if we want to read it well.

The journey into the text of Hebrews will turn into a journey into life itself. As we shall see, Hebrews envisions the Christian life as a journey toward perfection, toward God's promises and God's rest. In some ways the theology of Hebrews emerges from a change in the structure of time that is created by Jesus. The coming of Christ as Son, high priest, pioneer, and perfecter opens up to his followers promises that God made long ago. The Son's arrival creates a crisis in God's relationship to Israel. Suddenly the covenant with Israel is "old" (Heb. 8:9, 13; 9:1). There is a "new" covenant (Heb. 8:8, 13; 9:15). Much of the theology of Hebrews explores the relationship between this old covenant and the new one. The new both depends on and supersedes the old.

The arrival of Jesus creates a temporal crisis not only between the old and the new but also between the present and the future. Even if Christians have, through Christ, gained access to God's rest, they do not have that rest now. Even if Christians, through Christ, can become perfect, they do not enjoy perfection now. Today is not the time of rest; today is the time of journey, of growth, and especially of hope. The theology of Hebrews is built upon hope in these still-future promises. This hope must be lived out in the midst of the sufferings and terrors of life.

Even though Hebrews uses many images and ideas that are somewhat alien to modern ears, in other ways Hebrews is pursuing the most fundamental and persistent of all Christian questions. At the heart of most Christian theology, and certainly at the heart of Hebrews, is the notion that the coming of Christ makes things new. Now that Christ is here, many things must be different. But it is not entirely clear what has changed and what remains the same. The coming of Christ undoubtedly changes what is possible for human life. A new reality is available to us. In most theology, and assuredly in Hebrews, the forces of the cosmos have been realigned. For instance, the role that angels and temples should—and do—play in our lives is completely transformed. Even the role God plays in our lives is recast. Much of Hebrews is a wonderful exploration of what is new.

However, Hebrews is also a wonderful exploration of what remains the same. The new reality that arrives with Jesus Christ is not wholly new. This new time belongs to the past. In fact, the past in some ways gives birth to the new. Part of the genius of Hebrews is how it weaves together the old and the new. And as we have noted, Hebrews will also weave this new present together with a new future.

In some ways, then, according to Hebrews, Christ changes everything. Christ changes the past, the present, and the future. Furthermore, Christ changes how the past, present, and future do and do not belong to one another. Hebrews writes a new cosmic narrative.

Hebrews takes its readers into some of the most difficult places in all of theology. In order to understand this new Christian reality, we must wrestle with the inveterate problems of human sin, blood, the efficacy of sacrifices, the holiness of God, the persistence of suffering, the equal persistence of hope in the midst of suffering, the paradoxical nature of faith, and even the possibility of human perfection. Coloring every moment of this theological journey is a prevailing confidence that everything will finally work out. Our Christian belief that God in Christ is and will be victorious is declared in Hebrews to be fundamentally true.

However, in order to understand this new reality, Hebrews asserts that we must do hard theological work. We must go on a demanding theological journey. In the imagery of Hebrews 5:11–14, the writer declares that it is time to move from milk to solid food. "Let us go on toward perfection, leaving behind the basic teaching about Christ" (6:1a). Hebrews is an invitation to readers to go on a difficult and rewarding theological journey.

Outline of Hebrews

1:1–4   Core confession
1:5–10:18   The superiority of Jesus
   1:5–4:13   Jesus' superiority to angels and Moses
      1:5–14   Jesus as Son is superior to angels
      2:1–4   Exhortation to pay attention
      2:5–18   Jesus as pioneer in suffering
      3:1–6   Jesus as Son is superior to Moses
      3:7–19   Exhortation to not harden hearts
      4:1–13   The promise of rest
   4:14–10:18   Jesus' superiority as high priest
      4:14–5:10   Jesus the great High Priest
      5:11–6:20   Exhortation not to fall away but to go on toward perfection

Jesus the High Priest

At the heart of Hebrews resides a notion of Jesus as the great high priest. As the outline indicates, the image of high priest shapes most of 4:14–10:18. In some ways, this concept is the central theological idea in Hebrews in the sense that Hebrews devotes more attention to it than to any other single theological image. An exploration of Jesus as high priest is, therefore, a natural place to begin our theological account of Hebrews.

Our reading of Jesus as high priest will shape our reading of the rest of Hebrews. It does not seem to be the case that the concept of high priest functions as the real theological center in Hebrews. The image of high priest does not seem to organize or produce the other theological images of the text. Hebrews contains too many potent theological forces to have a controlling theological center. Nevertheless, our reading of Hebrews suggests that the forces put in place by this image of Jesus as high priest transform all the other theological images in the text. The high priesthood of Jesus is the best entry into the wonderfully diverse theological images in this book.

Perhaps the most natural way in antiquity to think about how the human world connects to the divine is through temples, priests, and sacrifices. Temples are a potent symbol of both the distance and the intimacy between humans and God (or the gods). On the one hand, gods and humans are of a wholly different order; they do not belong together. Gods are immortal, powerful, remote, holy, and—in the case of the God of Israel—perfectly righteous and just; humans are none of these things. On the other hand, gods and humans constantly enter into relationship with one another. In fact, every single temple in the ancient world is a monument (literally) to some kind of agreement between humans and a god. Although the kinds of agreements associated with these temples were incredibly diverse, there are certain minimal generalizations we can put in place for our reading of Hebrews.

The God of Israel and the gods of Gentiles were the source of both blessings and curses. The safety of the city, the fertility of the land and the family, the health of the people, fortunes in war and business, love and marriage, in fact nearly everything important in human life was dependent in some way on the beneficence or maleficence of the gods. The countless inscriptions on ancient temples and the complex biblical stories of God and Israel all testify to the wonder and terror of the relationship between humans and their gods. As every reader of the Bible knows, when God is pleased with Israel, God blesses, and when God is displeased, God punishes. For our purposes we should note that temples, priests, and sacrifices work at the very center of these blessings and curses.

Access to the blessings of God comes through properly offered sacrifices. This is the core assumption of Hebrews (9:11–14; 10:14, 19). But it is an assumption that undergoes considerable transformation. When the notion of priesthood is combined with the basic confessions about Jesus, a unique account of both Jesus and priesthood results. Jesus is the priest who nullifies all other priests, temples, and sacrifices (7:11–12, 18; 10:1–4). The perfect priest is the last priest.

But it is not the case that Hebrews merely asserts that Jesus is a new high priest or even the perfect high priest. Rather, the author undertakes a subtle and complex exegetical argument. The key move is the application of Psalm 110:4 to Jesus. Psalm 110:4 reads: "The LORD has sworn and will not change his mind, 'You are a priest forever according to the order of Melchizedek.'" Hebrews understands the "you" of this psalm to be Jesus. Thus, according to Hebrews, God declares to Jesus, "You are a priest forever, according to the order of Melchizedek" (see Heb. 5:6; 7:17).

The fundamental role of Psalm 110 in this argument signals two key aspects of Hebrews. First, the author is not simply walking the streets of the ancient world, looking up at temples and speculating about Jesus and these temples and their priests—not even the Jerusalem temple. In fact, Hebrews never uses the precise word for temple. Instead, the author is walking the syntax of the Old Testament. His journey is through a particular set of priesthood texts. His argument is an interaction between the story of Jesus and that of the Old Testament. Second, Jesus is not simply the best of the Jerusalem priests. He is not even one of them. He belongs to a completely different order of priesthood—that of Melchizedek (5:6; 7:17). Thus, he is the perfect priest, not in being more of what was already present in the world of priests, but in being different. His perfection lies in his uniqueness.

The center of Hebrews, from 4:14 to 10:18, elaborates upon this concept of Jesus as high priest. Although its literary structure is quite difficult to follow, the core ideas are clear. In fact, part of the literary style of this section is that of repetition. Key ideas are restated over and over, with slight nuances added, so that core ideas become almost unavoidable. What every reader notices is a structure of contrast—a contrast between the old priesthood with its laws, its sacrifices, its priests, and its effects and the new priesthood of Jesus.

The old priests are human descendants of Levi who are chosen by other mortals to serve God in the holy tabernacle (Heb. 7:5). These priests every day return to the temple to repeat sacrifices over and over again (9:6; 10:1). Since they themselves are polluted by sin, they need to offer sacrifices for themselves (5:3; 7:27). They use the blood of various animals (9:12–13). Finally on the Day of Atonement they make sacrifice for sins that might remain unaccounted for through the normal course of sacrifices (9:6–7). The author of Hebrews draws these descriptions of the Levitical priesthood directly from texts in Leviticus and Numbers (esp. Leviticus 15–16; Numbers 9–14). At first Hebrews treats these priests as mostly positive, although they are superseded by the better Jesus. But eventually Hebrews declares that the whole course of the old law and its priests is a failure (10:1–10). The problems are many.

The opening problem is simply that Jesus is so much better. Jesus is an eternal priest (Heb. 7:3, 24); he needs no succession, no tribe to support him (7:3). In fact, according to the law he cannot be a priest at all, since he is from the tribe of Judah (7:14). Jesus is not chosen by humans, but by God's own oath (7:20–22). The old priests must repeat everything every day (9:6). Jesus does it once and for all (7:27). The old priests go into a temple that is a shadow, a sketch, of the heavenly one (8:5); Jesus goes into heaven itself (9:24). Jesus needs to make no sacrifice for himself, since he is himself perfect (7:27). In fact, in a wonderful twist, he is himself the sacrifice (9:12). Jesus is both the sacrificer and the sacrificed, both priest and offering. Thus, Jesus offers not the blood of animals but his own blood, the blood of the perfect offering (9:12–14). The explicit problem with the Levitical priesthood seems to be simply that of weakness—Jesus is a more potent priest. And now, instead of this flawed priesthood, we have a perfectly potent, eternal high priest in the heavens. The new is better. We have better promises, better results, better rewards.

At this point in our account of Hebrews, we have friendly interaction between Old Testament images of sacrifices and the story of Jesus. Although there is a tension between the old and the new, this tension seems positive. What once was a pretty good priesthood has been replaced by a perfect priesthood. It is as though the author is engaging in a little theological experiment: Let's think about Jesus by means of these priesthood texts. And indeed such an experiment deepens and transforms our understanding of Jesus. As nearly every reader of Hebrews has insisted, some such theological enrichment seems to be one of the book's major accomplishments. We can now think about the blessings of Jesus while walking streets with temples over our heads, and especially while walking through the temple regulations in the Old Testament.

But the tension between the old and the new that creates this nice Christology is not as gentle as this. The old does not fall naturally into the new. Jesus is not simply an extension, a perfection, of the old. This tension includes real conflict, even incompatibility. On the one hand, the author of Hebrews carefully applies the positive functions of the old priesthood to Jesus, and this application assumes some value in the old. On the other hand, the replacement of the old with the new includes the notion that the old never worked at all. We see in this conflict how the author deals with one of the oldest problems in the New Testament—the connection between the story of Jesus and the story of Israel. Christians have always felt obligated to explain how Christianity can both depend upon and transcend Judaism at the same time. Hebrews creates a complex interaction between the story of Jesus and the Old Testament.

Ultimately, the author seems to argue that the old priesthood really did not work: "For it is impossible for the blood of bulls and goats to take away sins" (10:4). In fact, Hebrews mounts a series of arguments against the effectiveness of the old priesthood that go beyond the more gentle admonition that it is less effective than the new. In 7:11 the author suggests that the identity of Jesus reveals the true character of the Levitical priesthood. The status of Jesus as high priest in itself means that the old priesthood is flawed. "Now if perfection had been attainable through the Levitical priesthood ... what further need would there have been to speak of another priest arising according to the order of Melchizedek?" (7:11). If the one priesthood worked, there would be no need for another. The fact that Jesus functions as priest, while being of a different order than the Levitical, means that the Levitical cannot be sufficient in itself. Or perhaps, as we shall see below, it is more of an exegetical argument (see 7:1–28). The story of Melchizedek in Genesis 14 and Psalm 110 shows that the Levitical priesthood was always and still is secondary to the Melchizedek priesthood. Thus, the Levitical priesthood has always been flawed.

In chapter 9, Hebrews gives a brief description of the layout of the desert tabernacle as it is recorded in Exodus (9:1–5), but then moves to Leviticus 16 and the account of the Day of Atonement (9:7–14). Hebrews notes that the priests go into the "first tent" every day (9:6), "but only the high priest goes into the second, and he but once a year" (9:7). From this account the text draws a striking conclusion: "By this the Holy Spirit indicates that the way into the sanctuary has not yet been disclosed as long as the first tent is still standing" (9:8). Most readers see a reference to a well-known Jewish tradition that the sections in the tabernacle, or later in the temple, mirror the divisions between heaven and earth. The separateness, the inaccessibility, of the Holy of Holies is a symbol of the separateness of heaven from earth. But instead of concluding, as most Jews would, that this mirroring of cosmic structures adds value to the architecture of the tabernacle, the author of Hebrews concludes that this symbol of separation denotes the general ineffectiveness of all sacrifices performed in the first tent.

And here the argument becomes even more subtle. It is not that sacrifices in the first tent have no force at all. Such a conclusion would undo the positive connection between the first priesthood and the second. The first must have value of some kind. Instead, the text builds on the distinction between the inner and the outer. These sacrifices in the first tent can only touch the outside of things, just as they are conducted outside. They "deal only with food and drink and various baptisms, regulations for the body" (9:10). But they "cannot perfect the conscience of the worshiper" (9:9). At this point Hebrews is touching upon the classic early Christian complaint about the force of the Jerusalem temple: how can the killing of animals clean the heart and soul of a human? Such a question was not, of course, unknown to Jews and Gentiles who frequented ancient temples. But the Christian conclusion is a radical one. In Hebrews, all temples, including the one in Jerusalem, become irrelevant.

In fact, in chapter 10, Hebrews seems to reject completely any value for the old sacrifices, asserting that "it is impossible for the blood of bulls and goats to take away sins." Two arguments support this radical conclusion. First, "the law has only a shadow of the good things to come and not the true form of these realities" (10:1). It is not clear whether the text is drawing on the du-alisms of Greek Platonism or on classic rabbinic distinctions between above and below, or on apocalyptic notions of before and after. But it is clear that a radical distinction is being drawn between the old law and the new. The old law is only a shadow of the real, thus it lacks power over sin. Second, the need to sacrifice over and over again demonstrates by itself that these sacrifices have no final power over sin. Thus, they cannot "take away sins" (10:4). This in it-self is a conclusion which dismantles all temple systems. They have no real power.

All of this leads to what many readers think is the clearest statement of the status of the old priesthood. Hebrews 10:5–7 quotes Psalm 40:6–8: "Sacrifices and offerings you have not desired …; in burnt offerings and sin offerings you have taken no pleasure" (10:5b–6). The Old Testament is peppered with sim-ilar critiques of sacrifices. But these critiques are never final or absolute. More poignantly, the quote from Psalm 40 continues: "Then I said, 'See, God, I have come to do your will'" (10:7a). Hebrews reads the "I" of verse 8 as refer-ring to Jesus. It is Jesus who has come, and it is Jesus who is announcing that God does not want sacrifices. As Hebrews argues in 10:8–9, this psalm sets temple sacrifices in opposition to the will of God. It is not only the case that God does not want sacrifices unless other things are done first or as well; God does not want sacrifices at all. The Jerusalem temple is contrary to the will of God.

Hebrews does not seem to believe that the temple has always been contrary to God's will. In Hebrews' reading of Psalm 40 it is the arrival of Jesus which changes the status of the temple. There is a "before" and "after" which is put in place. Before the arrival of Jesus, the temple was not contrary to God's will. But it is now. As Hebrew notes in 10:9, "He [Jesus] abolishes the first in order to establish the second."

This is a classic example of early Christian eschatological (end time) thought. The messianic age has begun. The messiah has come. Promises are being fulfilled. Time and the cosmos have changed. With the arrival of Jesus, there is an old and a new. The old and the new are embedded in one another yet are distinct from one another. This collapsing of time is one of the most potent theological engines in the New Testament. It is found everywhere, and it shapes Christian thought from the New Testament until today. Hebrews will have more to say about this.

This series of arguments about the old Levitical priesthood and the new priesthood of Jesus has long resisted systemization. Even our quick readings above make it obvious that the author is using a variety of categories and methods of argument in order to connect and disconnect these priesthoods. Nevertheless, all these arguments assume the basic efficacy of temples, priests, and sacrifices. Hebrews assumes that humans relate to God by means of blood. Even Christians depend upon blood, properly spilled, to enter the new Christian reality. The coming of Jesus does not end the force of blood and sacrifices; it makes those forces eternal.

Hebrews assumes that God is holy and that only a holy person can approach God. Hebrews further assumes that properly spilled blood can make a person holy. Christians have a better covenant because they can claim a better sacrifice. Jesus makes for a perfect sacrifice. He is the perfect priest. He spills perfect blood. He spills it in the perfect place. Finally, all this perfection of the sacrifice makes personal perfection, both moral and cultic, possible for Christians.

Christianity and Dualism

One of the ongoing questions about Hebrews concerns the origin and force of the many dualisms in the text. As we shall see, many of the arguments in Hebrews are built upon some sort of dualistic structure. In fact, the priesthood arguments sketched above depend on a series of dualisms—the old and the new, the human and the divine, earth and heaven, shadow and substance. Readers have long noted that how one reads these dualisms determines how one renders the overall theology of Hebrews. But it is not clear how these dualisms should be understood. Some readers think the core dualism is the distinction between heaven and earth. Others suggest that the core distinction is between shadow and substance; still others suggest the human and the divine. I suggested above that the core dualism is a "before" and "after" put in place with the arrival of Jesus.

One way to decide how to read these dualisms in Hebrews is by making a decision about their proper historical context. But, as noted earlier, this is not always easy to do. Part of the difficulty of deciding about context depends to a great extent on how specific one wants to be. Thinking in large-scale terms, most scholars could safely say that Hebrews belongs to the diverse world of early Christianity with influences from Judaism and Greco-Roman thought. However, a background as large and diverse as this offers little guidance to the task of reading. Thus, historical critics want to be more specific. They want to know which part of early Christianity, which part of Judaism, and which part of the Greco-Roman world. As the attempt to comprehend the proper historical background becomes more focused, it also becomes more difficult to be confident in one's decision.

In general all we can do is find hints in the text itself. Rarely do we have outside confirmation. Thus, we look for ideas, words, syntax, and forms of argument that remind us of similar ideas, words, syntax, and forms of argument in other documents. It is a process of perceiving connections. While such a process is admittedly subjective, it is not purely so. The textual evidence cannot be read just any way we want. To make an absurd point: Hebrews was not written by Aristotle. But some people do indeed perceive connections where others do not. In the case of the dualistic arguments about priesthood in Hebrews, three proposals seem to receive the most attention these days. Each proposal leads to a different kind of reading of Hebrews.

1. Whenever we encounter dualism in an ancient text, we immediately think of the various Greek philosophical dualisms that flow out of Platonism. In the case of Hebrews, we think especially of the Hellenistic-Jewish dualisms in Philo of Alexandria. Philo was a well-educated, wealthy Jew who lived in Alexandria from c. 20 B.C.E. to 45 C.E. In Philo's writings we encounter a complex interaction between Greek philosophical ideas, especially those of Plato, and early Jewish thought, especially scripture. When scholars read Philo and Hebrews together, they find an impressive number of linguistic and theological connections. Many of the connections are simply singular images, but more pervasive connections are also found.

Philo, for example, conceived of the world as a reflection of the eternal. In typical Platonic fashion, he built upon notions of an interaction between divine and human wisdom that structures the cosmos. Such ideas seem at work in Hebrews' Christological notions, such as 1:3 and in the description of the tabernacle in chapter 8. In fact, both Hebrews and Philo speak of the heavens and the earth in a dualistic structure that seems very Platonic.

We can, therefore, conceive of the author of Hebrews as a Platonic Christian, a predecessor of later Alexandrian Christians such as Clement and Origen. Conceived this way, the generative structure in Hebrews is not temporal but spacial or even philosophical. What Jesus manifests is the hidden, eternal truth in the shadowy, temporary forces on the earth. The key is to connect this opening to the eternal. The problem with the old priesthood is not that it precedes Jesus; the problem is that it is a weak shadow of true substance, which is Jesus. Thus, the only "new" in the coming of Jesus is that what was once hidden is now revealed.

2. The second proposal seems to have somewhat more support than the first. One theory of deciding context is that the shorter the distance one travels for the parallel the better. We do not need to go to Athens or Alexandria, or even to a Greek philosophical school, when the literature of Hellenistic Judaism can easily explain the dualisms in Hebrews. Thus, many readers sug-

gest that there is nothing in Hebrews that needs a Platonic explanation. Hebrews, in fact, seems typical in its imagery and thought structures when compared to a large number of ancient Jewish and Christian texts. For instance, the Old Testament itself supplies motifs of above and below, then and now, and even shadow and substance. We cannot really specify one philosophical or theological or literary school as the only proper milieu. Hebrews is simply a Jewish Christian text swimming in the imagery of the ancient world. It is indeed more Hellenistic than rabbinic; but then so is most everything else. What is unique about Hebrews is not the historical framework of its thought but the peculiar arguments it creates. What we have is a Hellenistic Jew thinking about Jesus and priests.

In this scenario, the dualisms of Hebrews are simply representative of the dualisms in much of ancient Jewish and Christian thought. If there is a driving distinction, it would be the dualism between God and humans: God is holy and humans are not. The coming of Jesus has solved this ancient incompatibility.

3. The third proposal of how to discern Hebrews' context produces a quite different reading from the first two. This theory insists that we remember, first of all, that the writer is Christian. The specific confessions of Christianity provide the major forces and data of his argument. The author is not, in his mind at least, either Jew or Gentile. He is a follower of Jesus. Thus his key passages are the Christological confessions that appear throughout his letter. When we think of the text this way, the dualisms between the old and new priesthoods derive not from the dualisms of Hellenism or the Old Testament but from the internal dynamics of the Christian confession. Thus the primary force in these arguments comes from the new situation inaugurated by the arrival of the Messiah. The author is thinking, first of all, in terms of new age and old age, which creates a dualism that can be further funded by various Hellenistic and biblical dualisms. If we need to find non-Christian parallels, we might go to apocalyptic texts of Qumran and Hellenistic Judaism. But the primary place we search for context is within other early Christian writings. We then describe the author as a quite traditional, Christian, apocalyptic theologian, who is thinking about the new age of the Messiah and what that does to the traditional notions of temples, priests, and sacrifices. Exactly where the line would be between tradition and innovation is not only unknowable, it is intentionally being erased. In fact, it is the erasure of that line that structures his theological method.

All three of these scenarios are plausible, although each is structured differently. I confess, however, that for me a combination of the second and third proposal works best for Hebrews. When I envision an early Christian author who lives in the enormously rich culture of the Greco-Roman world with its diverse fund of Greek philosophy and Jewish theology, and who is dedicated to rather traditional forms of early Christian confessions about Jesus, then Hebrews reads well.

If we think this is the proper historical setting for Hebrews, then we will tend to organize our reading of the text around Christological themes. This will indeed be our preference in what follows. But we also need to be careful here. For some reason it belongs to the nature of scholarship to want to control and master texts. We scholars dislike messiness; we want order; we want to know what idea orders what other idea.

However, texts sometimes resist our imposed orders. That resistance is important. When we have to labor as hard as we do in our reading of Hebrews to tidy up a text, perhaps the text is in its original voice untidy. Perhaps the genius of Hebrews' exploration of priesthoods is the diversity of imagery that it holds in one syntax. Perhaps to make one image submit to the dominance of another is to misread. In fact, this is precisely what I think. The author of Hebrews likes all his ideas about priesthood, and no single one of them holds the key to the other. Thus, Hebrews' theology of the priesthood of Jesus is diverse, unsystematized, and even a bit chaotic. It is also, again in my opinion, wonderfully creative.

A New Age

We have argued that the most helpful place to begin a theological reading of Hebrews is with its explorations of the priesthood of Jesus. The central role of the concept of Jesus' priesthood in the overall theology of Hebrews justifies, to some extent, our use of it as an entry into the theology of the text. But there is also something inadequate in what we have done thus far.

Even if this notion of Jesus the priest is the most prominent theme of the letter, it derives its meaning from its connection to other ideas in the letter. We have tended to pull it from its context and address it on its own. And it would be more adequate to connect this concept of priesthood to the other images and ideas that surround it in Hebrews.

Furthermore, the image of the priesthood of Jesus is not just an idea; it is an image that plays a particular role in the overall rhetoric of Hebrews. That is to say, it has a literary function in a particular literary argument. The image of priesthood belongs to a certain sequence of images and a certain rhetorical structure. We need not only to embed this single idea in the complex of ideas around it; we need to embed the words themselves within the words of the text to which they belong. That is to say, we need to comprehend the literary force of Hebrews as a whole before we disconnect any theological ideas from it.

Thus, if we return to the syntax of Hebrews, looking for what the text of Hebrews does with this image of high priest, we find a fascinating literary and theological program. We have already noted that the author draws several conclusions from this image of high priest. Jesus accomplishes perfection in his capacity to take away sins once and for all. Jesus is able to cleanse the conscience of the believer. But there is much more.

Nearly every reader of Hebrews—in fact, I can find no real exception—notices a constant literary pattern of proclamation followed by exhortation. The author first establishes a theological truth and then draws a moral conclusion of some kind. Basic to the literary style of the letter on both a large scale and a small scale is this constant pattern of theological argument followed by parenesis based on that theology. For instance, many readers outline the letter according to this basic format.

Theology. Jesus as superior to the angels.   1:1–14
    Exhortation. Pay attention.   2:1–4
Theology. Jesus as pioneer in suffering.   2:5–18
        Jesus as superior to Moses.   3:1–6
    Exhortation. Do not harden your hearts.   3:7–4:13
Theology. Jesus as High Priest.   4:14–5:10
    Exhortation. Call to perfection.   5:11–6:20
Theology. A high priest of the order of Melchizedek.   7:1–10:18
    Exhortation. Let us approach God.   10:19–39
Theology. Examples of faith.   11:1–40
    Exhortation. Follow Jesus.   12:1–13:17
Epistolary conclusions and benediction.   13:18–25

In spite of the obvious oversimplifications in such an outline, the basic pattern does indeed seem appropriate to the letter. In fact, the pattern runs deeper than this outline indicates, for even within these sections, this pattern occurs on a smaller scale. For example, 4:14–16, classified above as "theology," actually contains two brief sequences of "theology" and "exhortation." Verse 14 is, in one sentence, such a sequence: "Since, then, we have a great high priest, who has passed through the heavens, Jesus, the Son of God [theology], let us hold fast to our confession [exhortation]."

Finding this pattern of proclamation and exhortation to be pervasive in Hebrews is no real surprise. This pattern is one of the most common in the New Testament, and it frequents most theological argument. "If this is who God is, then we must…" The fact that such practical conclusions about how we are to live can be derived from these theological arguments shows that the theology built here is not simply theological play. It is not just a thought experiment. The author is articulating in these arguments the truths about who God is, who Jesus is. These truths about God show us the basic reality of the universe. The world works this way, because this is who God is. Therefore, let us live accordingly.

Hebrews devotes enormous attention to explaining what this "accordingly" might mean, to articulating how our situation has already changed and our behavior should change because of the event of Jesus. We already noted that having Jesus as high priest means that we need no more sacrifices on our behalf. No longer do the old temples and sacrifices connect us to divine blessings. Hebrews gives a powerful Christological reason for this shift. It is not that priesthood and sacrifices no longer matter; it is that Jesus is always, even now, the perfect priest and sacrifice. Therefore, go no more to temples.

Yet this negative conclusion does not mean that God is no longer a God connected to sacrifices. In fact, it means just the opposite. Since Jesus is the eternal high priest, God is forever connected to the ancient Old Testament dynamics of sin, expiation, priest, sacrifices, and sacred space. Most of all, if Jesus is an eternal high priest, then the terrors of sin and God's holiness become fundamental theological issues. Hebrews then must explain how we are to live in this new reality of an eternal priesthood.

By pursuing this pattern of proclamation and exhortation, we can begin to reconstruct how the author of Hebrews thinks we should conduct ourselves in this new age. He concludes his exploration into the priesthood of Jesus with an extensive "therefore." In 10:19–39 Hebrews details a series of exhortations that are couched as the proper response to having Jesus as high priest (12:14–13:19 gives a somewhat more general series of exhortations).

It is difficult to summarize a set of exhortations such as these, since their diversity resists general categories. But apart from just reading them through over and over, we can make a few comments. The section begins with an explicit conclusion, "since we have a great high priest over the house of God, let us approach with a true heart in full assurance of faith" (10:21–22a). The first issue would have been an obvious one to the ancients: if temples are no longer open to us, there seems to be no way to get near to God. Heretofore, it has been through the sacrificial, cleanliness, monetary, and prayer systems surrounding temples that we achieve the ear of God. We have always understood that we must perform the temple liturgies if we want God's blessings. Now, however, as Christians we are denied these liturgies. Instead, we are told to come to God wherever we are, not with a liturgical dance (such dances are now irrelevant), but with a clean heart, conscience, and even body. Jesus cleans them all always.

Thus a psychological and geographical transformation is accomplished. We do not need extensive obeisance. We do not need the endless humiliations and obligations of temple liturgies. Jesus gives us direct and immediate access to the most holy places of God. And the holy places of God are not places. No travel is needed. Faith, in the heart, is all that is needed. If there is a journey, it is a journey taken by the heart within the geography of the heart.

"Let us hold fast to the confession of our hope without wavering, for he who has promised is faithful" (Heb. 10:23). With this statement, Hebrews touches upon some of the other most powerful themes of the letter. Every phrase in this sentence evokes fuller treatments elsewhere in the letter. Much of the diverse exhortation in Hebrews could be summarized as pleas and warnings to hold fast to the confession without wavering. What Hebrews means by "the confession" is not perfectly clear. Some readers suggest that this text is referring to such nice summaries as 1:1–4. Others suggest that those summaries, coupled with the diverse Christological arguments of the letter, constitute the content of the confession. Still other readers suggest this text may also be referring to standard early Christian confessions that remain unstated in the letter. For instance, 6:1–2 refers to such general confessions. The imprecision of the language here and in the rest of the letter, which results in this scholarly uncertainty, suggests that the author is not being particularly precise or exclusive in his reference to "confession." It is not that the content of the confession does not matter to us; the letter devotes considerable attention to tracing a proper Christology. It is, instead, that the content may well take diverse forms.

In any case, the emphasis here is on holding fast and not wavering. In fact, this call to hold fast and not waver recurs so often that many readers conclude this is the immediate cause for the writing of the letter (e.g., 3:6, 14; 4:14). The repeating refrain to hold fast suggests a community that is not doing so. And if the author's response is not simply a plea to hold fast (after all, he works hard to provide his readers with helpful theological ideas), he does, nevertheless, repeatedly plead with them. His plea takes several forms. He will, for instance, provide positive examples of others who held fast (10:4–40). He will also provide negative examples (3:16–19). All those examples will issue in direct exhortation to imitate or not imitate the example. Apart from these examples of faith and non-faith, he builds various exhortations explicitly upon the theology in the letter. A perfect example of such intertwining of theology and exhortation follows immediately upon this verse (10:23) in 10:26–31.

Several ideas, all of which surface again in the letter, are combined here. On the one hand, God is still a God of righteous judgment. Whatever it means to have Jesus as high priest, it does not mean that righteousness and judgment have been stripped from the character of God. God still announces that "Vengeance is mine, I will repay" (10:30). The tone here is that of warning. The passage in fact concludes on a chilling note: "It is a fearful thing to fall into the hands of the living God" (10:31).

On the other hand, this same passage begins with a comforting invitation to the presence of God: "Therefore, my friends, since we have confidence to enter the sanctuary by the blood of Jesus ... let us approach with a true heart in full assurance of faith" (10:19, 22). The passage begins with this wonderful invitation and ends with a warning about how fearful it is to fall into the hands of the living God (10:31). Two seemingly incompatible images of God are hereby combined in one theological argument. It is only by way of this striking combination that the force of the high priesthood of Jesus can be conveyed. Jesus gives us access to a fearful God.

If we return to the syntax of 10:23, we can follow the reasoning. We have to hold fast; we must not waver. Two forces are in place here. First, there is the Christological force of Jesus as high priest which opens a new kind of access to our terribly righteous God. Second, our response to this new opening has the power to invoke both God's blessings and God's curses. Thus, in a rather controversial sentence the author asserts, "For if we willfully persist in sin after having received the knowledge of truth, there no longer remains a sacrifice for sins, but a fearful punishment, and a fury of fire that will consume the adversaries" (10:26–27). It is best to take this as meaning what it appears to mean, in spite of Pauline-inspired protests. Whatever Jesus has accomplished in becoming high priest, it has not made the character of our lives irrelevant. In fact, it seems instead to have made our lives more relevant.

Our lives are more relevant because the coming of Jesus has raised the stakes. As the author notes in 10:28–29, "anyone who has violated the law of Moses dies without mercy." But if that is true, "how much worse punishment" awaits those who "spurn the Son of God." All the "better" and "more" arguments that the author constructed about Jesus as high priest come into play here. Not only are there better promises and more mercy, there seems to be more severe judgment as well. Now that the Messiah has come and the confessions about him are being proclaimed, all our decisions for or against the call of God have become intensified in their ramifications. Both sides of the relationship between humans and God becomes more potent. God is both more merciful and more righteous. Now that Jesus is high priest, our acts have both more wonderful and more terrible consequences.

Midrash

Apart from the obvious problem of focusing our readings thus far on the arguments of 4:14–10:39 and thereby ignoring almost half of the letter, even within those chapters a curious misreading has occurred. Hebrews builds its case, not upon a set of theological truths that the author simply asserts, but upon a series of exegetical arguments. At the heart of Hebrews 4–10 is a series of Old Testament texts. Some readers suggest that these chapters are actually structured as a midrash on Psalm 110, Genesis 14, and Jeremiah 31. Midrash is sometimes used almost as a technical term to refer to exegetical readings of text in the style of the great Jewish Midrashim. Here, however, the term midrash has a more general meaning of "interpretation" or "interpretation in classic ancient Jewish style." It is argued that the primary theological engine in Hebrews is a collision and integration of the Jesus story with some key Old Testament texts. Hebrews is reading the Jesus story through the lens of these texts and it is reading these texts through the lens of the Jesus story. What we have is a creative interaction of early Christian confessions about Jesus and the Old Testament. Thus, we need to understand Hebrews, first of all, as exegesis.

There is something undeniably true about these assertions. Certainly, if we remove these Old Testament texts from Hebrews, the entire argument of the letter unravels. More importantly, these texts do indeed seem to fund the argument. It is, of course, the Melchizedek texts that are the most striking. Melchizedek is mentioned only twice in the Old Testament—in Genesis 14 and Psalm 110. No other New Testament text uses this image of Melchizedek as a way to understand Jesus. Hebrews is unique. This does not mean that the author of Hebrews is the first early Christian to think about these Melchizedek texts in relationship to Jesus. It only means that Hebrews is the first text still in existence that does so. What other people might have thought, said, or written outside of these texts is beyond our reconstruction.

Three times the author cites Psalm 110:4, "You are a priest forever according to the order of Melchizedek" (5:6; 7:17, 21). He reads this text as God's speaking directly to Jesus in the second person. God is designating Jesus as a unique high priest. We have already traced much of that uniqueness. If there is a starting point or foundation to the priesthood argument of Hebrews, this text must be it. Jesus is named by God as high priest. This changes the way we must understand Jesus. Furthermore, Jesus is not high priest according to the Levitical order but according to the order of Melchizedek. As we have seen, this changes almost everything about the Levitical order and the place of temples and sacrifices in the lives of Christians. Thus, the syntax of Psalm 110:4 dictates the basic configuration of the priesthood argument. If we want, we can hang the core of the argument here.

However, Hebrews does not simply cite this one sentence and then imagine a theology based upon it. The author follows this Melchizedek through the canon. It is as though the author treats Melchizedek as a real figure with a life of his own. Thus, he does not read just this one sentence about Melchizedek. Everything said about Melchizedek becomes relevant. Thus, we do not seem to be dealing here with proof texts in the negative sense, wherein someone hunts down a biblical text which says, more or less, what that person already knew was true. The author seems to be submitting to the full force of this Melchizedek figure. Thus, he turns to Genesis 14, which is the only other place we encounter this figure.

We must admit that his reading of Genesis 14 is very creative. At a minimum we can say that he reads Genesis 14 through the lens of both Psalm 110 and his confessions about Jesus. What he believes about Jesus must be true. But what he reads in Psalm 110 and Genesis 14 must also be true. So he cannot misread one in the name of another. He must read them all well, and they all must cohere.

The author's reading of Genesis 14 is remarkable for the care and detail it manifests. He begins with a brief citation.

> This "King Melchizedek of Salem, priest of the Most High God, met Abraham as he was returning from defeating the kings and blessed him"; and to him Abraham apportioned "one-tenth of everything."
>
> (7:1–2a)

This is a puzzling citation, since it does not exactly match any text we possess. We can recreate this text by combining parts of the Masoretic text (the Hebrew Old Testament) with parts of the Septuagint (the Greek Old

Testament). But, we do not really know whether Hebrews is quoting imprecisely or whether the text the author possessed read this way. In any case, Hebrews builds its argument on the text as it is cited here.

The interpretation begins with two etymological notes, both of which depend on a knowledge of Hebrew. "His name, in the first place, means 'king of righteousness'; next he is also king of Salem, that is, 'king of peace'" (7:2b). The first etymology is pretty accurate. Melchizedek in Hebrew means "my king is righteous" or "righteous king." "King of righteousness" is more or less the same. Most ancient Jewish readings of "king of Salem" treated Salem as a place name. But it depends on how the Hebrew is pointed. To render "Salem" as "peace" is not so much wrong as it is a minority reading. Only Philo seems to share this reading of Salem as peace. In any case, surrounding the name Melchizedek are the classic biblical categories of righteousness and peace. Jesus, like Melchizedek, thereby becomes the locus or agent of righteousness and peace. This is crucial, of course, to the theology of Hebrews.

More creatively, the author notes the lack of proper introduction of Melchizedek in Genesis 14. He arrives on the scene without any note of his proper pedigree. "Without father, without mother, without genealogy, having neither beginning of days nor end of life, but resembling the Son of God, he remains a priest forever" (Hebrews 7:3). Readers have long complained that, just because the text does not bother to mention the father and mother of Melchizedek, this does not mean he has none. However, Hebrews seems to be pursuing something more mysterious than any simple historical reading such as this might suggest. The point seems to be that, in the syntax of these texts about Melchizedek, God is giving hints about the truth of Jesus. The main exegetical move (apart from combining Genesis 14 and Psalm 110) is the identification of the "you" of Psalm 110:4 ("You are a priest forever, according to the order of Melchizedek") as Jesus. According to Hebrews 5:6 and 7:17, God names Jesus in Psalm 110 as a priest according to the order of Melchizedek. Furthermore, if Psalm 110 is referring to Jesus, then Genesis 14 is as well. When these two texts are combined and attached to Jesus, Jesus becomes an eternal high priest, a priest forever.

Hebrews takes us even further into the details of the Genesis story. It notes that Abraham "gave him a tenth of the spoils" (7:4). This means that Abraham acknowledged him (Melchizedek and Jesus) as high priest. Hebrews then suggests that "one might even say that Levi himself … paid tithes through Abraham, for he was still in the loins of his ancestor" (7:9–10). This is pretty clever. Levi, through his ancestor Abraham, paid tithes to Jesus, thus acknowledging the superiority of the priesthood of Jesus. Hebrews pushes still further and notes that Melchizedek blessed Abraham. "It is beyond dispute that the inferior is blessed by the superior" (7:7). Thus, these readings emphasize that Jesus and the new covenant are superior to the old.

These rather clever notations on the Genesis text lead, as we might expect, to a series of conclusions about the priesthood of Jesus (7:11–28). Without intentionally downplaying all the diverse points included here, most of which build upon the "better" and "more" dynamic so crucial to the theology of priesthood, one point is particularly helpful in illustrating how Hebrews is reading these texts.

In the midst of his reading of Genesis 14, the author cites Psalm 110 twice. In 7:17 he cites the psalm in its usual form, namely, "You are a priest forever, according to the order of Melchizedek," in order to emphasize the non-Levitical nature of this new priesthood. But in 7:21 the citation is a bit different, because he cites only the first half of Psalm 110:4. In that first half, God takes an oath, "The LORD has sworn and will not change his mind, 'You are a priest forever'" (7:21). Upon this first half of the verse Hebrews will build theological images of a divine oath that undergirds the priesthood of Jesus. But this change in how the text is cited also shows that the author is not simply raiding a text for an image or two that might be helpful in reinforcing an argument already built with other tools. He seems to linger on this Old Testament text. His argument seems to be coming out of the ancient texts rather than being simply imposed upon them. If Jesus really is a priest of the order of Melchizedek, then we need to learn who this Melchizedek is. We need to read the texts about him carefully and slowly. The author of Hebrews does just that. And his careful reading is his theology, as much as the theological statements he derives from those readings are his theology. His theology is, in part, the act of reading the Old Testament.

This seems even clearer in his reading of Jeremiah 31. His longest continuous citation of a text is his citation in 8:8–12 of Jeremiah 31:31–34. Perhaps the best way to describe the author's reading of this passage in Jeremiah is to assert that he thinks every sentence of it is true. Not only is every sentence true, but every sentence is about the new covenant in Christ. Every sentence describes life now. The concepts of rejection of the old covenant, the coming of the new, the writing of the new on minds and hearts, the new intimacy between God and people, the new knowledge by people of God, the victory of mercy, and the final forgetting of sins will all feed into the author's description of the new life. It would be a misrepresentation of the force of these texts to describe their role as simple reinforcement, as though the author, by living in the new age, knew the full character of the new covenant and found this text as a fortuitous description of this new life; as though he stumbled into this text and thought it was a good match. These texts must be given more force than this.

The question of what comes first, the new reality in Christ or the new reading of the old texts, then seems unanswerable. It is not the case that readers must simply adjust their perception of reality to the predictions and images of these ancient texts. Nor is it the case that we must comprehend our new reality correctly, then return to ancient texts hoping we can read or misread them in such a way as to make them match. Such a dominance of one by the other undoes the basic force of the argument. What makes these exegetical

arguments work is the very possibility that ancient text and modern reality cohere. Thus, even if we suspect that the author found these texts out of a preceding experience of life in Christ, that there was some kind of recognition of
fit that initiated these readings, it would be a mistake to think that his modern
reality is simply overwhelming the voice of the ancient text. It seems more accurate to say that each feeds the other. He does indeed seem to learn details
about his own new life from details in the ancient text.

The resulting interconnectedness of Old Testament texts and Christian
theology leads many readers to assert that this Christian rereading of ancient
texts is the basic theological method of the letter. Hebrews thus becomes a
classic early Christian attempt to hold together the truth of the "old" revelation with that of the "new." The elasticity with which Hebrews reads the Old
Testament, and the diversity of pathways constructed between the old and the
new, mean that no simple formulas for how to connect Old Testament and
New Testament, such as promise and fulfillment, or typology, or analogy, or
even old and new will suffice. Hebrews charts a complex intertwining, a dependence and independence, between the time before Christ and the time after. Therefore, if there is a model for the modern reader here, it is probably
that the task of reading must be taken up again by us, with a fidelity both to
ourselves and to the text equal to what we find in Hebrews.

Beginning at the Beginning

At this point, we have focused our reading of Hebrews on chapters 4–10.
Many readers of Hebrews have argued that these chapters form the theological heart of the letter and that the real creativity of the letter also occurs here.
Thus, in one sense chapters 4–10 are the natural and proper place to center
one's readings.

However, when people read texts, they normally do not start in the middle
as we have done. Typically, they start at the beginning. The beginning sets up
the middle, tells us how to read the middle, gives us ears to hear the middle.
And the middle sets up the end. We should, at a minimum, before we draw
too many conclusions, read a text from beginning to end. Thus, we need to
read the rest of the letter, perhaps even by beginning at the beginning.

Several surprises occur in the opening verses (1:1–4). First, the letter does
not start like a letter. There is no sender and no recipient. Perhaps this "letter" is not a letter. On the other hand, the "non-letter" ends like a letter, with
classic final greetings. Readers then stumble at the very first in trying to decide what kind of document Hebrews is.

Through the centuries, readers have been divided in their opinions. Some
suggest that it is not really a letter but a theological essay written to the church
at large, or at least to an audience larger than one church or one destination.
They say it was intended from the beginning to become part of a collection of

Christian literature that could be read by anyone. Others argue that, despite the lack of opening salutation, Hebrews is a real letter with a specific address. Who the author is, who the recipients are, and what the occasion for writing was, produces much debate. But, they say, it is still a letter.

This uncertainty over genre leads to an uncertainty over the traditional title of the document. This text, even in our earliest references to it and in the earliest manuscripts, is titled "To the Hebrews." Whether this is or is not a letter, the title is curious. We do not know how or when or why it became the title of the document. All we know is that it was called this as early as the second century.

Thus, when we begin at the beginning, questions of setting, authorship, and destination immediately surface. If we want to know who, to whom, when, and why this letter was written, we must wait until we read more. The beginning gives conflicting hints.

> Long ago God spoke to our ancestors in many and various ways by the prophets, but in these last days he has spoken to us by a Son, whom he appointed heir of all things, through whom he also created the worlds. He is the reflection of God's glory and the exact imprint of God's very being, and he sustains all things by his powerful word. When he had made purification for sins, he sat down at the right hand of the Majesty on high, having become as much superior to angels as the name he has inherited is more excellent than theirs.
>
> (1:1–4)

It is surprising how quickly the letter throws the reader into theological argument without warning or preparation. The opening verses are seen by many as an excellent summary of the theology of the letter, or at least of the Christological part of that theology. But the letter has a complex and a bit disconcerting beginning. We are thrown into a quite complex discussion of the relationship between Christ and angels. Readers who want to understand the literary structure of this text are immediately puzzled. It is not clear how we should read this opening theological piece.

Three suggestions seem to get the most attention. Two of them find their key in the curious comparison of Jesus to angels which opens the letter. Jesus is "as much superior to angels as the name he has inherited is more excellent than theirs" (1:4). A series of biblical quotes follow which make the consistent point that the Son is better and has higher rank than the angels. Although an indirect hint is given about the coming presentation of Jesus as high priest in 1:3 ("When he had made purification of sins, he sat down at the right hand of the Majesty on high"), Jesus is not treated as high priest here but as Son.

From this some readers surmise that the veneration of angels must be the immediate problem. The author begins with a confession universal in the early church, namely, "Jesus is God's Son." He then builds on that universally accepted confession an argument about the relative status of Jesus and angels.

These same readers divide on why there might have been a problem with angels. In any case, this apparent problem with angels leads directly to two of the three suggestions about the immediate cause of the letter.

1. Some readers note that we have problems with angels elsewhere in the New Testament. Colossians 2:18 mentions the worship of angels and in 1:15–20 devotes energy to asserting the superiority of Jesus over all cosmic powers. The problems and the responses seem similar. Perhaps Hebrews was written about the same time as Colossians. Perhaps they both originated from the Lycus valley region, where we might imagine a general problem with Christians turning to old temple procedures, Jewish or Greek, to mollify the powers of the cosmos. Thus, Hebrews, first addresses the problem of rank in the cosmos and then the problem of temples and their sacrifices. The argument is that we need to turn neither to the Jewish temple or its replacements in the synagogue nor to Greco-Roman temples to deal with the ongoing problems of Christian life. Jesus is higher than all angels and is the perfect high priest.

2. Others contend that we do not have to go to Colossians to find an explanation of the problem of angels, since Hebrews 2:2 states the reason explicitly. Jewish tradition, probably in an effort to protect the transcendence of God, frequently maintained that the law was given to humans by angels. Paul also seems to know this tradition (Gal. 3:19). Thus, when Hebrews 2:2 connects angels and the old law, it is because the author of Hebrews is confronting the fact that Christians are wandering back to their Jewish roots. Belief in Jesus has not solved all their problems; in fact, it has made some things worse (Christians must suffer). And they are now drifting back to the synagogue. When the collectors of the early Christian manuscripts added the title "To the Hebrews" to our text, they were probably reading Hebrews in this way. Such a setting provides a nice context for the midrashic structure of the letter. If your audience is Jewish and perhaps you are a Jew yourself, you would naturally seek to understand Jesus by way of the sacred texts. You would read the Jesus story and the Old Testament together. This is, of course, precisely what Hebrews does.

3. These first two suggestions are a bit overly precise, overly determined. It is not clear that there really is a dire threat to the fidelity of the community such as these scenarios suggest. Hebrews seems to be written out of more calm than this. It reads more like exploration than refutation. Consequently, most readers point to 5:11–6:12 as the best evidence of the immediate cause of the letter. The letter is a call to move from "milk" to "solid food." "Therefore let us go on toward perfection, leaving behind the basic teachings about Christ, and not laying again the foundation" (6:1a). Of course, all Christian communities would have problems and weaknesses, and the two scenarios above may correctly identify them. But this is not a community in crisis. The real criticism in the letter of its readers is less that they have abandoned the basic teachings and more that they have become stuck in them. They need to move on to a more sophisticated theology and a more perfect moral life.

I find the last suggestion to be the most successful. However, all three suggestions are plausible. This means that it becomes difficult to establish precise details of the origins and purposes of the letter. Given the range of these scenarios, we could date the writing of Hebrews anywhere from about 60 C.E. (any earlier is hard to imagine) to 95 C.E. (when *1 Clement* quotes it). Places of origin include Palestine and almost anywhere else in the Roman world. We can assert with some surety that the author is a hellenized Jewish Christian, but that does not tell us very much. Thus, when we read Hebrews a certain formal ignorance about origin must be maintained.

The Road to Perfection

Part of the wonder of Hebrews is the diversity of theological concepts and images it employs in its arguments. Obviously, our reading of Hebrews thus far has not given full account of the enormous richness of this text. Without pretending to articulate completely every theological moment in this text, we shall attempt a more complete gathering of theological images in what follows.

In particular, by focusing where we have thus far, we have downplayed the force of the future, of divine promise, in the text. We noted at the beginning that the advent of Jesus creates a new dynamic both between the past and the present and between the present and the future. The main force of the arguments about Jesus as high priest in 4:14–10:18, at least in regard to the structure of time, is on the relationship between the past and the present. In some ways, the rest of Hebrews focuses on the relationship between the present and the future. Furthermore, in its explorations of the future, Hebrews draws on theological traditions and concepts that are not expressly derivative of priesthood theology. In particular, Hebrews finds its language of divine promise in a different part of the canon.

In Hebrews 3:7–9, after the series of superiority arguments that open the letter, the author quotes Psalm 95:7–11. He draws several conclusions from this text. First, even though God calls you, God will reject you if you reject God. This was true for ancient Israel and it is still true for his Christian readers. While this argument may be disturbing, it comes from a rather straightforward reading of the Psalm. However, Hebrews 4:1–11 represents a much more creative reading, which takes us to one of the most powerful and persistent points the author wants to make. If God swore in his anger that these disobedient Israelites "shall not enter my rest," this means that God's rest is still there, yet to be occupied. To swear this means that God has prepared rest for someone; to swear this means that Israel did not enter. Therefore, "the promise of entering his rest is still open" (4:1). God has an unfulfilled promise. This promise falls upon the early Christians. The conclusion is obvious: "Let us therefore make every effort to enter that rest, so that no one may fall through such disobedience as theirs" (4:11).

This promise of rest is a fundamental image in the theology of Hebrews. Most theology is built, to some extent, on God's promises. Most theology includes the conviction that the future will be better than the present. Most theology also includes the notion that what we have seen of God so far is not all that we shall see. Most theology then invokes the power of hope because we are trying to live now, based on a future we do not have. Hebrews builds on these familiar convictions in unfamiliar ways.

Perhaps the key move here is a Christological one. Christian readers have long been troubled by a series of statements that the author makes about Jesus. "Although he was a Son, he learned obedience through what he suffered; and having been made perfect, he became the source of eternal salvation for all who obey him" (5:8–9). "It was fitting that God ... should make the pioneer of their salvation perfect through suffering" (2:10). These statements have troubled orthodoxy because they suggest that Jesus did not start out being perfect, that he had to acquire perfection by obedience and suffering (see also 2:17–18; 7:28).

Perfection is acquired through a journey, a journey of obedience and suffering. Jesus is the pioneer, the one who leads the way, who opens the way, who makes those who follow perfect like himself. Jesus is still high priest, but he becomes high priest at the end of his journey. At one point he "was made lower than the angels," but was "crowned with glory and honor because of the suffering of death" (2:9). He had to endure life as a suffering human before he could be eternal high priest. As high priest, Jesus offers permanent forgiveness of sins, but only to those who follow him on this journey of obedience and suffering.

Readers have long noted that Hebrews treats Christians as a pilgrim people, as though we are still the wandering people of God, suffering now, but looking over across the Jordan into the promised land. And there is indeed suffering now. In 10:32–39, the author reminds the readers of their "hard struggle with sufferings" (10:32). Sometimes they themselves were "publicly exposed to abuse and persecution" (10:33); sometimes they were "partners with those so treated" (10:33). They "had compassion for those who were in prison, and you cheerfully accepted the plundering of your possessions" (10:34). Becoming a Christian does not seem to have made their lives better, if by "better" one means easier and safer. Christians suffer, not just because all humans suffer, but because Christianity itself is a journey through suffering.

The theological conflict is severe. On the one hand, God has promised rest. On the other hand, right now we have the very opposite of rest. We have social and political terror. It is natural then to look to other powers. Even if Jesus is the one who bestows final rest, it is not clear who bestows it now. We know that angels and temples and sacrifices and gods and goddesses have such powers. It makes good sense to seek their aid in the meantime, in the time before the end.

Hebrews responds not by declaring that these powers cannot help us. He may, in fact, believe that they could. He responds with a combination of promise and threat. Suffering is the road to rest. Look at Jesus' own story. He suffered, then he rested. The promise awaits. But if you waver, if you drift to other powers, God will cut you off from rest. "It is a fearful thing to fall into the hands of the living God" (10:31).

We are not alone in this journey. Not only has Jesus preceded us but so has a "great cloud of witnesses" (12:1). Hebrews' account of these witnesses in chapter 11 has proved to be the most powerful and popular passage in Hebrews for Christian readers. There are Abel, Enoch, Noah, Abraham, Isaac, Jacob, Joseph, Moses, Rahab—in fact, "time would fail me to tell of Gideon, Barak, Samson, Jephthah, of David and Samuel and the prophets" (11:32). All of these people remained faithful even though they did not receive their promises. This is what faith is: to live on the basis of promise. Faith, if it is faith, must have an aspect of not-having. If we have already received the promise, it loses its character as promise. Promise must remain beyond us. Faith is the continuing on even as the promise recedes. In fact, not only must the promised rest remain as promise, the present must be shaped by suffering. This is the life of faith.

"Now faith is the assurance of things hoped for, the conviction of things not seen" (11:1). Faith is a journey towards perfection. Faith is a journey towards a promise. Faith is a journey through suffering and obedience. Jesus is the pioneer and the high priest of that journey. But our ancestors, all of whom are pre-Christian Jews, can also show us the way. Our task is also to help others on the journey.

The classic Christian ethics that we find outlined in chapters 12 and 13 take shape in the context of this journey. The diverse imperatives in these chapters resist an easy summary. They range from such general Christian maxims as "Let marriage be held in honor by all" (13:4), "Keep your lives free from love of money" (13:5), "Pursue peace with everyone" (12:14), and "Let mutual love continue" (13:1), to imperatives that seem more particular to the motifs of journey and priesthood: "Endure trials for the sake of discipline" (12:7), "See to it that no one becomes like Esau" (12:16), and "Let us then go to him [Jesus] outside the camp and bear the abuse he endured" (13:13).

On the one hand, these imperatives seem to be animated by the gentle character of much of early Christian ethics. This common pattern of "mutual love," of support for one another both spiritually and materially, of submission to the general needs of the community, of a strict sexual ethic, probably has its ultimate origin in the mouth of the historical Jesus and its more proximate origin in the many collections of Jesus sayings of which the Sermon on the Mount was (and is) the most influential. Hebrews seems to participate fully in this gentle, gracious, communal ethic which so many early Christians enjoined upon themselves.

The ethic of Hebrews also seems to be animated by more particular theological notions. Your journey will ultimately bring you into the presence of the living God. This should give you pause. "You have not come to something that can be touched, a blazing fire, and darkness, and gloom, and a tempest"

(12:18). "For indeed our God is a consuming fire" (12:29). God is still the God who demands perfection. Only perfection can come into the presence of God and not be consumed by the consuming fire. This is why Jesus is the high priest. This is why his priesthood has this unique character: it can make you perfect, if you follow Jesus in suffering, obedience, and faith. Yet the journey is difficult. You are suffering now. And if you survive this suffering and hold to your faith, you will then come before the God of consuming fire.

> Therefore, since we are surrounded by so great a cloud of witnesses, let us also lay aside every weight and the sin that clings so closely, and let us run with perseverance the race that is set before us, looking to Jesus the pioneer and perfecter of our faith, who for the sake of the joy that was set before him endured the cross, disregarding its shame, and has taken his seat at the right hand of the throne of God.
>
> (Heb. 12:1–2)

Let us follow this Jesus, looking through our suffering to the promised rest, and gently help each other on the way.

Conclusion

Hebrews displays one of the classic ways Christians like to do theology. We take Christian confessions to a passage in the Bible and read the passage as though both the passage and the confessions we bring to it are true. In our readings, we try to surrender the truth of neither. We let both voices interact in ways we cannot fully control or anticipate.

Hebrews brings a sense of the temporal dislocations occasioned by the advent of Jesus to an intriguing set of biblical texts. The choice of texts cannot have been purely accidental. We must imagine that Hebrews reads these particular Old Testament texts because the results of the readings are somehow persuasive and helpful. These texts enable the author to work with the right set of theological issues. Thus, there is a certain utilitarian quality to the choice of texts.

However, there is a remarkable sense in all of these admittedly creative readings of Old Testament texts that the texts are always given their proper voice. For all the cleverness of Hebrews' reading of Psalm 110 or Psalm 95, there is no sense of misreading in the cleverness. The theology of Hebrews emerges, at least in part, from a respectful encounter with the syntax of these texts. The theology of Hebrews cannot exist apart from these texts. Part of what is being affirmed, in fact, is that our confessions about Jesus and the words of these texts cohere.

Furthermore, the core questions that Hebrews brings to these texts are some of the fundamental questions of Christian theology. For all the diversity of questions and issues that surface in Hebrews, they all derive from the newness created by the event of Christ. The reality of Christ changes things. The coming of Christ changes how the powers of the cosmos are configured. The coming of Christ changes the proper force of temples and sacrifices. Christ changes how certain texts should be read. He changes time—the past, the present, and the future. He changes how past, present, and future connect and do not connect to one another. He changes how people should live. And he changes our perception of hope, sin, God's righteousness, and salvation itself.

In pursuing these questions using these Old Testament texts, Hebrews creates a remarkable model of Christian theology. Christology, ethics, and exegesis are woven together in wonderfully productive ways. In doing this, Hebrews creates some of the finest passages in the New Testament.

However, the reading of Hebrews that we have given here also raises awkward issues for modern Christians. There are views of the self and of God in Hebrews that do not carry much credibility with many in the church. Hebrews has an uncompromising view of human sin and of the problem this raises for our relationship with God. In Hebrews, on the one hand, God is a God of absolute righteousness. On the other hand, people are absolute sinners. This creates an impossible conflict between God's righteousness and our sinfulness. This conflict is so absolute that, according to Hebrews at least, only blood and sacrifice can deal with the impasse.

This view of both the self and God seems overly severe to many of us today. Certainly, people are sinners, and certainly God is righteous. But people are not all that bad; we are both wonderful and terrible. And God is not only full of righteousness, God is full of grace, forgiveness, and understanding. Perhaps most of all, many of us do not understand why anyone would need atoning blood in order for there to be reconciliation. We do not ascribe such power to blood, whether it is Jesus' blood or not.

Connected to this absolute view of our sin is Hebrews' optimistic view of the future. Hebrews imagines human perfection and a time of perfect rest. Perhaps we should admit instead that humans will never be perfect; there will never be perfect rest. It is better to imagine humans as a combination of good and evil. We have always been and always will be some such combination. If we should improve, it will only be ever so slightly. Christian theology should not look to a perfect future with perfect Christians. We do better if we build our theology on a more balanced and realistic account of who we are and what the world is. Let us not despair too much over the sin in us, and let us not count too much on the grace in us. Finally, it is dangerous to live our lives believing in an absolutely secure victory for God. If we assume that there will be perfect rest and perfect righteousness in our future, we may abandon our responsibilities to create and order human history. We should not entrust the future solely to God. God has called us to build righteousness and justice here. Our task is not to wait but to work.

However, we might wonder if Hebrews can be so easily dismissed. Perhaps we, and not Hebrews, are the ones who misunderstand human evil. Maybe human sin is much more serious than we like to admit. Perhaps our puzzlement

over blood is part of the often-commented-upon Western hypocrisy about violence. Today may be the most violent time in human history, and yet you and
I dare not think about blood.

Most of all, I think Hebrews would say that we underestimate both ourselves and God. Whether or not the best words are "perfection" and "perfect
rest," at the heart of faith is a sense that there is more. Hebrews speaks to that
sense, which most believers have, of a better tomorrow. It speaks of a God
who has promised humans perfect rest. It points to the possibility of more. We
can be more. We can be more because God has promised that we shall be. We
should not give up on ourselves so easily. This "more," it seems to me, is a
good word to us.

2

James

"Faith without works is dead" (James 2:26). Christians, and perhaps all humans, have tried to maintain some kind of distance between their deeds and their true selves. We often have a certain disappointment with our acts. We think we could have done better. And we like to imagine that these dreams of a better self are who we really are. We want to believe that we are not fully identical with our acts.

In the arena of theology, we have wanted to maintain some kind of separation between faith and deeds. We think we can believe without fully living out the implications of our belief. We often lose our nerve or give in to temptation. But this failure of deed does not mean that we do not truly believe.

The letter of James critiques and complicates all such distinctions. In fact, James locates our true selves in our acts, not in our words or our thoughts or our feelings. We are what we do. It is our words not our deeds that deceive us. It is only in an actual deed that we fully manifest what we truly believe. The reason our deeds do not match our confessions of faith is that we do not truly believe our own confessions. What we believe is fully and completely displayed in what we do.

The letter of James offers one of the most compelling and influential accounts of Christian ethics in all of Christian literature. It is a bold and insistent call to live the moral life. James has had a long and powerful influence on how Christians imagine their moral lives. But for all the wonders of his ethics, James has also attracted controversy. His letter is famous (and infamous) for its insistence that faith must live in works and that wisdom is less an act of knowing than a life of doing. In James, righteousness is not the automatic result of faith but is carved out of the deeds of your life. His elevation of works to heights equal to that of faith has led to many complaints, such as Luther's famous designation of James as "a right strawy epistle."

Two passages, above all, sit at the center of this controversy (James 1:22–25; 2:14–26). Twice in his brief letter James separates doers of the word from non-doers, although in each instance the non-doer is described differently. These two passages, which have been read and debated so often, may indeed hold the key to the theology of James. They are, therefore, an excellent place to begin one's reading.

35

Doers of the Word

The oft-quoted passage in 1:22–25 distinguishes "doers of the word" from the "merely hearers," while the much-debated passage in 2:14–26 distinguishes "works" from "faith." The initial challenge in 1:22 seems straightforward enough: "Be doers of the word, and not merely hearers who deceive themselves." This admonition leads into the well-known analogy of people who look in a mirror. Mere hearers are like those who look in a mirror, see themselves, then on leaving the mirror forget who they are.

Like many analogies, this one is a bit puzzling. Analogies always work on a creative combination of likeness and unlikeness: X is like Y, even though X and Y are different. And readers must create a map of likeness and unlikeness to make the analogy work. However, readers of James have puzzled over just where the likeness occurs in this mirror analogy, or at least what the extent of the likeness might be. Fortunately, 1:25 draws the basic map of the analogy: "But those who look into the perfect law, the law of liberty, and persevere, being not hearers who forget but doers who act—they will be blessed in their doing."

At first reading, this seems clear enough. We hear the word; the word tells us who we are; it draws a picture of the righteous life; we, in turn, must do what the word tells us to do; we must draw with the deeds of our lives that picture of ourselves spoken to us in the word. James will paint some of the details of that picture later in the letter.

However, this text has proven to be less clear than it first appears. We are not certain precisely what "word" means in these expressions. Christian readers have naturally tended to understand the "word" as the gospel. But then, it is not clear what "gospel" might mean in James. Furthermore, the "word" in verse 22 seems in verse 25 to be called "the perfect law, the law of liberty." Thus, word appears to be both gospel and law. Thus, if the key for James is the doing of the word, we must first know what this word is. And our initial readings suggest that "word" in James may not mean what it often does in Christian theology.

In the second passage (2:14–26), wherein James seems to focus on this doing of the word, the terminology changes from the verbs "do" and "hear" to the nouns "works" and "faith." This is, as every reader admits, a complex passage, which is animated by a series of four analogies interspersed with declarations about faith and works. The passage begins with two questions that seem to imply the basic theses of the verses that follow: "What good is it, my brothers and sisters, if you say you have faith but do not have works? Can faith save you?" (2:14). The presiding issue is salvation. What saves us? The working categories for these questions are faith and works. Faith and works seem to belong together, to the same questions, to the same persons, to the same moments. But in belonging together they remain crucially distinct.

The explicit declarations make a similar point.

So faith by itself, if it has no works, is dead. (2:17)

Show me your faith apart from your works, and I by my works will show you my faith. (2:18b)

You see that faith was active along with works, and faith was brought to completion by the works. (2:22)

You see that a person is justified by works and not by faith alone. (2:24)

For just as the body without the spirit is dead, so faith without works is also dead. (2:26)

Without becoming too entangled in the subtle differences that might exist in these declarations, a basic geography of faith and works can be constructed. While faith and works are distinct, neither can exist without the other. It is assumed in these sentences that works grows out of faith. Exactly how is not made clear. It is also assumed that one can at least think about faith apart from works, since it is this proposition which is apparently under attack. In slightly different ways, each sentence insists that faith needs works, that works belong to faith and that faith without works is, well, "dead."

For all the controversy and confusion these passages have produced in Christian theology, they are wonderful entries into the theology of James. The necessary interconnectedness of faith and works, which is articulated in these passages, in many ways comprises the heart of the theology of James. Believing and doing, in his theology, belong to the same moment. The many Christian readers who have wondered whether James is not, to some extent, contradicting Paul's separation of faith and works are, in fact, reading James correctly. (Whether they are reading Paul correctly or not is another question.) Jesus, in the letter of James, is not the one who died for our sins. Jesus is our teacher. Furthermore, he is not a teacher of universal moral truths; Jesus is the teacher of the "perfect law" (1:25). The gospel and the law are one and the same in James. Salvation comes not purely from a Christological act but from our own deeds of obedience.

James thereby focuses the reality of faith and salvation on the interaction between one human and another. Faith is always ethical. It is in our behavior toward other people that our faith lives. It is in the interconnectedness between one person and another that salvation becomes possible. The letter of James demands righteous behavior. Furthermore, it sketches for its readers a fairly clear picture of that behavior using classic Old Testament images such as righteousness, justice, and peace. It draws especially on a set of Jesus' sayings that apparently come from the same tradition as does the Sermon on the

Mount. In fact, the theology of James reads a lot like the theology of the Sermon on the Mount. In this focus on our relationship to the other, James articulates one of the most persistent themes in Christian thought. Many Christians through the centuries have argued that faith, law, salvation, righteousness, and the kingdom of God find their real place in the encounter with another person. James takes us deep into the possibilities and temptations of how one person treats another.

In this account of the Christian life, James includes treatments of several classic Christian problems. He will discuss the violent disparities between the rich and the poor. He will address the ongoing Christian love of the things of the world, noting that this love divides us from our love of God. He will address the problems of suffering and of the many trials and temptations of faith.

Much of the ethic in James has a universalistic cast to it. The ethic comes in the form of general maxims and exhortations that could be followed by both Christians and non-Christians. Nevertheless, the ethic of James is not a free-standing ethic in which the imperatives are self-justifying. This ethic is built upon a particular vision of who God is. It is God who makes this life possible. If the task of being a Christian is the task of living the law of liberty in our lives, we can only do so because God supplies us with what we need in order to live this life. For instance, we can know the content of this law only because God has revealed it and because Jesus has taught it. We can only live this law because God gives us the wisdom and power to do so. And ultimately we can and should live this law only because God's righteousness and final judgment stand behind it.

Outline of James

1:1   Opening salutation
1:2–18   Trials and temptations
1:19–27   Doers of the word
2:1–7   Partiality toward the rich
2:8–13   Fulfilling the whole law
2:14–26   Faith without works is dead
3:1–12   The dangers of the tongue
3:13–18   Wisdom from above
4:1–10   Conflicts and humility
4:11–12   Warning against judging one another
4:13–17   Boasting
5:1–6   Warning to the rich
5:7–11   Patience and suffering
5:12–20   Call to prayer

Universal Ethic

Crucial to our understanding of any text is our first impression of it. First impressions function as a kind of anchor, almost as a corrective, to the more aggressive readings that often follow. Once we begin to pull a text apart, to dig behind it, to overwhelm it with various reading strategies, a text can cease to look like itself. It is always important to remember what impressions result from an initial reading of the text, since those first readings tend to adhere closely to the surface structures of the text.

Initial reactions to James are remarkably consistent, at least among Christian readers. And the most common initial reading is the one signaled above: James promotes an inviting and challenging ethic. In fact, James not only promotes this ethic, James insists on it, placing it at the heart of the gospel and everyone under the threat and promise of judgment. This focus on ethics has been perceived as the primary force and importance of James. And any reader of James must come to terms with this ethic. However, this focus on ethics, along with the declaration that faith without works is dead, has troubled Christian readers, who wonder how to square James with Paul. Christians have struggled to reconcile "faith without works is dead" (James 2:26) with "a person is justified not by works of the law but through faith in Jesus Christ" (Gal. 2:16). Paul and James seem to contradict each other.

We started this chapter with the two passages that not only have dominated post-Luther scholarship on James but that also have, from the beginning, highlighted the distinctiveness of James. These passages have occasioned a certain tension or even conflict in our initial reaction to the text. We shall try to keep this conflict in mind in the readings which follow.

We have argued above that a necessary moment in reading well is an attempt to understand the text as the original author wanted it understood. Thus, all the chapters in this volume devote considerable energy to hearing the text on its own terms. We try to understand the individual images in a text, first of all, in their relationship to the other images in a text. We even try to imagine what the author was thinking in the moment of writing. We have, of course, mentioned some of the problems with these attempts, and yet the endeavor remains necessary to any good reading. However, it turns out that James creates a unique set of problems for any effort to read it historically. Both the attempt to hear the author's organizing point of view and the attempt to comprehend the organizing system of the text prove quite difficult.

In fact, the most common reading by historical critics concludes that the text of James is a divided, composite text that cannot be gathered into a singular point of view. It has neither literary nor theological unity. The author was not attempting to promote a systematic theology. There is not a single organizing point of view behind this text. Perhaps one hand wrote it, but the role of that hand was simply to collect disparate materials into one text. So our reading of the text must reflect its divided nature. We should not try to cram the diversity of the text into one theology or one literary intention. Both the text and the original intentions of the author resist and undermine any attempt at a unified reading.

The reasons for this common historical reading are rather obvious. James reads like a loose collection of moral maxims and illustrations. It is unclear, on first reading at least, how these diverse maxims connect to one another and what might be the organizing literary structure of the letter. One topic leads to another without apparent cause. For instance, the letter opens with a call to joy in testing (1:2–4), moves to a comment on wisdom and true faith (1:5–8), then admonishes the lowly to boast in being raised and the rich to boast in being brought low (1:9–11). There is no explicit attempt to connect one theme to another. The whole letter moves in this unpredictable and jerky fashion.

The cause of this disconnectedness, say some historians, lies in the nature of ancient ethical exhortation. Ancient parenesis (ethical exhortation), whether Greek, Jewish, or Christian, is eclectic in form. It moves loosely from one topic to another. Even if a consistent theology or philosophy undergirds the ethic, that theology remains unstated. In fact, to detail that theology would distract from the ethics. Ethical persuasion works best with loose argumentation, diverse images, and eclectic rhetoric. Formal and systematic argumentation is less persuasive in moral discourse. Thus, even if James should have a consistent theology, that theology remains offstage. Therefore, it is not only laborious to reconstruct its theology, it is also virtually impossible to evaluate the results. Even if we should guess at the theology behind this text, there is no way to know if we have guessed correctly.

Many readers assert that James has no theology at all apart from standard Jewish and Christian notions of God as creator and judge (1:17–18; 4:11–12). And the occasional theological notions that surface in the letter represent nothing more than standard (and nearly ubiquitous) Jewish theological premises. Furthermore, these occasional images should not be combined into any system, no matter how loose.

Under such a reading, James becomes uniquely accessible to modern readers. It requires no special theological convictions. And, more importantly, its argument is couched in the form of universal ethical maxims, which in their very form address the general reader. It is the nature of the ethical teachings found in James that they want to escape their historical context. For example, when James announces in 1:27 that pure religion is "to care for orphans and widows in their distress," it is articulating a permanent theological truth not limited to the time and culture of its inscription. This saying has coinage for any person anywhere anytime. Its power depends on the creative insight of the reader, who as moral agent will perceive the universal truth in the words and seek occasion to live it in a new time and new place. In this sense, the truth of the saying for a reader may be that "orphans and widows" for them may not be orphans and widows at all, but street people and refugees. It takes a creative and committed moral agent to give life to these sayings.

To comprehend and live the call to care for widows and orphans does not necessarily depend on any theological point of view. Any Jew, Christian, Muslim, Buddhist, or atheist who pursues moral insight can be the hearer and doer of this maxim. Anyone can care for widows. It takes no particular religious convictions to do so. We can easily pull this maxim from James, disconnecting it from any theological notions, and from all other maxims, in the letter. The maxim in 1:27 is not grounded in the theological or ethical system of the text or the historical culture of James. Its universal intentions means that it is grounded in any sympathetic and wise reader. Any reader at any time and any place can be the proper destination for this text.

James is thus frequently understood as a gathering of timeless moral and religious maxims. Not only does it have no explicit theological system, it would be an impoverishment of its power and an abuse of its voice to articulate a theological or even ethical system for it. Each maxim, each argument, stands on its own. We should not try to connect, for instance, the condemnations of the rich to the admonitions on the tongue either by imagining a social situation in James's original audience or by creating an ethical or theological system that orders both maxims. They each live on their own. If they come together, it is just by way of the accidents of life.

James is thus best understood, in his scenario, as a collection. It is a historically fascinating collection because it pulls from so many sources. Much of it is standard Jewish ethics: concern for orphans and widows, conflict between rich and poor, images of the perfect law, and the classic Jewish terms of righteousness and peace. We hear the somewhat more Christian themes of remaining unstained by the world and the power of prayer to heal the sick. Of course, most, if not all, of the ethic is a combination of common Christian and Jewish themes: love of neighbor, humility, and so on. Some of it also seems to belong to humanity in general: "the tongue is a fire" (3:6).

Jesus as Teacher of the Perfect Law

Most readers hear the peculiar voice of Jesus himself in both the selection of issues and the way some issues are addressed in James. There is a series of echoes of or parallels to the Sermon on the Mount.

| James 1:2 | Whenever you face trials of any kind, consider it nothing but joy. | Matt. 5:11–12 | Blessed are you when people revile you and persecute you. Rejoice and be glad. |
| James 1:4 | So that you may be perfect and complete. | Matt. 5:48 | Be perfect, therefore, as your heavenly Father is perfect. |

James 1:5	Ask God, who gives to all generously and ungrudgingly.	Matt. 7:7	Ask, and it will be given to you.
James 1:22	Be doers of the word and not merely hearers	Matt 7:24	Everyone who hears these words of mine and acts on them.
James 2:5	Has not God chosen the poor in the world	Matt. 5:3	Blessed are the poor in spirit.
James 2:10	For whoever keeps the whole law but fails in one point has become accountable for all of it.	Matt. 5:19	Whoever breaks one of the least of these commandments ... will be called least in the kingdom of heaven.
James 2:13	Mercy triumphs over judgment.	Matt. 5:7	Blessed are the merciful, for they will receive mercy.
James 3:12	Can a fig tree yield ... olives?	Matt. 7:16	Are grapes gathered from thorns?
James 5:2–3	Your riches have rotted, and your clothes are moth-eaten ... You have laid up ... treasure for the last days.	Matt. 6:19–20	Do not store up for yourselves treasures on earth, where moth and rust consume ... but store up ... treasures in heaven.
James 5:12	Do not swear, either by heaven or by earth or by any other oath, but let your "Yes" be yes and your "No" be no.	Matt. 5:34–37	Do not swear at all, either by heaven ... or by earth. Let your word be "Yes, Yes" or "No, No."

This list could easily be extended. The teachings of Jesus recorded in the Sermon on the Mount (Matt. 5–7), which are themselves a complex and even original combination of traditional Jewish and Greek ethics, seem to form the loudest voice in James. James presents for us a glimpse of the ongoing vitality of the teachings of Jesus in the church. This reconfigured voice of Jesus may be the primary theological force of the letter.

Its theology would be this: Jesus is our teacher. This is not to say that Jesus in his teachings provides a theology, but that Jesus being teacher is the theology. Thus, if Jesus is the teacher, the voice, whose words we are to both hear and do, he provides an organizing force only by virtue of his name and not by providing a conceptual system. This would mean that the task of every Christian is to hear, learn, study, and then do the words of Jesus. James is not a collection of Jesus sayings in itself. It is already a meditation and adaptation of those sayings, an example of how to study those words. It is a living, serious attempt to learn and live the words of the Lord. Theology for us, then, is to do likewise.

There is, however, something misleading in this account. It makes Jesus sound like a universal moral teacher who has no history; it brings Jesus too quickly to us; it forgets, overlooks, and misrepresents the peculiar Jewish cast of James. If there is in the form and purpose of James a push towards the universal, a persistent attempt to escape the confinements of the first century, a call to any human as reader, there is also an embeddedness in first-century Judaism. As readers have always noted, the God of James is the traditional God of the Old Testament. This God is creator and judge (e.g., 1:17–18; 4:11–12); this God is committed to righteousness and peace (e.g., 1:20–21; 3:13–18; 4:6–12); this God answers prayers (5:13–18) and gives gifts (e.g., 1:5, 17–18; 2:5; 4:2–3). This is the God of Israel. The character of this God should not be passed over as irrelevant background. The ethic of James is not self-justifying; it is God's will and God's purpose for us. The God of Israel funds the ethic. Moreover, Jesus is not merely a teacher of universal truths; he is the teacher of "the perfect law, the law of liberty" (1:25). Of course, this perfect law is both universal and true.

We can now nuance more adequately the basic theological framework of James: Jesus is the teacher of the perfect law of the God of Israel. There is, therefore, no distance between the words of Jesus and the words of the law. When scholars debate, whether "the word" we are to hear and do in James 1:22 is the word of God or the word of Jesus, whether it is Old Testament law or the sayings of Jesus, they are dividing what cannot be divided. The words of Jesus are the law, and, as the law, they belong to the history of Israel and the God of Israel.

It becomes clear, then, why we cannot decide whether James is more Jewish or more Christian. Some readers see James as a collection of common Jewish ethics sprinkled with a few Christian terms. Others see James as a meditation on the sayings of Jesus sprinkled with a soft background of Old Testament terminology. The question of whether James is Jewish or Christian cannot be answered because it is both. That is its core affirmation. Jesus is the teacher of the perfect law.

The eclecticism of James is constitutive of its theology. James gathers in one passage a loose quote from Deuteronomy, a creative rendition of a Jesus saying, a generalization about God, an example from everyday life, and a dizzying variety of commonplace maxims and specific exhortations. This coming together in one place of all these voices is the theology of the letter. Furthermore, this gathering cannot be final. If Jesus is the teacher of the perfect law, then we need more than the text of James. Other sayings of Jesus, other lines from the Old Testament, other words of the perfect law will be needed. James is only one moment in this process of theological gathering.

However, not just any gathering will do. Some words are more important than others.

A Letter

James begins like a letter. This in itself embeds it in a specific moment. Letters are sent by specific people to specific people at a specific time. Letters belong to the sender and the recipients, in different ways, but they do not belong to us. Thus, in our attempt to read this text fairly and well, we want to identify with the sender and recipient. This means we have the hard labor of historical reconstruction. We want to know who the author was, why he wrote, what he knew and did not know. We want to know, perhaps above all, how he wanted this text to be read. We have similar interests in the recipients. We want to know who they were and how they would have read the letter. We look for data to feed our historical imaginations. But it is the case with James, as with many ancient texts, that these historical reconstructions are tentative. It is difficult to get enough data in which we have much confidence.

> James, a servant of God and of the Lord Jesus Christ, to the twelve tribes in the Dispersion: Greetings.
>
> (1:1)

The letter begins in standard Greek form: author to recipient, greetings. But the greeting in James does not tell the modern reader much. It is not clear who this James is. Two Jameses are listed among the Twelve: James the son of Zebedee and brother of John, and James the son of Alphaeus. We know very little of either. According to Acts 12:1–3, James the son of Zebedee was martyred by Herod Agrippa I in the early 40s. We know nothing of James of Alphaeus apart from his name and his listing among the Twelve. The most famous James in early Christianity was, of course, James the brother of Jesus. About this James we know a good bit more. He is inscribed as a key figure in the controversies between Christians in Jerusalem and Antioch (Acts 12:17; 15:12–21; Gal. 1:19; 2:9, 12). Descriptions of him in both Acts and Galatians (and in later tradition) indicate that he believed that Christians should follow the law. Such a portrait fits well with what we have seen thus far in James.

Perhaps our James is one of these three, or perhaps our James is a person unknown to us. Most scholars today think that the author of our text was none of the three Jameses named above. The letter reflects a quality of Greek and a stage in the development of early Christianity that do not fit easily with any James we know. All three of these people named James would speak out of early Palestinian Christianity. However, it is unlikely that our letter is either early or Palestinian. It is more likely that the author was a person unknown to us whose real name was James or who was pretending to be James the brother of Jesus.

Many readers suggest that an unknown James, who calls himself "a servant of God and of our Lord Jesus Christ," writes to "the twelve tribes in the Dispersion." His self-designation is a natural one for an early Christian. It is a bit puzzling why an unknown James would write a letter to "the twelve tribes in the Dispersion." An unknown might designate himself this way when writing to friends or to people who know him. But his audience is too general. In fact, most readers think that an address of such imprecision means that this cannot be a real letter that was actually delivered. All of this leads many readers, including me, to decide that this unknown writer is writing under the name of James the brother of Jesus. Nevertheless, if an unknown person is indeed writing under the pseudonym of James the brother of Jesus, it would make sense to actually call himself "brother." Instead, he designates himself a "servant" of Jesus and not brother. This awkwardness leads some people back to the suggestion that James the brother of Jesus wrote the letter himself. He called himself "servant" rather than "brother" out of modesty.

It is not clear how much help for the task of reading any of these suggestions might provide. The results are too tentative, and, even if true, provide little guidance for how we are to read. We are left with reconstructing information about the author and the recipients from hints in the text of James. We can, of course, place them both in the shifting background of early Christianity, and that helps some.

Consequently we must focus on the letter itself for guidance in how to read it. The letter itself suggests several possibilities. (1) Readers have always noted that James has the salutation of a letter but lacks a typical epistolary greeting and benediction at the end. It has a sender but a destination that is too general. Some readers feel that this compromised form indicates that this was not a real letter, but a general treatise, an ethical essay, addressed to any Christian reader. (2) Others think that the mention of the twelve tribes of the Diaspora indicates a Jewish Christian audience. (3) Still others think they see a specific community, the character of which can be reconstructed from the letter.

These choices give us some interesting and important reading options. If, for instance, James is a letter sent to a specific community with specific problems, then both the problems and solutions inscribed in it belong first of all to the peculiarities of that community. The advice, in spite of its generalized form, may have more limited intentions. The imperatives may belong to the specific difficulties in one community long ago. In which case, we should be careful about applying them in unaltered form to ourselves.

No matter what one's choice among the preceding options, the question remains as to whether there is some internal logic to the diverse moral exhortations in the letter. Even if there is not a full theology articulated here, there may be a thematic order of some kind. The reading of James given in this volume suggests that we do not have here just a chaotic gathering of loosely related themes, but an ordered and coherent interconnection among these themes. In fact, my opening account of James as a disordered gathering runs contrary to our most natural reading instincts. Readers look for order, for coherence, for compatibility. Even if we, the readers, do not need system, we want connectedness of some kind from one passage, from one theme, to another.

Some readers suggest that there is a literary order rather than a thematic order in James, an unfolding of the argument that follows good rhetorical norms. There have been frequent attempts to discover a governing rhetoric in the letter. There are undeniable repetitions and parallelisms in the letter. Any casual reading notices these. Some readers go further and find a sophisticated pattern of inverse parallelism that governs both the larger structure of the letter and the order of individual passages. But most readers find such a pattern too subtle and too infrequent to be convincing.

There is, nevertheless, a prevailing conviction among readers that a view of James as a chaotic gathering of disconnected themes is inadequate. Something approaching a coherent and consistent ethic is offered here.

Wisdom, the Word, and the Law

As we saw above, James seems to equate the law with the word. The hearing and doing of this law, this word, is an essential moment in salvation. In our account of James 1:22–25, we understood "the perfect law, the law of liberty," as the torah, the Old Testament law. Many Christian readers resist this equation. If this "word" either is or includes the sayings of Jesus, then traditional theology, which wants to separate Old Testament law from the sayings of Jesus, resists reading "word" as "torah." Furthermore, it is difficult to understand how the law, which undergoes such serious critique in Paul, can be named "law of liberty." It is more adequate theologically to see the "law of liberty" as the commandments of Jesus, not as Old Testament law. But this separation undoes, in my opinion, the prevailing rhetoric of the letter. It is precisely the rolling together of Jesus' sayings, Old Testament law, and general maxims that forms the argument of James.

James may also equate this law of liberty with wisdom. Wisdom is a gift of God (1:5); it comes from above (3:17); and it issues in the righteous life (3:17–18). Word and wisdom are often identified in Jewish theology, so it would be easy to equate the two here. But, perhaps it is more adequate to see word and law as something external into which one can look (1:25), while wisdom refers to an internal gift from above, which enables us to understand and live the word.

There is, in any case, in James the conviction that the road to righteousness comes from outside of us. We do not find ourselves in ourselves. We find ourselves in a law, a word, which comes from above, from outside of us. We see ourselves, recognize ourselves, in our portrayal in this law. Then in the understanding and doing of this word, empowered perhaps by divine wisdom, we become that true self, that righteous self. We can even read, study, and learn this self, since it exists in words.

The vision of the self here is less of someone who thinks a certain thing, who believes a certain way, or who even possesses internally a certain set of virtues. What is envisioned here is a self who behaves a certain way. The imperatives in James relate less to describing what kind of person we should become and more to how we interact with others. This is one of the reasons words of Jesus, wisdom, and Old Testament law must be intertwined. The public nature of the law, the social realities of righteousness, and the indebtedness of one person to all other persons is assumed here. A certain set of interactions among persons is commanded here. The word, wisdom, the law of liberty all create relationships and obligations. The goal in James is not to create a series of holy and self-sufficient individuals. The goal is far more social and communal than that.

Thus, the emphasis on doing as opposed to merely hearing does not come from a philosophy of the self wherein we are what we do, although such a philosophy might be assumed here. The emphasis is on classic Jewish righteousness. Thus, true religion is "to care for orphans and widows in their distress" (1:27). This naming of orphans and widows may be understood as shorthand for the whole set of prophetic concerns for justice and righteousness. Of course, these orphans and widows are still real orphans and widows for whom we must care.

Reading further in 1:27, James also describes true religion as keeping oneself "unstained by the world." This cannot be a call for ascetic withdrawal, a command to retreat from the world and its social and political complexities. We cannot manage righteousness and justice if we are in retreat. Instead, we should read 1:27 through the lens of 4:1–5:6. The world is the place that evokes our desire for things. We want "something and do not have it" (4:2). This wanting leads to conflict, hatred, and even killing of other people. Our love of the world leads us to make the world a place of violence and injustice. The law of liberty, on the other hand, draws a portrait of the world as full of peace and righteousness. Thus, if we want the world to be good, we must keep ourselves unstained by it. We must keep ourselves free of the desires the world provokes in us.

There is no opposition here between the needs of the world and the commandments of God. Rather, our love of the world undermines the proper needs of the world. Thus, there is considerable irony in the assertion, "Do you not know that friendship with the world is enmity with God? Therefore whoever wishes to be a friend of the world becomes an enemy of God" (4:4). When we love the world, we love it selfishly for the things the world can give us. In a way, only God truly loves the world because only God sees its potential for justice and righteousness.

This view of God is the classic view of Old Testament prophecy. God has intentions for us, for society. God has revealed and is revealing those intentions. God will judge us all by the bar of those intentions. James assumes this complex background of Old Testament theology. For the most part, he evokes it only in brief allusions. But we misunderstand the force of the word that we are to hear and do if we disconnect this word from the creating and judging God of Israel.

All of this creates the very traditional configuration of commandments and judgment. Thus, the question "Can faith save you?" (2:14) comes in the context of judgment. We are saved only by God at the final coming of the Lord. Salvation is eschatological, because salvation comes at the end (the eschaton) (5:7–11). Today, if we do the word, we can have "a harvest of righteousness" which "is sown in peace for (or by) those who make peace" (3:18). But we cannot have final salvation. Not yet.

Thus, James invokes the common Jewish and Christian theme of patience, of waiting, of expectation. The series of exhortations, warnings, and promises in 5:7–11 show how traditional the theology of James is at this point. "Be patient … until the coming of the Lord" (5:7a). "Strengthen your hearts, for the coming of the Lord is near" (5:8b). "The judge is standing at the doors" (5:9b). We are pointed to Job (5:11) and the prophets (5:10) for their endurance, their capacity to wait, and promised that God is "compassionate and merciful" for those who endure (5:11).

Thus, salvation comes to those who hear and do the law of liberty. Salvation comes from outside. It is not a state we are in now. We do not find the way to salvation by an inward journey. We hear the public word. We learn it. We perform it in wisdom. We endure. God, in turn, rewards us with salvation.

The problem with faith on its own is that it is not yet obedience and thus it is not yet righteousness. Faith is probably necessary, although there is some room for debate here. But "works" seems to be the dominant category. And it also seems to be the individual and not the community or the society that is judged. There is a certain individualism that is put in place in comparison to the great prophetic critiques, which tended to address Israel or Judah as a whole. This is consonant with the wisdom motifs in James. Wisdom tends to focus on the individual in ways that prophecy does not. But it is also the tendency of the time in which James was written. The first century of the Christian era, the time of the early Roman Empire, was a time when the individual was increasingly being addressed in independence from his or her community.

James mirrors this focus upon the individual but in distinctive ways. The great prophetic visions of community, of public life, are not lost. Thus, James is not trying to create the balanced, perfect, and virtuous self. James seems minimally interested in the internal geography of the self and its harmony, or lack thereof. James catches the individual in her or his public moments. James focuses upon how people treat their neighbor, the rich, or the poor. James points to how each person reacts to trials and persecutions. The concern of James is the individual as the individual turns toward the other. Thus, the righteousness and the peace envisioned here live in the traffic from one human to another.

The Rich and the Poor

Given these assumptions of prophetic justice and given the attention on how one person treats another, the discussion of the rich and the poor acquires particular weight (1:9–11; 2:1–7; 5:1–6). Nothing can display our secret allegiances to the world as much as the differences in how we treat the rich and the poor. James puts this division in our behavior at the heart of his challenge to us. Many readers think this discussion in James reflects a real problem in the community or communities to which James is writing. This could, of course, be the case, but it is impossible to reconstruct the facts. We might say, a bit cynically, that every Christian community everywhere has always had and will always have this problem. So even if a specific event elicited the discussion in James, the problem is universal.

James addresses the poor (or "the believer who is lowly") only in passing, admonishing them to "boast in being raised up" (1:9). But he addresses the rich twice (1:10–11; 5:1–6) and devotes his longest argument to brothers (and sisters) who show favoritism toward the rich (2:1–13). In these three passages we can see how the theology of James works. We can see how diverse the theological voices in James really are.

The first admonition to the rich is rather mild, at least in comparison to what follows. The rich are admonished, in contrast to the lowly, to "boast ... in being brought low" (1:10). The reason given is rather disconcerting: "because the rich will disappear like a flower in the field" (1:10). How to read this "being brought low" is rather unclear. The warnings in chapter 5 sound eschatological; they appear to be final judgment warnings. But it seems unlikely that the rich are being admonished to boast in their low status on judgment day. Thus, most readers imagine a social leveling that is occurring in Christian communities. The rich and the poor are drifting toward having the same status in the community, or at least to the point where their relative wealth is not a factor in their status.

This reading suggests that the final leveling that will occur on the day of judgment, when God's righteousness is realized, is being anticipated now in the community. In the imagery of James, the withering of the rich on the day of judgment is being accomplished and celebrated now. In this imagery of social reversal, we are touching on one of the most powerful and pervasive themes in early Christianity. Although the prophets provide many details of this social, political, and economic reversal which the coming of justice shall accomplish, the more proximate source of the imagery is the teachings of Jesus. The promise of the first being the last, the blessings on the poor, the woes on the rich, the story of Lazarus, and much more in the Jesus material evoke this prophetic portrait of justice and its reversals.

Scholars have coined the term "eschatological community" to describe those who live in anticipation of the end in the present. Christians were trying to live out of end-time realities now. Throughout the New Testament we can see traces of this experiment in social leveling. To what extent this radical egalitarian vision was ever realized in real life is unclear. Certainly by the time we get enough data in the second century to draw social portraits of early Christian groups, we discover groups with extensive hierarchies based on economic and political status. The absolute social leveling of the kind evoked in James has become either an ideal that animates a compromised justice or an ideal that provokes renegade communities to withdraw from the mainstream.

Furthermore, it is not even clear in James what is being envisioned. There are still poor and rich in the community, although the rich fall under dire warnings. There is no program of Marxist exchange. It seems to be more a sense of the moment of Christian gathering having a special dynamic. Here, when Christians gather, there is no favoritism, no division of rich and poor. Here, when Christians gather, all status acquired out there is shed. Status here has to do with loving your neighbor as yourself.

The theological forces here are complex. In 5:1–6, classic prophetic condemnations of the rich are gathered into the most startling denouncement of the rich in the New Testament. There seems to be no room to maneuver here. "Weep and wail for the miseries that are coming to you" (5:1). "Your riches have rotted" (5:2a). "Your gold and silver have rusted," and that rust "will eat your flesh like fire" (5:3a). "The wages of the laborers who mowed your fields," whom you defrauded, "cry out" (5:4a). And their cries reach the "ears of the Lord of hosts" (5:4b). "You have fattened your hearts in a day of slaughter" (5:5b). The great prophetic cry for justice and the brutal imagery of that cry are here applied in full force to the rich.

The question then becomes, exactly what are the rich expected to do? The only advice is "to weep and wail for the miseries that are coming to you" (5:1). The rich are not told to sell all they have and give to the poor, although it sounds like good advice. The rich are simply and terrifyingly condemned.

The admonition against partiality in 2:1–13 offers quite different reasoning. To our ongoing favoritism towards the rich and our ongoing ostracism of the poor, James asks two questions. First, "Has not God chosen the poor in the world to be rich in faith and to be heirs of the kingdom?" (2:5). In one sense, the question contains its answer and its argument. God has chosen the poor. However, by speaking in this indirect manner the precise theology of God's choosing of the poor remains unstated. This sparse argumentation is typical of James. Theology is invoked in shorthand. James assumes a larger fund of knowledge and imagery than it actually inscribes. It assumes readers who know other texts and other arguments. There are, of course, many ways we could narrate God's choosing of the poor. The Old Testament and the sayings of Jesus offer numerous options. James may have one option in mind, although it seems to most readers as though he does not care which we choose. The fact that there is a variety of possible sources here, the fact that the background of the question seems uncontrollably diverse and full, adds weight to the argument. We know in many forms the truth implied in the question. Yes, God has chosen the poor. The conclusion to this first question, as is typical of James, remains unstated, perhaps because it is so obvious: If God has chosen the poor, why do you choose the rich?

The second question is of a different order. Rather than turning again to this fund of theology, the argument evokes the social experience of the readers. "Is it not the rich who oppress you? Is it not they who drag you into court? Is it not they who blaspheme the excellent name that was invoked over you?" (2:6–7). These three questions call to mind the injustices which the rich inflict on others. The most curious is the last, wherein the rich are described as blaspheming "the excellent name that was invoked over you" (2:7). It is possible to imagine different scenarios here. Many readers see these questions, especially the third one, as evidence that early Christianity was a movement of the poor. The "name," we assume, is Jesus. The blaspheming could be either of Jesus himself or of the poor who bear the name or both.

All of this creates an image of the church that is composed of the poor or at least of the not-rich. In which case the condemnations of the rich are for the ears of the poor. The rich will never read them. These verses would be like condemnations of Edom in the Old Testament, which are for Israel and not Edom. However, the scenario of the rich entering the Christian gathering in 2:2–4 and the admonition against favoritism need some connection to a real social possibility. Thus, it becomes difficult to dismiss the possibility of a mixed community, a community composed of the poor, the in-between, and at least some rich. There seems to be not only poor and rich in this community but an in-between who are neither poor nor rich. For example, the reader of this section is transcribed as neither the poor nor the rich but as the one who is called to live with both. Perhaps we are to imagine a situation analogous to that in Corinth (1 Corinthians 6), where believers are taking other believers to court. According to James, it is the rich who take the poor to court and not the poor the rich. In fact, the rich not only take the poor but also the in-between. We can assume the rich do this because things go well for them in court. As always in human history, justice in the Roman era was not perfectly blind.

The connection of the critique of partiality in 2:1–7 with the declarations about the law in 2:8–13 is debated by readers. Those readers who see James as an unharmonized collection warn against creating connections between ideas where none exist. However, most readers today see some literary order in James and thus most see 2:8–13 as theological support for 2:1–7. In which case, the opening statement of the law, "You shall love your neighbor as yourself" (2:8), has immediate application to the poor. We are to love the poor as ourselves. We notice again that the recipient of this word seems not to be the poor but the one called to love the poor. This commandment is not treated, in the argument that follows, as the first or second commandment, or even as a summary of the law; it is treated simply as one tenet that must be obeyed, as are all tenets of the law.

It is hard not to hear the voice of this historical Jesus in all of this. Although the command to love neighbor does not, of course, originate with Jesus, the command becomes his in Christian circles (Lev. 19:18; Matt. 22:39). We cannot say it or hear it without perceiving the face of Jesus. For Christians, Jesus is the speaker of this commandment. But as the speaker he is, in James, neither summarizing nor overcoming the law. He is simply giving voice to or highlighting one old commandment. Once again, in James it is not possible to separate the words of Jesus from the Old Testament law. The words of Jesus fold into the law, so that Jesus becomes a speaker of law. This does not, I think, reduce the status of Jesus in the mind of James; it elevates him. Whatever Jesus says is law. There can be no higher status for a teacher. And here, he says once again, "love your neighbor." And while 2:1–7 makes us connect neighbor and the poor, the subsequent verses connect the command to other voices in the law. The command begins with a specific application but quickly drifts to a general truth, so that the passage can end with the admonition to speak and act "as those who are to be judged by the law of liberty" (2:12). In this way, a specific obligation becomes a platform for reminding readers of many obligations.

In these comments we can recognize the familiar question of how much an argument belongs to its original context and how much it belongs to us the reader. I argued first of all that in James the proper referent for the command to love neighbor is a command to the "in-between" to love the poor. In this reading, we can track what for James is the proper destination of a word of the Lord. It is to be heard, learned, and lived. The command to love neighbor belongs, in this instance, to "our" relationship to the poor. James applies the command to a real situation with real people. These people are not us and the situation is not ours. Thus our reading embeds the command in the past, in a moment not proper to us the modern reader. In this way we are excluded from the force of the text.

On the other hand, as we read further into the argument about the love command, that command slips from its anchorage among the Christian, Roman poor. Its status as general command reemerges. Its destination becomes unforseeable. Its destination becomes the responsibility and task of the righteous and wise believer. And suddenly the line between the past of the text and the present of reader disappears.

Trials

If you prefer the poor to the rich, the powers of the world will not like you. If you act as though God's kingdom will really come and the present political, economic, and social order will be overturned, the powers of the world will not like you. If you should really love your neighbor as yourself, always, the powers of the world would be properly astonished and probably would not like you much. I admit the last scenario is hard to imagine, since no one seems to be able to love all the time. In spite of my hesitation, such a scenario is inscribed in the syntax of James, although not as existing condition but as a possibility. A command must assume the possibility of obedience.

In any case, James imagines its readers as in conflict with the powers of the world. It is difficult to reconstruct the precise nature of this conflict. We know so little about persecution of Christians in the first century. First-century Christians refer to it; so we know that persecution of some kind occurred. But these references are usually couched in the traditional theological language of either Jewish martyrdom or the passion of Jesus. The historical details are left unstated. Such is the case here. Whether the conflict emerges in some way out of the theological outlooks I suggested above is uncertain. Christians typically perceived themselves as outsiders, as people who had left the Roman world. This sense of separation led naturally to all kinds of aberrant behavior, aberrant at least in Roman eyes. This behavior in turn led to all kinds of conflict. What kind of conflict may lie behind James is beyond our reconstruction.

The conflict is, in any case, important to the letter. The letter begins with a reference to it (1:2). Many readers, in fact, understand the naming of the recipients as "the twelve tribes in the Dispersion" as already hinting at the problem of conflict. The body of the letter begins with the formidable challenge that "whenever you face trials of any kind, consider it nothing but joy" (1:2). This seemingly self-contradictory command reminds most readers of a series of passages in the New Testament that connect joy and suffering (e.g., Rom. 2:2–5; 2 Cor. 6:9–10; Phil. 2:17–18; Col. 1:24). Most often in such passages one rejoices or boasts in sufferings because sufferings connect one to Christ. Through this connection, the Jesus narrative of suffering and resurrection becomes ours. However, James does not connect us mystically to Christ in this way. Instead, for James, suffering is a teacher.

The fact that James does not use the term "suffering" but the term "trials" in 1:2 is significant. The term "trial" could be translated "test" or even "temptation." Reading more slowly, we note that the testing in verse 2 becomes clarified in verse 3 as "testing of your faith." Readers have debated whether the "trials" mentioned here refer to real persecution or just to the variety of disappointment, challenges, and contradictions that life deals to any attempt to believe. In 1:2 this testing is further defined as being "of various kinds" or "of any kind." All of this suggests to most readers that James is keeping his reference general; he wants to evoke all kinds of sufferings. The reader is perhaps called to fill in the blanks. We all have experiences of trials and temptations that we can bring to this text. And the syntax of James gives room for a great variety of such experiences.

This testing of our faith is asserted to be a good thing in which we should rejoice (1:2). It is a good thing because it leads us, through endurance, to perfection and completeness (1:3–4). This is awkward logic for most modern

Christians, but it would not have been so for early Christians. The path to perfect virtue was much discussed and pursued in the ancient world. Romans, Greeks, Jews, and Christians all articulated, in an endless variety of ways, the path to virtue. Life, or at least the ethical life, was a journey from vice to virtue. This journey was ruled by cosmic or divine laws. It was assumed that we can even teach each other the road to virtue. James takes for granted the coherence and attractiveness of this journey. The coherence of this journey to virtue is part of divine providence. God has organized human life, the soul, the world, and time itself so that people can learn virtue. This acquisition of virtue, as even we still know, was not easy.

First of all, James assumes faith. He never tells us the content of that faith except indirectly. It certainly includes belief in God, in God's promises and threats, in the law, and in the sayings of Jesus. These beliefs set one on a journey. Life is full of tasks and possibilities, of visions of peace and justice, of the possibility of righteousness even for us. I assume that part of what we must believe is that these Christian forces come together properly in order to lead us to righteousness and salvation. The forces of the Christian life guide us on this journey.

Life in the world, on the other hand, resists this journey. James will give two examples of how it resists us in this journey. This resistance teaches us and trains us; it leads us to endurance and to patience (5:7). The capacity to continue in the life of faith, when the dreams of faith, the visions of the kingdom, seem not only remote but absurd, is an essential moment in the life of faith. Faith is this patience, this endurance. As James will admonish in 5:7–11, Christians should think about the prophets and Job, about how they combined suffering and patience, how they showed endurance. Thus, without this testing, faith cannot become faith. We need the terrors of life in order to become complete Christians. When your faith is tested, rejoice, because this is the proper path of faith.

Disconcerting to many readers is the assertion in James 1:13 that God tempts no one. The problem here is obscured a bit in most English translations. As most commentaries point out, the word translated "trial" in 1:2 and "temptation" in 1:13 is actually the same Greek word. A curious conflict emerges. Trials are not from God, yet they are good. We are asked to rejoice in something that is the direct result of our sinfulness.

This apparent contradiction in James's treatment of "trials" has provoked several responses. For people who view the letter as an unharmonized collection, the contradiction is ours and not James's. James is simply combining disparate material. It is our misguided attempt as readers to harmonize and systematize that produces the conflict. The Greek word means both trial and temptation. The passage in 1:2 is using the meaning "trial"; the passage in 1:12 is using the meaning "temptation." Don't try to read them together. They are addressing different issues.

Some readers see James simply playing with the dual meaning of the word. He wrote them both and intends the double reference. He is actually referring to two different things even though he uses the one Greek word. We should be cautioned against reading the passages together.

Recent attempts to insist on the literary coherence of James have led to a rather creative suggestion. Part of how we typically read is by determining who believes what. We assign the various opinions in the text to various persons. Also part of how we read is by submitting to the rhetoric of a text. A text does things to us, not only by way of its ideas, but by its organization, tone, and argumentative structure. James may be playing a rhetorical game in which these contradictions play a necessary part. Producing conflict in the reader may be part of James's rhetorical strategy.

If we read this way, we can dissolve contradictions in the text by assigning the contradictory texts to different sets of people. The problem for the author of James is that some Christians believe the classic Jewish line that suffering and trials lead to wisdom. James states this incorrect belief in 1:2–4, then corrects that belief with the proper idea in 1:12–18. You think, incorrectly, that suffering leads to wisdom. But in truth, suffering leads only to suffering. Wisdom comes from God. Ask God for wisdom; do not try to wrestle it from the experiences of life. Do not ever say that God sends you the terrors of life in order to teach you something. These terrors are evil and come from sin. God did not become God, did not become perfect, by enduring temptation. Nor does God tempt or try you. God gives only good things. This correct view is stated in 1:12–18.

Embedded in James are wrong and right ideas. The good reader can identify them and does not confuse them.

Although this is often a wonderful way to read, it does not seem to work in this case. There ought to be some indication on the surface of the text that this idea is good and that idea is bad. This reading requires that we know a sociological secret in order to read correctly. Most modern readers reject this rather elegant solution.

Instead, let us take the text at its word. Let us assume that, since 1:2 and 1:12 are using the same Greek word, they are talking about the same thing. This would mean that trials and/or temptations are both the occasion for growth and have their origin in our sinful desire. Furthermore, the same thing (trials) can lead both to perfection and to death. Actually, this reading works, especially if we include 4:1–10 in the discussion.

Read this way, James appears to create a complex role for trials and temptations in the life of faith. First, we are enticed by the world. We fall in love with the world. Our sinful desires make us want (1:14; 4:1–10). These wants align us with the powers of the world. When thus tempted, our faith is tested. The future righteousness of God, the not-yet of the kingdom, seems ridiculous in light of our desire for the things of the world. This is the test of faith.

It does not come ultimately from the evil of others who hate the good in us. It comes from the evil in us that hates the good in us. We do not overcome this love of the world by simply rejecting it or by choosing the good in us. The choice is for something else external. Wisdom comes from God (1:5–8). All the good things we need come from God (1:17–18). The true test is over which external source is able to bless us: God or the world.

In this reading we can comprehend the warnings against being "double-minded" and against "doubt" (1:6–9). To be double-minded is to waver between the things of the world and God's kingdom. To be double-minded would be to try to love the world both for the status and comforts it gives us and for the righteousness God intends for it. To be double-minded is to not make the choice, to compromise our allegiances, to deny the necessity of choosing, to assert that the conflict between the things of the world and the things of God is not the ultimate choice. This double-mindedness is not, however, merely a choice between the world and God. It is not just a choice between caring about justice on earth and caring about rewards in heaven. It is a choice between contrary destinies and purposes for the world. A choice for God, in James, is a choice for justice in the world. A choice for the "world" is a choice for treating the world as my own possession. Doubt is to abandon our visions of the kingdom. Doubt is to deny the power of God's future. To doubt is to decide that what is true now is the only truth. Doubt is to kill the future.

One reading of 5:1–11 complicates the above picture. If we continue to look for coherence and connection from one section of James to another, then chapter 5 includes the suffering inflicted on believers by the rich into this geography of patience. We detailed above the theological terrors that await the rich in the syntax of 5:1–5. The rich fall under all the powers of God's righteous judgment. Their sins, as detailed here, parallel almost exactly the sins of desire, of double-mindedness, in chapter 1. They use the world to accrue wealth and status for themselves. They choose the world to keep their treasures. In so doing they deny God's future. They exemplify what happens when you give in to doubt. When we are tempted, when our faith is tested, we can become like the rich. In a sense we can choose riches even if we do not become rich. If we love the world for its stuff and not for its righteous future, we become the rich.

In this reading, the exhortation for patience, for ongoing belief in "the coming of the Lord," in 5:7–11, follows naturally upon 5:1–6. The presence and behavior of the rich toward us is also a test of our faith. The example of the prophets fits nicely here. Even if some of their suffering came from internal doubt, from love of the world, some of it also came from evil persons. The rich "murdered the righteous one" (5:6). The rich seem to be the source of violence in the world. This is, of course, exactly what 4:1–3 maintains. James asks, where do "conflicts and disputes" come from? It answers, "You want something and do not have it; so you commit murder" (4:2). Wanting the things of the world leads to violence. The rich love the things of the world.

The rich are the violent ones, even if their violence takes place in the gentility of the court.

Ultimately, the real terror in James is that we are the double-minded. We are the potential rich. We are our own murderers. The question of whether the rich ever hear this condemnation in 5:1–6 becomes moot. The rich person in me hears it. The condemnations are, then, for me.

Unless ... unless we ask God for wisdom, unless we look into the law of liberty. If we do, if we can live the vision of ourselves and of the world that this law teaches, then our lives will be a harvest of righteousness and peace (3:18).

James does not regard this as an easy choice. We need all the powers of the Christian life ordered on our behalf. We need God's ongoing various gifts to us; we need especially God's gift of wisdom; we need endurance, patience, peace, and righteousness; we need the words of Jesus; we need the words of the law. We need to learn and practice all of this. This means we also need teachers. We need people to teach us both the what and the how. In fact, it sounds as though the highest calling would be to become one of those teachers. If I were a teacher, I would have status, status in the right place, in God's kingdom, not the world, but status nonetheless.

Teachers

"Not many of you should become teachers" (3:1). We hear this advice from Matthew 23:8–12 where both Jesus' exclusive status as teacher and some kind of egalitarian ideal are in play. James gives two reasons that are different from those in Matthew and different from each other. The first is rather sobering: "You know that we who teach will be judged with greater strictness" (3:1). This otherwise unknown glimpse into the final judgment is coupled with a warning about the impossibility of perfection: "All of us make many mistakes" (3:2). Thus we should not be teachers, because the role is too important. Much of the theology of James is built upon words: words of the law, words of Jesus. Teachers speak and interpret those words. It is words that show us the righteous life. It is through words that God speaks to us. It is through words—words of the law, words of Jesus, and words of teachers—that God guides us. It is as though James is asking, Who are you to speak such sacred words?

This leads to a fascinating passage on the tongue (3:3–12), wherein its power to rule the whole body is asserted. Without exploring the details of this passage, in which some of the analogies are not especially felicitous, as readers have long complained, the point is fairly clear. Words have power over the speaker and the hearer. Words play a unique role in human life. Thus the tongue rules the body, both for good and for bad (3:5). With the same tongue we bless God and curse God's works (3:9–10). "The tongue is a fire" (3:6). It burns others with its power; it burns all of nature. It will itself be burned (3:6). A teacher is a tongue, a speaker, a source of words. Being a teacher looks less and less attractive.

In fact, that seems to be the point: to discourage us from seeking the role of teacher. Teaching is too hard and the judgment is too severe. However, the advice in 3:13–18 softens the edges. The syntax of 3:14 suggests that part of the problem in being a teacher is that it comes from "selfish ambition." There seems to be no status in the community equal to that of teacher. Given the theology of James, we can see what high regard a teacher must enjoy among his readers. This high status is seductive, drawing believers away from gentle love of neighbor and toward envy, selfish ambition, boastfulness, falseness, disorder, and wickedness of every kind (3:16). The path toward virtue is disrupted by the honors of teaching.

Thus, instead of showing your wisdom with the felicity of your tongue, "show by your good life that your works are done with gentleness born of wisdom" (3:13). Desire for teaching is of the same order as love for the world; it is perverting what should be good by our selfishness. Such wisdom is "earthly, unspiritual, devilish" (3:15). In contrast, the "wisdom from above" is "first pure, then peaceable, gentle, willing to yield, full of mercy and good fruits, without a trace of partiality or hypocrisy" (3:17).

The guiding vision in all of this is the standard Jewish and Christian reading of the law. The law articulates for us a world of peace and righteousness. This world is composed of the gentle, communal virtues that frequent Jewish and Christian ethics. Love for the status of teaching, desire for the riches of the world, and doubt sponsored by the trials of life work to frustrate that world and our commitments to it. We can surround ourselves with the many powers of the Christian life—the words of the law, the words of Jesus, the ongoing gifts of God, wisdom from above, good teachers, a gentle community, the examples from the past, and especially our faith in God's coming kingdom—and those powers can outfit us for the journey toward virtue and steel us with endurance and patience.

Thus, the ethic enjoined here is empowered and compromised by its relationship to the future. On the one hand, when we are doers of the word, the present can become a time of virtue, of gentleness, and perhaps even of peace and righteousness. We must be committed to living these virtues no matter what it costs us in the economy of the world. On the other hand, these virtues, these moments of peace and righteousness, do not seem to be fully anchored in the present. Their home, their destiny, their purpose is the future. They come from above. They come from outside. Thus, this is an ethic caught between the present and the future. It is an ethic that wagers on God's ultimate victory. If God's kingdom does not live in the future, then this ethic lacks sufficient warrant.

We seek righteousness less because we can envision it or understand it or find it, and more because God is implicated in its possibility, or because the possibility of God suggests that righteousness is also possible.

God and Jesus

Thus, the frequent reading of James that finds therein a standard Greek ethic with an extraneous dressing of theology is not adequate. Virtue and God cannot be separated this way in James. In fact, all virtue is from God. As James explains, "Every generous act of giving, with every perfect gift, is from above, coming down from the Father of lights" (1:17). Thus, any act that partakes of righteousness, of peace, is a moment of God's kingdom. God is the righteous one. The equation is absolute in both directions. And the character of God that is explicit in James is the God who funds such righteousness.

So little is said directly about Jesus that most readers refuse to construct a Christology of James. And it certainly is the case that we cannot even remotely imagine a Christology of the Trinitarian or cosmological type. Furthermore, it is unclear whether the various references to "Lord" refer to God the creator or to Jesus. Even the phrase "the coming of the Lord" is not clearly a reference to Jesus, since God is depicted as coming or arriving in many Jewish texts. The only incontestable references to Jesus are those where his name actually occurs; and these two instances (1:1; 2:1) tell us little. However, we have seen that the sayings of Jesus, in particular the Sermon on the Mount, have an undeniable impact on the theology of the letter. James sees the law, the law of liberty, through the lens of this Jesus material. Jesus is the teacher, the speaker of the law, the one who sorts and orders the law. If the references to "Lord" in 5:7–11 are to Jesus, which seems likely in a Christian text, then Jesus functions theologically much as he does in the Sermon on the Mount. He is the true rabbi, the teacher of righteousness. We, his followers, are to learn, study, teach, and live his words. He will then judge us. The teacher will judge the students on the last day.

Jesus then is a key figure in God's intentions for righteousness. We do not have Jesus' own righteousness imputed to us, as we do in Paul. Jesus' death seem to have no function, except perhaps as an example of patience and suffering (5:11). But Jesus' life has tremendous influence because Jesus taught the law of liberty. We can look into this law and find our way to peace, righteousness, love, and salvation.

The Wise Reader

To some extent, every text needs a creative reader in order to make it speak. Silence is part of the character of every text no matter how often or how well that text is read. However, an ethic such as that articulated in James needs more than a creative, sympathetic, and insightful reader. To understand the text is not yet to give this text its voice. James wants to live in the particular deeds of its readers. It only speaks when someone visits a widow.

Part of the reliance on the reader comes from the character of formulating a general ethic. General rules exist in particular acts. We should carry these general exhortations in our heads and hearts, hunting for moments in our lives in which to apply them. A proper capacity for knowing when and how to live this ethic is wisdom. Thus, a prayer to God for wisdom is a prayer for ongoing insight into how and when to obey.

Moreover, once we declare that righteousness belongs to God, it becomes beyond both our reach and our knowledge. We cannot hammer out righteousness through some sort of social or personal system. James does not draw a picture of a righteous and just society. James does not even draw a full portrait of the perfectly virtuous person. James describes instances of righteousness wherein one person treats another person as God envisions. This ethic lives in the encounter between one person and another. In this way, it is never finished and can never be fully articulated. It exists only in the opening of the face-to-face. It exists in the possibilities of how I treat this neighbor right here in front of me, or this real enemy. To read James well, we must sketch out this law of liberty in the unpredictability of our relationships with other people. This takes a creative, wise, and faithful reader.

3

1 Peter

The heart of 1 Peter is a sustained and profound exploration of Christian suffering. In this analysis of suffering, 1 Peter takes its readers deep into one of the most puzzling aspects of Christian life, in fact, of human life itself. Suffering has long resisted all attempts to grasp it. Humans not only struggle to live in and through the suffering in their lives, we struggle to understand what suffering really is. Christians, in fact, have argued, in what seems to be a contradiction, that suffering is both a sign of God's absence and a sign of God's presence.

On the one hand, suffering seems so evil. The terrors that humans endure seem so brutal and contrary to God's intentions for us. Thus, we have often contended that suffering cannot be God's will because God is above all a good God who gives good gifts. When God's kingdom comes, all the terrible suffering of humans and of creation itself will cease. God will wipe away our many, very real tears. This awful suffering that terrorizes human life is, then, a unique sign that God is not here. And our task in life is, with God's help, to banish suffering from human history.

On the other hand, Christians have also argued that the terrors of suffering, even the evils of suffering, are a mysterious sign of God's presence. We have noted that in the New Testament a—if not the—primary manifestation of God occurs in Jesus' passion, in his suffering on the cross. The terrors of suffering in some mysterious way manifest the face of God. And we, if we belong to Jesus, must partake somehow in this divine suffering; we must endure a taste of the evil Jesus endured. We can only reach the resurrection through the crucifixion. The glories of God's kingdom follow upon the judgments of God's kingdom. Thus, our suffering, no matter how terrible, is a sign of our connectedness to Jesus Christ. We can even find joy in this suffering. And our task in life is not to banish suffering but to find God's redeeming face in its midst.

Furthermore, both of these options obscure the complexity and diversity of experiences that we name with the word suffering. Surely not all suffering is the same. To suffer imprisonment for a violent crime against another human cannot be equated with Jesus' suffering on the cross. We suffer all kinds of

ways for all kinds of reasons. Most of us suffer internally from time to time because our dreams of fame or success or wealth or security are frustrated by the
forces of society and history. We want things for ourselves that we cannot
have, and this causes us grief.

Sometimes our dreams are animated less by such self-centeredness and
more by our affection for others. We want good things for people we love; we
even want good things for all people. And the constant tragedies that afflict
human life cause us grief. We dream of God's kingdom and its blessings, but
that kingdom does not come. Such internal frustrations are almost innumerable in their complexity and variety. Christians have long puzzled about how
to sort these diverse accounts of suffering. We wonder which suffering connects us to Jesus and which does not, and how we might know the difference.

Furthermore, Jesus in his passion did not suffer only psychic frustration.
His body was tortured. He endured physical pain. And the violence against
him finally killed him. Early Christians endured not only internal frustrations
and griefs, they endured violence to their bodies, and to their families and
friends. They watched as their mothers were killed. Their bodies were torn by
torture; they were fed to lions; they were burned alive. They suffered these
persecutions not for doing evil but for doing, in their minds at least, the good.
Perhaps it is only such extreme violence against righteous behavior that constitutes real Christian suffering, that connects us to Jesus.

First Peter may well contain the most sustained analysis of suffering in the
New Testament. It arrays an astonishing range of theological images and admonitions to this question of suffering. First Peter looks deep into the heart
of suffering; it explores its complexities and contradictions; it connects experiences of estrangement, abuse, and legal attacks to a deep fund of early
Christian traditions. In doing this, it provides us with a unique resource for
understanding suffering and for living in its midst. This analysis has been and
still is the primary voice of 1 Peter in Christian theology. First Peter has been
mined over and over for its justifiably renowned wealth of insights into suffering. And we shall explore those insights here. We shall pursue those insights in part because suffering is so clearly the key issue of the text. Almost
every reader agrees. But we shall also pursue those insights because this has
been the traditional Christian entry into this text. Prior readings of a text, especially prior readings from circles close to our own, have a claim on us. There
would be a certain irresponsibility and dishonesty in feigning ignorance of
these prior readings.

In recent years a second theme, a second theological question, has come to
the forefront in our readings of 1 Peter. The letter opens by designating the
recipients as "exiles in the dispersion." This naming signals an ongoing discussion of the estrangement these Christians feel from the society around
them. They perceive themselves as outsiders, and non-Christians perceive

them as outsiders. This outsider status impacts, of course, the experience of suffering and abuse that these communities are enduring. But this status also raises directly the question of how and to what extent Christians should conform to the customs of their surrounding culture.

This is, of course, still a pressing question for Christians. Christians today debate to what extent they should be good citizens and adopt the prevailing norms of the culture around them and to what extent they should disengage themselves from the culture and pursue peculiar Christian customs. First Peter will pursue a complex give-and-take on this question.

At the heart of 1 Peter's response to this question of how to live as Christians in a non-Christian culture is an insistence on "good behavior." Christians, no matter what the setting, no matter what the moment, are to practice "good behavior." The context for this admonition is, of course, complex, and we shall pursue it in what follows. Nevertheless, this basic admonition for "good behavior" has become the classic Christian response to the question of Christianity and culture. On the one hand, in this admonition we find one of the most fundamental Christian assertions: we are to practice Christian behavior no matter who we are dealing with or what the context might be. We deny ourselves permission to abuse the outsider. If we are abused or hated, we cannot return that behavior in kind. We must respond even to our enemies with "good" deeds.

On the other hand, as fundamental as this response has become, it has also occasioned much debate. Christians have enormous differences of opinion here. We do not agree on what constitutes "good" behavior or on who should decide what is good and what is not. Especially we do not agree on the role that outsiders and the standards of outsiders should play. Thus, we debate whether outsiders, working with their own criteria of what is good, should perceive our behavior toward them as "good." First Peter makes a fascinating proposal on this question.

Finally, 1 Peter is stunningly rich in its theological and ethical language. Any reader of 1 Peter finds the text to be complex, inviting, stimulating, and challenging. It seems to draw on an enormous range of early Christian traditions. It combines those traditions into one text without collapsing the diversity of those traditions into one program. Thus, readers of 1 Peter constantly become sidetracked. A Christological image, which may be used in part to support or explain an ethical imperative, will have echoes and meanings beyond its relationship to that imperative. This has led some readers to doubt the theological or ethical unity of the letter. Other readers have, from time to time, attempted to combine all these diverse images into one theological system or to submit them to one controlling theological image. However, 1 Peter resists such a simple collapse. It is a rich, diverse, and complex gathering of theological and ethical images.

Outline of 1 Peter

1:1–2   Opening salutation
1:3–12   Born to a living hope; suffering and glory
1:13–2:10   The holy life
   1:13–16   Call to be holy
   1:16–21   The blood of Christ
   1:22–25   The eternal word and love
   2:1–10   Christ as a living stone. Be a holy people
2:11–4:19   The suffering of Christ
   2:11–17   Aliens who live honorably in the world
   2:18–25   Slaves and suffering of Christ
   3:1–7   Wives and husbands and the suffering of Christ
   3:8–12   Unity and love
   3:13–22   Suffering for doing right
   4:1–6   Turning from the old life
   4:7–11   Virtues before the end
   4:12–19   Sharing in the suffering of Christ
5:1–5   Charge to the elders
5:6–11   Final exhortations
5:12–14   Greetings and benediction

The Particular Voice of 1 Peter

Our reading of 1 Peter has long labored under the problem of being read through the lens of Paul. To some extent, this is no surprise, since it seems as though the entire Bible has suffered, in Protestant circles at least, from being read through Pauline categories. Most modern readers, in any case, admit that the particular voice of 1 Peter has been muffled or even misheard because we have typically transposed its theology into a Pauline framework. Perhaps the most important shift in the way we read 1 Peter has resulted from readers who freed its voice from the hegemony of Pauline theology. They point out that, although 1 Peter has many terms and phrases in common with Paul, these are not used in Pauline ways. They further note that, although 1 Peter moves from cosmic images to everyday ethics, from theological indicatives to moral imperatives, as does Paul, it actually has a different set of images and imperatives, and it does not connect them in a Pauline way. They note finally that if we read 1 Peter while intentionally resisting Pauline categories, we find a very distinctive and quite non-Pauline voice.

This strategy of reading 1 Peter in isolation from Paul raises one of the great problems and issues in how to best read biblical texts. One text is always read in light of other texts, but it is not clear to what extent we should read one text in light of another and to what extent we should labor to hear each text on its own. We have, of course, no definitive answers here. We cannot read or understand any single text in perfect isolation from all other texts or from all of our own ideas. Without other texts and without our own understanding of the world, no text can speak. However, when we impose ideas and structures on a text from outside, we risk effacing and dismantling the intentions of the text. The noise of our own ideas silences the voice of the text. In the case of 1 Peter most readers think that its particular voice has long been silenced by the power of the ideas and structures we brought to it as Christian readers. Thus, there is a conscious attempt among most modern readers to read (or to begin reading) 1 Peter as a singular voice and to find its intentions and its theology solely from the rhetoric of this single text.

But this is no easy task. As noted above, 1 Peter resists our attempts to systematize it. It manifests a diversity of images and forms of argument that disclose no obvious governing system or idea. Typically we have tried to control the diversity of this text using the four ways historical critics typically try to control texts. First, we have looked for a controlling or central theological idea that governs the rest of the ideas. Numerous ideas have been proposed for this governing role: new birth, election, holiness, hope, suffering as grace, and so on. But none of these ideas or images seems to have such a governing force. The numerous theological images do not seem to interact in such an ordered way. It is not that the gathering of theological ideas and images in 1 Peter seems to be chaotic and totally unordered. Almost all readers find an effective compatibility among these diverse images. They somehow belong together even if they do not fall into a neat system or hierarchy.

Second, we have looked for a literary, rhetorical order. Perhaps there is coherence to the progression of the argument that can manage these diverse images. Early attempts to find such a rhetorical unity actually found the opposite. Two difficulties emerged. To begin with, 1 Peter 4:12 appeared to many readers almost like the start of a different letter. Verse 11 is a doxology reminiscent of the conclusion of many Christian letters. And verse 12, on the surface at least, seems to introduce a new topic. Although both 1:1–4:11 and 4:12–5:11 address the question of suffering, they may be talking about quite different things. The first part of 1 Peter (1:1–4:11) addresses suffering that results from alienation from society and verbal abuse by that society. The second part (4:12–5:11) addresses, or may address, the different experience of being hauled into Roman courts. The first part deals with the many problems of alienation; the second part deals with actual, official persecution. Thus, 1 Peter may not even be one letter.

A further difficulty is that the internal rhetoric of the letter seems repetitive. It does not move from topic to topic in any recognizable order. Instead, it constantly repeats images and arguments, adding slight nuances as it does so. Thus, any attempt to outline the course of the argument in 1 Peter foundered. Some readers concluded that 1 Peter was a more or less careless gathering of diverse traditions around the poorly defined topic of suffering.

However, recent readers have rejected this conclusion. Readers have noted the considerable similarities between 1:1–4:11 and 4:12–5:11. Pulling them apart seems unjustified. Furthermore, the possible reference to official allegations in 4:12–16 hardly indicates a new situation. It is better understood as another aspect of the complex issue of Christian alienation and suffering that 1 Peter explores. Furthermore, what appear to be repetitions in 1 Peter can be better read as developments. Readers now tend to find in 1 Peter a gradual unfolding of the issue of alienation and suffering, in which the repetitiveness functions to reinforce and expand. Readers also note that ancient parenesis, and perhaps modern as well, prefers a certain repetition. This repetition assists in the power of persuasion. Thus, 1 Peter may not have a clear rhetorical outline, but it does have an appropriate and effective progression of ideas. This is, in fact, the way we shall read 1 Peter in what follows.

The third way readers have tried to find order in 1 Peter is by identifying an underlying and unifying social situation that inspires and grounds the letter. This has proven to be, in some sense, quite easy to do. The general setting of the letter seems obvious. We have an intense instance of the well-known Christian experience of alienation from both the Jewish world and the Greco-Roman world. This alienation is occurring on all kinds of levels, internal and external, private and public, spiritual and physical. This alienation derives from and feeds into these Christians understanding of themselves, God, Jesus, history, salvation, and almost everything else. There is a lot we can say about this fundamental early Christian experience.

However, the precise nature of the problem in the communities of this letter is more difficult to determine. The details are covered over with general references to "suffering." And the analysis of 1 Peter is devoted not so much to a description of the problem as to an articulation of the response. What matters is not the details of an instance but how that suffering connects to Jesus, to the theological traditions of the community, and to the proper way of living as a good Christian. Thus, the setting of the letter must remain a bit unfocused.

Fourth and finally, undergirding all these other attempts to find order is a fundamental pursuit of the face and intentions of the original author of 1 Peter. As we have noted before, part of the task of reading is meeting our obligation to the intentions of the author of the text. However, as was the case with Hebrews and James, reconstructing a portrait of the author of 1 Peter has proven to be controversial. The main question is, of course, the relationship of the text to the apostle Peter. Some readers argue that Peter himself is the author. Others suggest that Peter has no connection at all to the text; his name was added by an unknown author to give apostolic weight to the text. Others pursue something in between. On the basis of 5:12, "Through Silvanus, whom I consider a faithful brother, I have written this short letter," some readers suggest that Silvanus, the companion of Paul, wrote this letter at the behest of Peter. Thus, we have ideas and intentions of Peter funneled through the mind of the Pauline Silvanus. Others suggest that an unknown author, who worked in the tradition of both Peter and Paul, wrote the text.

The data here are difficult to sort. Without rehearsing the pros and cons of all these possibilities, it is perhaps best to conduct our reading of 1 Peter with a certain modesty about our knowledge of the author. As is the case with most of the texts discussed in this volume, the forces of origin of the text are not clear. My own opinion is that the last scenario suggested above is the best. But even that is a bit misleading because it sounds as though we can name the shape of the tradition with more authority and definition than is actually the case. It is not clear what would be passed down as originating from either Peter or Silvanus or Paul. We do indeed have a gathering of fundamental and fairly common early Christian traditions. And this gathering does not appear to be a haphazard one.

We shall read 1 Peter as an intentional and effective combination of traditions and images. It is an assemblage of theological conceptions in which all the pieces are needed in order to make the text function. There does not seem to be one master image. We cannot begin with any one proposition and deduce the rest. The many pieces of this text have independent force and origin. Furthermore, the gathering is not chaotic or even confused. If there is not hierarchy or system, there is at least compatibility and fit. A particular place is constructed. It is these named forces coming together, interacting, which make the Christian life. We need them all. Or at least they all come together in order to help us understand and live in the midst of intense alienation and suffering. The reading that follows is a general account of a loose but successful coherence among some powerful ideas. The results are unique and compelling.

New Birth

First Peter opens with a blessing to God because God "has given us new birth into a living hope" (1:3). There is a prevailing and persistent sense in 1 Peter that these Christians have become new people. They are people who are starting over, who are connected both to the cosmos and to society in a fundamentally new way. This new birth funds both their new hope and their alienation and suffering. This new birth funds a new way of living that is characterized by good deeds and by the eschewing of their former vices.

The theological syntax that gathers around this image of new birth is common to early Christianity. Early Christianity often connected this image of new birth to baptism. First Peter 3:21 mentions baptism in such a way that it is reminiscent of this new birth imagery. Thus, many readers suggest that the underlying context and rhetorical format of 1 Peter is that of baptism. Indeed, much of the imagery in 1 Peter is typical of what we will find in later baptismal homilies. However, most readers think that the references to baptism are insufficiently explicit to cast the letter as a baptismal homily.

Nevertheless, a baptismal context is helpful and proper here, even if baptism is not the controlling image. God has acted to create new people. Baptism is one of the ways of thinking about that. First Peter reads baptism through an analogy to Noah's ark (3:20–21). God saves us through the water. There is here a sense of being pulled out, of being rescued, of a divine act that changes our status. What exactly happens to us in this baptism cannot be easily summarized. First Peter will arrange a variety of images around this new birth. But in 3:21–22, which contains the only explicit image of baptism, baptism connects us to a change in the structure of the cosmos that God has accomplished through the resurrection and ascension of Jesus Christ. Jesus is now at the right hand of God and the powers of the cosmos are subject to him. We are connected by way of baptism to this Jesus, who was also snatched from the grip of death. It is intriguing and essential to the theology of 1 Peter that our connectedness to Jesus' ascension comes not through the magic removal of dirt or sin, but through an appeal to God for a good conscience (3:21). That is to say, the fundamental force of ethics, of good deeds, surfaces here.

First Peter draws the equally classic and nearly universal connection between new birth and the "word of God" in 1:22–25. Furthermore, the fundamental role of good deeds is again affirmed. This passage hints at one of the real creative theological proposals of 1 Peter. Holiness is carved out by good deeds. Here we are told to make our souls holy by loving one another. New birth is not simply a divine act to which we submit. As many readers have noted, 1 Peter has a cooperative view of salvation. It takes God and a human to save that human. We carve out holiness through the ongoing act of loving others. This new holiness, this new capacity to love, is then connected in this passage to "the living and enduring word of God" (1:23). Grounding the Christian life in God's word is common among early Christians. We live out of, in, on the basis of, and under the power of God's word.

So general and prevalent is this connection that it is not clear to most readers what 1 Peter might actually mean here. It is, naturally, not perfectly clear what 1 Peter means by "word of God" nor precisely what connection is invoked by saying we are "born anew … through" this word. The clipped nature of this language is what encourages readers to fill in the gaps with Paul. However, as we noted above, we need to be careful employing larger explanations from Paul to explain curiosities in the text of 1 Peter. Furthermore, 1 Peter on its own may provide sufficient hints as to how to read this. We get a brief definition of the "word" in 1:25: "That word is God's news that was announced to you." "Word" here is oral proclamation of the gospel about Jesus Christ. Based on this passage alone, it would not seem to include the text of the Old Testament. But elsewhere 1 Peter certainly includes the Old Testament as authoritative word. First Peter affirms (1:10–12) that it was the "Spirit of Christ" or the "Holy Spirit" that was speaking in the Old Testament. Thus, "word" seems to include the Old Testament and the emerging early Christian traditions. It may even include the text of 1 Peter itself. Whether it is included in the penumbra of "word" or not, 1 Peter certainly illustrates how the "word" should function in our lives. There are words we should learn, read, hear, explore, understand, obey, submit to, re-articulate, and speak to one another. It is this engagement with these words that supplies our Christian lives.

This dependence on the word leads to one of the most creative images in 1 Peter. In 2:1–2, after a brief reference to ridding oneself of certain vices (again we see the key role of ethics), 1 Peter returns to the image of new birth. But here we are depicted as babies suckling our mother's milk. "Like newborn infants, long for the pure, spiritual milk, so that by it you may grow into salvation—if indeed you have tasted that the Lord is good" (2:1–2). The image here is wonderfully effective. We are babies at our mother's breast. We "taste" that the Lord is good. Just as mother's milk tastes good and enables the baby to grow, so also the "word" tastes good and enables us to grow.

There is a sense of exclusiveness here. We are new people. We are disconnected and alienated from what used to feed us. We are starting over. We have not just returned to our mother's breast; we have been reborn to a new mother's breast. And it is only this new mother's milk that can nourish us. We need, then, to gather around this new word, which comes to us as words, and drink it as babies drink milk. It will feed us and we shall grow "into salvation." We can sense in all of this both the wonders of this new birth and the radical sense of disconnectedness from the old life. New birth is a wonderful opening to a new world filled with the goodness of our new mother's milk; all of which leads us to hope and salvation. But new birth also leads to alienation, abuse, persecution, and suffering.

We can discern in this 1 Peter's view of the conflicted nature of the Christian life. We are born anew to a radical hope. The surety of this hope is explored in a wonderful variety of ways in this letter. We are also born to a life of alienation and suffering. A Christian life without both is not a Christian life.

Exiles and Aliens

> Peter, an apostle of Jesus Christ, to the exiles of the Dispersion in Pontus, Galatia, Cappadocia, Asia, and Bithynia.
>
> (1:1)

The initial naming of the recipients as "exiles" signals an ongoing and central focus of this letter. The outsider status enumerated in this letter is portrayed as being essential to the self-understanding and the behavior of Christians. You are now outsiders. You must understand why and what this means for how you live.

Twice in the letter the recipients are named as exiles (1:1; 2:11), but in 2:11 the term "exile" is coupled with the term "alien." There is some debate over the proper reading of these words. Some readers have pointed out that the terms are actually technical designations of a certain legal status in ancient cities. They should properly be translated something like "visiting strangers" and/or "resident aliens." These names are intended to evoke the complex problems of citizenship in the ancient world. In the Greco-Roman world, your citizenship belonged to the city of your birth. If you moved to a new town, you did not automatically become a citizen of that town. Instead, your legal status was something less than that of an original citizen. Questions of voting, holding office, owning property, inheritance, marriage, and so on were affected by this partial status. It is this status that is being evoked here.

Under this reading, the problem evoked in this naming is the uneven legal status of Christian groups. The legal status of Christianity is one of the complex stories of the early church, especially the first-century church. By the middle of the second century, and certainly by the third, we can track the story of the persecution of the church with some confidence. But in the first century we lack data. The best evidence we have are these ambiguous and stylized references from Christians themselves, such as we have in 1 Peter. We know from these references that Christians are having problems with abuse of some kind from outsiders. We know they connect these problems to Old Testament suffering and martyrdom texts. And we know, furthermore, that they interpret these problems in light of the passion and sufferings of Jesus. But we cannot reconstruct precisely what either Roman neighbors or Roman authorities might have been doing to Christians in the first century.

Our uncertainty over the precise social and political background, coupled with the stylized character of the references to suffering, leads most readers of 1 Peter to restrict their reconstruction of the facts to persecution of a general kind. The background here needs to be soft, a bit unfocused. The text pushes us towards a theological analysis of a social situation that we cannot completely reconstruct. In fact, some readers see the references to suffering and alienation as coming first of all out of a theological experience, out of meditation on certain texts and certain traditions, and not out of a real political experience. These readers suggest that what supplies the alienation language is the common Christian experience of belonging more to heaven than to earth. All Christians feel, or should feel, alienated from the world around them because their values and their destiny belong to heaven. The terms "exiles" and "aliens" refer to a spiritual status. First Peter is invoking and prescribing the life of the Christian sojourner who journeys from this alien land of human history to a home in the heavens with God.

However, such a strictly spiritual reading of 1 Peter is difficult, if not impossible, to maintain. The same should be said of a strictly social reading that brackets all questions of the spiritual life. The core theology of 1 Peter is the essential connectedness of the social and the theological. It not only refuses to divide the self into political and spiritual realms, into external and internal parts, it articulates a unity of the social and the theological. A social moment is a theological moment; a theological moment is a social moment. Thus, when 1 Peter moves from talking about the suffering of Christ (2:18–25) to how wives should behave with husbands (3:1–6), there is, in a sense, no shift in topic. The suffering of Christ and the behavior of a wife toward her husband belong to the same syntax, to the same order of life.

The most direct comment in 1 Peter on the cause of the tensions between Christians and outsiders is in the exhortation in 4:1–6. Here we can see this wonderful overlap of the theological and social. Since Christ suffered, we should be like Christ, both in Christ's suffering and in Christ's ethic. We should be free of sin; we should live "no longer by human desires but by the will of God" (4:2). These classic theological images feed into an intriguing social comment. "You have already spent enough time in doing what the Gentiles like to do, living in licentiousness, passions, drunkenness, revels, carousing, and lawless idolatry. They are surprised that you no longer join them in the same excesses of dissipation, and so they blaspheme" (4:3–4).

As we noted earlier, rebirth means that Christians submit to a new set of forces in their lives. These new forces disconnect them from the old forces that once governed them. This disconnection from the old leads to persecution or abuse from persons still aligned with the old. The general configuration of the social aspects of the situation is fairly clear. Roman society was an extremely religious society. Romans liked to claim that they were the most pious of all people. They even attributed their ongoing power to that piety. The many gods and goddesses who impacted the health and peace of ancient society placed many demands on ancient people. The quantity and the magnificence of ancient temples testifies to both the demands of the gods and the pious responses of antiquity. Coupled with the building of these temples was the requirement for fulfilling the necessary celebrations and offerings attached to each temple and each god. When a problem arose, whether it be famine, flood, warfare, sickness, or almost anything else, the gods were always implicated. Thus, part of the solution to any major problem was redressing some offense made to some god. Furthermore, the avoidance of such problems required the scrupulous keeping of all the public liturgies attached to these temples, gods, and goddesses.

Christians did not participate in these liturgies any more. Christian refusal to placate and petition these gods with the proper celebrations was perceived as endangering the health of the city and even as hatred of humanity. Furthermore, these celebrations touched so many parts of ancient life that a refusal to engage in public worship would alienate one from much of ancient public life. This simple refusal to engage in public worship would make Christians feel like outsiders and be perceived as such.

The language of 1 Peter suggests that Christian alienation resulted not only from this fear of idolatry but also out of new moral rigor. It sounds as though the problem with the old life was not simply a fear of the idolatry that frequented it, but a fear of the immoral character of the behavior associated with that old life. First Peter makes a radical moral distinction between the old life and the new. The old is defined as living "by human desires"; the new as living "by the will of God" (4:2). This conflict between human desires and God's will forms part of the basic character of the Christian life. We must constantly choose between living by our will and living by God's, between the forces of the new life and the forces of the old. Thus, at the core of the Christian life resides a rejection. This rejection creates alienation and animosity. But without this ongoing "No" there is no Christian life.

It is not clear what is precisely envisioned in the imagery of living "by human desires" (4:2). Nearly every moralist in antiquity, whether Greek, Roman, Jewish, or Christian, fought against the power of human desires. This language of human desire is, in fact, more Greco-Roman in origin than biblical. First Peter is, thereby, naming the non-Christian world with a term that world would not admit. No one wants to be described as living by human desire. To live by human desire is to live the immoral life. The many faces and forces of human desire produce the endless vices that ruin human life and human community. First Peter may be evoking here this whole panoply of vices in this shorthand "by human desire." Perhaps we are to imagine here the multifaceted vices listed in 2 Timothy 3:1–5. Human desire leads to endless evil and vice. Thus, the argument is that non-Christians, because they live by chasing their desires, live immoral lives. While Christians, who pursue the will of God, live the virtuous life.

However, the imagery in 4:3 does not completely square with such a reading. The list of vices in 4:3 evokes more the revelry attendant to religious celebration and less the general vices of life. Most of Roman life was typically sober and serious in character. But religious celebrations, whether official public festivals or more private parties, often tended toward the orgiastic. First Peter may not be naming all non-Christian behavior as immoral, but may instead be calling forth the excesses which frequented "idolatry." In this case, the alienation would be less absolute. We are not disconnected from all the forces of our former lives but from those forces tainted by idolatry. Such a limited reading of Christian alienation in 1 Peter, as we shall see, fits better with its insistence that Christians still submit to certain non-Christian forces.

First Peter's sense of alienation does not come from radical sectarianism, in which all things inside the community are good and all things outside bad. The "no" that animates the Christian life is more precisely focused than that. Thus, non-Christians ought to be able to recognize the virtues that characterize the Christian life as proper virtues. Thus, in 2:12 (and 3:16) when abusive outsiders see the "honorable deeds" which Christians practice, these outsiders will recognize these deeds as good and "glorify God when he comes to judge."

Despite the powerful "no" that Christians say to their old life, despite their sense of alienation, and despite the abuse inflicted on them by their former friends, there is a door open between Christians and non-Christians. In spite of all their differences, they share some core values.

We can also misperceive the nature of this "no" if we divide it from a perhaps more original "yes." The new birth language is crucial here. We are reborn to a new life which includes this "no." However, the language in 1 Peter is quite diverse on this yes and no. For instance, 1:18–19 professes that "you were ransomed from your futile ways inherited from your ancestors." Here the Christological act is less a call to something new and more a rescuing from an old evil. Again, it is not clear exactly what "your futile ways inherited from your ancestors" might mean. Denial of ancestral forces and obligations is a serious move. In fact, some students of the Greco-Roman world have argued that fulfillment of ancestral obligations was the single most fundamental human expectation in that society. Thus, the language here must be understood as quite aggressive. To characterize the Christian life as a denial of one's ancestral duties is to emphasize in a radical way the discontinuity between the old and the new.

Furthermore, the imagery 1:13–21 keeps shifting back and forth from ethical categories to cultic ones. We are admonished in classical ethical categories to "not be conformed to the desires that you formerly had in ignorance" (1:14). Instead, in classical cultic categories, we are to be holy (1:15–16). Our "futile ways inherited from our ancestors" (1:18) could be both ethical and cultic. But the image of ransoming (1:18–19) is clearly a cultic image. This overlap and interchange of ethical and cultic imagery means that an attempt to separate the two cannot succeed. As we shall see below, crucial to the theology of 1 Peter is the belonging together of cult and ethics, of holiness and good deeds.

Thus, our earlier attempt to describe the "no" as focused on idolatry and its accoutrements and not upon the whole Greco-Roman ethic may be placing a divide where it does not belong. We must in any case see the range of idolatry, of "human desires," of "the futile ways inherited from your ancestors," as inclusive of more than behavior attendant to public religious celebrations. The critique goes deeper than that.

In comparison to the ambiguity of the "no," the character of the "yes" in 1 Peter is more clearly articulated. The most obvious shift is in the name and character of the divine. "Blessed be the God and Father of our Lord Jesus Christ" (1:3). The divine is no longer perceived as the many gods and goddesses of the ancient Mediterranean world, with their majestic temples, rich treasuries, elaborate liturgies, and powerful stories of intervention. The divine is now the God of Israel, who is the Father of Jesus Christ. This God has no real temple. There are no public signs and commemorations of the greatness and beneficence of this God. Ancient temples were stunning sites, memorials to the greatness of these gods and goddesses. Ancient streets were constantly filled with their liturgies. Inscriptions in temples and on holy ways recounted their powerful interventions, for good and ill, in human life. This God lacks all of this. It is a stunning move to turn from these public and well-attested wonders to this nearly invisible God. First Peter can be thought of as an account of the forces and costs of turning from those gods to this one.

Both the blessings and the cost of such a turn are considerable. If 1 Peter falls short of the pervasive sense of celebration for the gifts of God, which we find in Ephesians, Colossians, and elsewhere, it is not because it lacks all sense of the good gifts of this new God. The letter, in fact, begins (1:3–21) with a celebratory narrative of those gifts. Many readers find this opening narrative to be an excellent summary of the theology of the letter.

This God, through the resurrection of Jesus Christ, gives "an inheritance that is imperishable, undefiled, and unfading, kept in heaven for you" (1:4). This secure inheritance is the basis of our "living hope." First Peter touches here a fundamental dynamic in Christian theology, perhaps in all Christian theology. We live on the basis of promise. We have not yet received the best thing God gives us. There is a gap between now and the future that constitutes the Christian faith. Faith requires hope. Celebration of God's gifts involves waiting. It is hard to imagine a Christian theology without this sense of incompleteness, of not yet.

Faith in 1 Peter, perhaps like all faith, exists in the midst of a lack, of a certain emptiness. The rewards for this costly faith are, in part, future rewards. It belongs to the character of all faith to endure an absence. To have all the gifts fully present would deny something in the basic nature of what makes faith deserve the name faith. Christians have long noted that faith exists in this temporal dislocation. Faith lives in a contradiction between present and future.

This dislocation has occasioned much Christian thinking on the pilgrim character of the Christian life. Our hope, our destiny, is neither this place nor this moment. Our proper destiny is both in a different place and different time. Thus Christians are on the move, on a journey, to another place and another time. Hope itself engenders aspects of alienation. Hope looks elsewhere than here. And the one who hopes must feel a certain discontent with this moment here. The one who hopes never quite fully submits to this moment. The one who hopes belongs elsewhere. All faith then gives birth to some sense of alienation. All believers are exiles and strangers.

However, the dislocation in 1 Peter is partial. The alienation is not absolute. Our belonging to the future does not fully negate our belonging to the present. Our affections for tomorrow do not undo our affections for today. Thus, we shall see a powerful commitment in 1 Peter to this life here. We are not simply waiting to get this life over with and to move on to heaven. We can be holy now. We can love now. We can carve out good gifts now in the ethics of our life, even if we do so trusting in a future we cannot yet have.

But the present is also a problem. It is not simply an empty place in which we must wait. It is not only a place where we can carve out good deeds; it is a place of suffering and abuse. In 1 Peter, faith holds to promises of salvation and glory, but it lives every day in the grips of suffering.

Thus, 1 Peter characterizes the new life of faith in this new God to be both a life of hope and a life of suffering. The letter does not simply admit suffering to the geography of faith as a necessary evil. Suffering is not an unfair imposition on the life of faith. According to 1 Peter, suffering is necessary to faith. In 1:6–7 we see a brief hint of one of the key contributions of 1 Peter to Christian theology: Suffering is a positive force in the formation of our faith.

Christians, according to 1 Peter, are called to a life formed by complex and often conflicting forces. Faith, hope, alienation, abuse, suffering, love, and holiness come together to form the Christian life. This gathering is never a simple one. Complex and competing obligations are put in place.

The Good Outsider

If there is a "no" at the heart of Christian faith, if there is a necessary alienation from the standards and forces of the non-Christian world, this "no" must impact how Christians live in the midst of a non-Christian society. Many Christians have concluded from this "no" that Christians should pursue an absolute sectarian option wherein all contact with outsiders is avoided, wherein we Christians name ourselves as light and outsiders as darkness. These Christians sometimes suggest that Christians should love only each other and not outsiders. To love outsiders would be to love evil. But other Christians insist that the "yes" of love must outweigh this sectarian "no." They insist that Christians should practice radical love and inclusiveness no matter who the person or what the moment.

Christians have, of course, not only espoused all of these scenarios and more, they have actively practiced them. In all the New Testament, 1 Peter gives the most sustained analysis of this question. For those of us who prefer simple answers, 1 Peter is frustrating. First Peter will maintain both a disconnection and a connection to outsiders, and it will offer a rather subtle script for how Christians live with non-Christians. This subtlety comes from a refusal of 1 Peter to ignore the complexity of our obligations and loyalties. There is no one single value that is relevant in these situations. Part of the power of 1 Peter's analysis lies in its capacity to maintain all these competing obligations without becoming confused. First Peter offers a coherent and ordered scenario for how Christians live in a non-Christian world, which enables them to live in this world without completely sacrificing one loyalty to another.

We have already encountered what may be the governing value in all of this. Christians are to practice "good" behavior towards outsiders. This standard will be applied to three different situations; in 2:3–17 to the question of the authority of Gentile political rulers; in 3:1–6 to wives living with problematic husbands; and in 3:8–22 to the experience of suffering. In all of these situations a similar analysis occurs, so that most readers feel that 1 Peter has some general and consistent principles that govern these analyses. In fact, many readers have suggested that these basic principles are effectively summarized in 2:11–12.

This passage begins by naming the readers as "aliens and exiles" and then warns them against the "desires of the flesh that wage war against the soul" (2:11). Thus it begins with an articulation of the break between the old and the new, of the distinction between Christians and non-Christians. But this is followed with an admittedly complex affirmation of connectedness.

> Conduct yourselves honorably among the Gentiles, so that, though they may malign you as evildoers, they may see your honorable deeds and glorify God when he comes to judge.
>
> (2:12)

In this one sentence we can trace the considerable tensions and complications that compose the relationship between these early Christians and their gentile neighbors. The sentence begins with the most fundamental and consistent early Christian response to this tension with non-Christian neighbors. We shall behave ethically, as good Christians, no matter what the situation. It is a question, first of all, of self-understanding and identity. We are people who perform good deeds. We are not, and can never be, people who intentionally do evil. This is practically the universal early Christian response to the complexities and seductions of living in the Roman world. The category of good has its own value which cannot be violated. So, whatever the precise shape of our response to outsiders, that response must deserve the adjective good.

In these various admonitions, 1 Peter alternates between two Greek words. Some translations maintain a distinction between them in English, as does the NRSV, which uses forms of "honor" for one and "good" for the other. Other translations render them both as "good." Together they form the classic terms used by Greeks for proper public behavior. Thus, "Conduct yourselves honorably among Gentiles" (2:12) may mean "submit to generally recognized public norms for ethical behavior when dealing with Gentiles." Some readers of 1 Peter dismiss as unlikely such a sweeping acceptance of external norms. The arbiters of what is honorable or not must be the Christians. However, such a divide misses the point. What makes this argument work is that certain behavior can be deemed by both Christians and non-Christians as "good." If not, then this sentence makes no sense. "Gentiles" must see this Christian behavior toward them and recognize it as good. There must be shared values here. Christians are not being called to dissimulation. They are being called to engage in a genuine good that "Gentiles," and perhaps all humans, also believe is good.

Thus, the admonition to behave honorably seems to have a dual purpose. On the one hand, the good is done for its own sake. Because Christians are good, they must only do good. Thus, the good is done as part of the self-understanding of Christians. On the other hand, the good is done as a witness to outsiders. These outsiders have maligned them as evildoers. Exactly what behavior has caused this malignment is unclear. It seems unlikely, though not impossible, that it would be the same behavior the Gentiles also name as good. One deed might occasion a believer being called both a doer of evil and a doer of good. Most readers, however, see a division here. Outsiders malign Christians for their rejection of the gods and goddesses of the empire. They consider this an evil deed. But the rest of the behavior of Christians, their overall ethic, the Gentiles recognize as good.

Such a reading fits with the final outcome, which concerns the giving of glory to God. The piety of the Gentiles leads them to name the Christians as evil. (Christians will be called atheists in later times because of their rejection of the gods.) However, the goodness of the Christians in their public behavior demonstrates to the Gentiles that something is wrong in their perception of Christians. It makes little sense for impious people to be at the same time good people. Perhaps they are not impious or evil people after all. Perhaps the question of the gods needs to be rethought. Behind this good behavior must lie a good god. The result is that these non-Christians will glorify God because this God produces good people. Christians, then, pursue good toward outsiders as witness to the goodness of their God.

Wives and Slaves

First Peter's account of good behavior toward outsiders has become the classic Christian position. And most of us find little controversial here. However, 1 Peter's account of slaves' behavior toward their lords and wives' behavior toward their husbands has been, or at least is in the modern Western world, exceedingly controversial. The New Testament contains a series of arguments that are usually termed "household codes." These codes exist in various forms in Colossians, Ephesians, 1 Timothy, Titus, and 1 Peter. They enjoin specific behavior on Christians in their classic household relationships. These codes are common in Greco-Roman ethics and will frequent later Christianity. In their fullest form, they prescribe the proper behavior between slaves and masters, wives and husbands, and children and parents. All six of these categories can be addressed.

Several aspects of these codes trouble many modern Christians. First, the basic structure of the ancient household, with its pattern of dominance and submission, with its approval of slavery, does not seem to be questioned or transformed. Christians simply take over from non-Christian society, with full approval, a dominance and submission model of the household. Modern Christians who believe in more egalitarian and democratic models find this ancient pattern troubling. Second, the admonition to slaves and wives to submit to abusive partners seems not only to be inadequate but even abusive itself.

Without pursuing the many extensive discussions that these "codes" have occasioned, we can point to the three core arguments which 1 Peter makes.

These three arguments, which support the submission to abusive masters and non-Christian husbands, show what is valued most by the author of 1 Peter.

The first two arguments are the ones we saw above. We submit to abusive lords and husbands because submission is itself a good thing. Submission comes out of the gentleness of Christian virtues. Thus, wives are to adorn themselves with "a gentle and quiet spirit" (3:4). They are to obey their husbands, because that is what good wives do (3:5) Sarah obeyed Abraham and we are children of Sarah (3:6). Thus, our self-understanding as good Christians leads us to do good in the face of abuse, to submit. Second, we submit as a witness. Our husbands who "do not obey the word" will be converted "without a word by their wives' conduct" (3:1). It is apparently less than virtuous for a wife to argue with her husband. Thus, she cannot preach the gospel to him against his orders. Instead, she will be the perfect wife, practicing perfect Christian gentle virtues. The husband will see the goodness of her behavior and will be "won over" (3:1).

We can see again how this argument rests on some values being shared by Christians and non-Christians. Whether this sharing of values actually includes a shared approval of the hierarchical structures of the ancient household is debated by readers. Some readers see 1 Peter as hunting for a good in the midst of the evil. We do good even when social structures are not good. Other readers see 1 Peter as giving approval to the structures themselves. All readers agree that 1 Peter does not offer a competing, more Christian structure. Such social rectifications seem beyond the proper role of Christians in 1 Peter.

Either reading has created much complaint among modern readers. If you live in an evil structure, to live in it well may be to further the cause of evil. To be the best soldier in an evil army is not a good. To be the most submissive of all slaves may not be a good. To be the quietest of all wives may not be a good. Christians have more obligations than blind submission. Christians also have a duty to refuse to further the cause of evil social patterns. Gentleness, peacefulness, and submission have their place. But they are not the only things we value.

First Peter's response to such complaints focuses on theology. After admonishing slaves to accept the authority of "harsh" masters, 1 Peter offers two theological arguments supporting the propriety of unjust suffering. The first argument is built on a common early Christian notion of accruing credit with God (4:12–19). The closest parallel to this argument of 1 Peter is found in the Sermon on the Mount (esp. Matt. 5:43–48). If we suffer when we do wrong, we are still in the normal economy of good and evil. Thus, 1 Peter will make the obvious point in 4:15–16 that not all suffering is Christian suffering. "But let none of you suffer as a murderer, a thief, a criminal, or even as a mischief maker" (4:15). Such suffering is deserved. As long as we are in that just economy, receiving good for good and bad for bad, no intervention by God occurs.

But if that economy is unbalanced or unfair, if we suffer evil for doing good, "if any of you suffers as a Christian" (4:16), a divine economy kicks in. We accrue credit with God. Thus, God's commitment to justice, to rewards for good deeds and punishments for bad, means that God will redress the injustices of human history. Thus, it is even good to suffer unjustly, for you will receive reward from God at the end.

The second argument is the more familiar Christological one. 1 Peter's admonitions to slaves in 2:18–25 is built primarily on a powerful Christological argument. "For to this [unjust suffering] you have been called, because Christ also suffered for you, leaving you an example, so that you should follow in his steps" (2:21). This statement is followed by a series of wonderful descriptions of the suffering of Christ, in which he models behavior for us. "When he was abused, he did not return abuse ..., but he entrusted himself to one who judges justly" (2:23). In this last phrase, Jesus is depicted as understanding the divine economy of unjust suffering. Jesus can suffer unjustly because he trusts God to be the final judge. This Jesus who suffered unjustly is the "shepherd and guardian of our souls" (2:25).

If all of this seems familiar, it is because these Christological moves have had a powerful influence on Christian theology and practice. Christians suffer because Jesus suffered. The suffering of Jesus does not end suffering; the suffering of Jesus engenders more suffering. Thus, if we in any sense belong to Christ, a good part of that belonging is the sharing of suffering. We suffer with one another and with Christ.

This Christological argument overwhelms the complaints that submitting to abuse is to further the power of the abusers. According to 1 Peter, such complaints are in error because they are calculating justice within the normal economies of human history. Yes, to submit to abuse, in the normal give-and-take between humans, is to permit evil behavior to win. However, God and God's judgment undo such calculations. The normal economies of justice and injustice that govern human history are not the real economies. The real power here is God.

This Christological argument has not, of course, ended all discussion among Christians. Some Christians respond that an absolute denial of our responsibilities for social justice is not a proper Christian response. Christians must pursue justice and righteousness in all its forms in every corner of life. Our calling is not simply to accrue credit with God but to further God's kingdom on earth. Furthermore, the historical Jesus did indeed suffer unjustly, but in his life and ministry he also pursued justice on earth. Thus, a suffering Christology such as this, while true, is unbalanced.

Actually, 1 Peter's proposals on suffering are even more difficult than what we have seen thus far. Suffering is not only something that God can transform into a good; suffering itself becomes, not just an unfortunate intrusion into the Christian life, but a necessary aspect of the Christian life.

Necessary Suffering

The most extensive comment in 1 Peter on suffering occurs in 3:8–22, the first part of which is a wonderful articulation of the Christological argument outlined above. Here we encounter again the Christological focus wherein Jesus' own experience of suffering for doing good creates the proper theological and ethical pattern for us. "Do not repay evil for evil or abuse for abuse; but, on the contrary, repay with a blessing. It is for this that you were called—that you might inherit a blessing" (3:9). When we break from the normal pattern of deed for deed, when we continue to bless others and do good to others while they return such behavior with abuse, we become connected to the Christ pattern. In this Christ pattern the principle of justice, of good for good and evil for evil, is given not only divine approval but divine assurance. If human history does not repay our good with good, then God will. In fact, this postponement of proper justice, this capacity to trust God to repay, this ability to live on faith and hope rather than on possession, is what makes the Christian life Christian.

At the conclusion of this section, where the passage focuses on the power of God to save us in the midst of suffering, the author makes an intriguing reference to baptism (3:20–21). The core Christological pattern of God saving in the midst of suffering is connected to Noah's ark and to baptism. The implications of these connections have long fascinated readers. The connection of the water of the flood to the water of baptism will become a familiar one in Christianity. The water of baptism becomes not a purifier in itself but a threat, the threat of death by drowning, the threat of abuse and persecution. Furthermore, a sense of exclusiveness begins to pervade our reading of 1 Peter. God saves through suffering. Perhaps the water of baptism is always a water of suffering. If so, then not only does God save through suffering, but only through suffering. Suffering becomes a necessary moment in the story of salvation. Thus, the Christ example of suffering is not mere example, but a necessary paradigm.

Connected to this is the notion of suffering as a purifier in 1:6–7 (and perhaps in 1:22). This frequent Jewish and Christian notion of the positive value of having one's faith put on trial is being intensified here. Given the reading above, we should probably read 1:6–7 not as a description of one of many courses the life of faith might take but as the one and only course. It is not simply that Christian faith can grow even in the midst of suffering. Rather, Christian faith needs suffering if it is to grow. The intensity of suffering forces the question of whether we really trust God to redress the unjust suffering in our lives. A real experience of suffering forces us to decide if we really believe that suffering for doing good connects us to the salvific story of Jesus. It is only in the intensity of suffering that our faith can really become faith. It is only in the gap between what should be and what is that faith can really be faith. Faith is like gold; it must pass through fire. The absence of justice is a good, for only in its absence can Christian faith grow.

The concept of suffering as a purifying fire leads to the striking notion in 4:12–19 of suffering as the beginning of divine judgment. This judgment is, of course, the final judgment in which the character of all persons and all things will be revealed. Furthermore, the revealing power of judgment is already occurring ahead of time in the fiery ordeal taking place among these Christians. This is a natural connection. If suffering reveals the true character of our faith, then suffering is of the same power as the final judgment. However, when suffering is not only an analogy to judgment but a species of it, the beginning of it, then suffering and God become connected in a new way. God is almost the author of suffering.

Few readers doubt the brilliance and power of 1 Peter's proposals on all of this. Instead, the questions focus on the sufficiency of the argument. Is this really an adequate account of suffering and God's righteousness? Is James more correct in 1:13 when it warns against too easily crediting God with temptation and trials? Isn't God the one who saves us from suffering and evil, not the one who sends it to us?

First Peter's arguments are not so simple as the above reading of 4:12–19 might suggest. It is not the case that suffering and God's presence can be absolutely equated. Suffering is also, in 1 Peter, a sign of God's absence. In fact, part of our suffering is that we do not presently see Jesus. As 1 Peter 1:8 notes in connection to our present suffering, "Although you have not seen him, you love him; and even though you do not see him now, you believe in him and rejoice." Our present suffering is hereby connected to our incapacity to see Jesus now.

The injustices of this life are not just the threatening waters of baptism through which God saves us. These injustices are signs of God's absence. God is still absolutely a God of justice. We cannot fully equate injustice with God's will.

If this is the case, then a tension exists in 1 Peter's account of suffering. No single proposition can hold the complex experience of Christian suffering. Suffering opens on a variety of theological powers and human conditions. First Peter does not collapse that variety. If anything, it adds to it, increases the tensions, and complicates our attempt to understand suffering.

Faith grows in this sense of God's absence, in this experience of suffering. However, because faith grows in this experience, God cannot be accounted as perfectly absent in either suffering or absence. God is both present and not present in suffering. God is both present and not present now. God is even present in God's absence. In the tensions and gaps created by this presence and absence, Christian faith takes on its fundamental character as Christian.

Be Holy: Love for the Community

> Now that you have purified your souls by your obedience to the truth
> so that you have genuine mutual love, love one another deeply from
> the heart.
>
> (1:22)

God's presence does not always have this paradoxical feel which it has in suffering; God's presence, according to 1 Peter, can be seen rather clearly in the holiness and morality of the community. Holiness is, of course, the classic category in antiquity for the presence and character of the divine. This is true for both the God of Israel and the gods of Greeks and Romans. Temples are holy places, whether the temple is in Jerusalem or Rome or Bithynia.

Christians have no temple. Thus, logically, they lack holiness. In fact, as we have seen, their refusal to frequent the temples of their cities would be seen as a refusal to partake of holiness, perhaps even as an attack on holiness. Their "atheistic" behavior would seem to be a rejection of the basic health, goodness, and holiness of society. Atheists are seen as hating both the gods and humanity. If we love humanity, then we must serve and worship the gods who bless and curse human beings. Christians have no holiness and no love.

First Peter makes the classic and nearly universal early Christian move. We Christians are a temple ourselves. In 1:13–2:10, First Peter details the theological forces that create the holiness of the community. The key is, of course, Christology. First Peter makes two Christological moves in this passage that initiate the holiness of the Christians. First is the sacrifice of Jesus. We are ransomed "not with perishable things like silver or gold, but with the precious blood of Christ, like that of a lamb without defect or blemish" (1:18–19). There are echoes here of the argument we encountered in Hebrews wherein Christ is not only the perfect sacrifice but also the eternal sacrifice. The blood of Christ ends the need for any more temples. Although 1 Peter does not explicitly say that the blood of Christ makes us holy, the context of both ancient sacrifice and the passage itself makes such a reading nearly unavoidable. Christians do partake of the power of temple sacrifices and their resultant holiness. However, our sacrifice occurred on the cross once and for all. Read this way, the flow of the passage makes sense; 1:16 quotes Leviticus 19:2: "You shall be holy, for I am holy." And 1:22 looks back on an accomplished holiness. We are holy based on the power of the "precious blood of Christ."

The second Christological move is also related to temples and the holiness of temples. But here the imagery is not of the sacrifices that occur in front of temples but of the stones of the temple itself. "Come to him, a living stone, … and like living stones, let yourselves be built into a spiritual house, to be a holy priesthood, to offer spiritual sacrifices" (2:4–5). Christ is the stone, the cornerstone, of a new temple (2:6–7). This stone is rejected by the builders of temples (2:7); it causes "them" to stumble (2:8). But this stone is now "the very head of the corner" (2:7). And we, when we belong to this stone, become "a chosen race, a royal priesthood, a holy nation, God's own people" (2:9).

The gathering of imagery here is impressive. The entire accoutrements and powers of temples are evoked here. A holy temple has a holy priesthood. A holy temple makes the nation around it holy. A holy temple is a sign that a people and a god belong to one another. A holy temple is composed of holy stones. We Christians, who have no temples, are a temple. In fact, we ourselves are all the accoutrements of a temple. Thus, when the early Christians walked through the sacred centers of their ancient cities and looked up at the grand temples around them, they were called to believe that they, and their Christian community, were themselves a temple. Temples had now become a people. People were the stones of this new living temple. It was a stunning theological move. And 1 Peter articulates it as effectively as any early Christian text.

However, the brilliance of 1 Peter lies not just in the elucidation of this living temple but in a re-articulation of the Old Testament understanding of holiness. Holiness is not a power or status that belongs only to the temple precinct or one's behavior in the temple. You cannot be holy only by offering proper sacrifice. Perfect liturgy does not make one holy. Holiness belongs to every moment of one's life. Holiness is an ethical category. Thus, if Israel keeps the temple and its priests pure and performs all the sacrifices and liturgies flawlessly but permits injustice in the land, then she is not holy. There is no holiness if there is no justice.

First Peter combines holiness and ethics in such a way that it becomes hard to distinguish them at all. There is a constant interplay between deeds and holiness in this section. Note, for instance, the flow of 1:13–16. "Prepare your minds" (1:13). "Like obedient children, do not be conformed to … desires" (1:14). "Instead, as he who called you is holy, be holy yourselves in all your conduct" (1:15). All our conduct is to be holy. This does not mean that we should spend all our time in church or in temple liturgies. It means "obedience."

Holiness comes from obedience to the "living and enduring word of God" (1:23). We make ourselves holy through our deeds. This is not to deny the efficacy of Christ's sacrifice. It is the realization of that sacrifice. The sacrifice makes us holy, but holiness is ethics. Holiness is not a status; it is a way of living. Thus, according to 1:22, we make ourselves holy by obedience to the truth. We become living stones by way of obedience. We become a holy nation, a royal priesthood, by having "genuine mutual love" (1:22). We partake of the blood of Christ (1:19) when we "love one another deeply from the heart" (1:22).

Thus, Christians do have holiness. They do have love for humanity. However, our holiness is not displayed in a temple. And our love is not displayed in our loyalty to the gods of these temples. Rather, our holiness is our love. Our love is our holiness. Christian temples do not sit on high points of the city; they do not abut the main streets; they do not have gleaming columns and majestic facades. Christian temples exist only in the good deeds of Christians. If Romans want to see Christian holiness, they must watch Christian behavior. If Romans want to worship this God of the Christians, they cannot go to any temple. Rather they will "see your honorable deeds and glorify God" (2:12).

Most modern Christians are astonished at the confidence early Christians had in the morality of their lives. First Peter builds a theology that asserts not only the possibility but the actuality of Christian love and compassion. Admittedly, much of the ethic in this letter comes in the imperative mood, as a request or a command. But the letter assumes the efficacy of the imperatives. Christians will indeed be holy, because they will indeed obey the word. They love each other.

The Universality of the Gospel

Honor everyone. Love the family of believers. Fear God. Honor the emperor.

(2:17)

Even in the details of the ethic of 1 Peter we can detect the tension between belonging and not belonging to the world around them. As we argued earlier, there is a "no" and there is also a "yes" toward the non-Christian culture that shapes Christian understanding. On the one hand, the Christian gospel is universal in its range. Everyone will be judged by the same God and the same standards. On the other hand, the Christian community has been already separated from the Roman world. They have been born again to a new life; they are new people. They are holy people in the midst of unholiness. They no longer belong. On the one hand, they reject the standards, loyalties, and gods of their old lives. This rejection, as we saw, leads to alienation and persecution. On the other hand, they witness to the goodness and holiness of the God of Jesus Christ through behavior that even outsiders deem good.

Similar tensions surface in the details of the ethics. We do not treat everyone the same way. We do not love everyone with absolute risk. Such radical love appears to be reserved for members of the community. That love is funded by mutuality. We love each other (1:22). We are not called to love any other with the same risk. Instead, we are called to "honor everyone" (2:17). We treat all persons with the proper virtues. We treat the emperor with the proper honor due an emperor (2:17). Slaves treat masters with recognized propriety (2:18). So do wives their husbands (3:1). We practice good behavior toward all. But we "love one another deeply from the heart" (1:22).

There is a certain distance between this kind of ethical calculation and the radical universal love most people find in the Sermon on the Mount. In perceiving this distance, we are touching on an ancient Christian debate. And we certainly cannot sort that debate here. In any case, most readers of 1 Peter detect a calculation of appropriateness in the ethic of 1 Peter. You do not risk absolute vulnerability toward outsiders. You assess the person before you and meet him or her with a virtue fitting for that person. A certain sectarianism is preserved in this kind of calculation. Of course, as we have seen, that sectarianism is compromised by a whole set of other forces.

First Peter gives no simple response to the issue of Christianity and culture. None of the classic models of "Christ against culture," "Christ of culture," "Christ above culture," and so on, seem to fit precisely. The text maintains a series of obligations and tensions that call one into and out of non-Christian culture in a way that fits no precise or consistent pattern. This is the text's real genius on this issue. Perhaps the only universal is that we are to practice good behavior toward all persons. Of course, it takes a wise person to know what the good is for this moment.

Conclusion

Our struggle to understand human suffering is not resolved by 1 Peter. And this letter does not give a conclusive answer to how Christians should relate to non-Christian culture. If anything, it increases the intensity and complexity of both of these issues.

First Peter reinforces the familiar contradiction at the heart of Christian experience of suffering. We noted at the beginning of this chapter that Christians have maintained that suffering is both a sign of God's absence and a sign of God's presence. Christians have evaluated suffering both as an unnecessary evil that should be avoided and as a necessary evil that produces a unique good. First Peter detects in suffering both the presence of evil and the presence of God. Suffering comes out of the evil in a world that hates Christians. Thus, suffering always belongs to evil. At the same time, God stakes a claim on suffering. Suffering is the beginning of God's judgment. Suffering is a necessary moment in the journey to salvation. Thus, suffering always belongs also to God. Neither of these truths can be surrendered. Suffering will always have a contradictory character in Christian life. And no one approach to it will ever suffice.

First Peter also reinforces the familiar contradiction at the heart of Christians' relationship to non-Christian culture. They have typically felt both disconnected and connected to non-Christian cultures. First Peter does not let us go either way with this. It intensifies both our connection and our disconnection. It articulates, with great insistence, the "no" at the heart of faith. But 1 Peter also articulates, with equal insistence, Christian obligations to non-Christians. There is both a "no" and a "yes" to non-Christians that Christians must always maintain. To say one without the other is to surrender part of one's Christian obligations. Again, as is the case with suffering, no one approach will suffice. These conflicting obligations must be sorted in each and every encounter by a Christian with a non-Christian.

The genius of 1 Peter lies in its capacity to gather diverse, even conflicting, concepts into one text. It gives full voice to the tensions that haunt theology. The tensions emerge both in the letter's treatment of individual topics and in the structure of the overall theology. We are unable to find a controlling image or controlling rhetoric that can master all the tensions in the theology of this text. There is a certain disorder in the text of 1 Peter that resists our attempts to order it.

It is certainly the case that modern Christians are less enamored with theological order than were our predecessors. We are less likely to think of good theology as a well-ordered hierarchy of theological truths in which one truth leads logically and coherently to the next. We are more likely to appreciate tensions and even illogic in our theology. First Peter is, in this sense, a very modern text. It does not have one central image from which the rest are derived. Its theology is more a gathering of theological truths, of theological forces. To subsume one image to another in our reading is to misread. In the midst of these diverse images, most readers perceive a coherency of outlook. But the coherency is not that of a single theological truth. It is a coherency of not forgetting the many theological truths that compose a good theology. It is the coherency of combining in one syntax a rich diversity of images.

This refusal to articulate simplistic solutions, this insistence on remembering the conflicts inherent to Christian faith, does not mean that 1 Peter is lost in despair and confusion. What we trust in the end is not our theology, even if what we say is true. What we trust is God.

> Humble yourselves therefore under the mighty hand of God, so that he may exalt you in due time. Cast all your anxieties on him, because he cares for you. ... And after you have suffered for a little while, the God of all grace, who has called you to his eternal glory in Christ, will himself restore, support, strengthen, and establish you.
>
> (5:6–7, 10)

This is the ultimate message of 1 Peter—in the midst of suffering, whatever its cause or destiny, trust in God, for God will "restore, support, strengthen, and establish you" (5:10).

4

Jude and 2 Peter

Jude as Theological Puzzle

Some texts do not quite fit the normal patterns for how a text works. They do not respond readily to our usual methods of reading. The standard ways we have read texts in this volume do not work very well when applied to the twenty-five verses of Jude. There is something about Jude that makes it hard to read.

We have employed a variety of strategies in our explorations of the other texts. For example, we have attempted to recreate the intentions and the patterns of thought that were present in the author at the moment of inscription of the text. We have tried to recreate the setting of the audience or the recipients of the original text. We have looked for literary patterns that order the rhetoric of each text. We have looked for controlling theological or ethical images that gather and manage the other images in the text. In general, we have explored the site of each text as a self-contained site, believing that we can identify all the things above (the author, the recipients, the rhetoric, the theology) in the sequence of the words before us. And we have tried to read these texts on their own terms to the best of our ability.

We have treated the words of each text as almost sacred in themselves. If we formed an image of the author, that image was subject to correction and even rejection by the text itself. If we built a theology out of our reading of a text, that theology was also subject to the rhetoric of the text itself. We have noted several times that texts tend to be more chaotic and slippery than the theologies we formulate around them. Rich texts, such as we have been reading, resist summary. As many readers have long noted, the Bible escapes and undoes our biblical theologies. Nevertheless, our various readings of these texts seem successful. And they certainly seem fitting to the texts themselves.

But Jude calls for a different kind of reading. Almost every reader of Jude notices that this text is a different kind of text. This difference makes it fascinating to read.

Outline of Jude

1–2   Opening salutation
3–4   The danger of ungodly intruders
5–16   Punishment of false teachers
    5–10   The stories of Egypt, Sodom and Gomorrah, and the fight for Moses' body
    11–13   Three more stories and a polemical description of the intruders
    14–16   The coming judgment
17–23 Warnings and appeals
24–25 Concluding doxology

Context

In some ways, the problems with reading Jude are just an intense form of the standard problems we have when reading texts. We have seen in our readings of Hebrews, James, and 1 Peter how difficult it can be to determine the proper historical context for an ancient text. In some ways the original setting of Jude is even more difficult to specify.

Who for instance is "Jude, a servant of Jesus Christ and brother of James"? Although there were several Judes in early Christianity (it was not an uncommon name), almost all readers of Jude think that the "Jude" mentioned here is one of the brothers of Jesus. He is named in Mark 6:3 along with James, Joses, and Simon as one of Jesus' brothers. Thus, under this reading, the James of Jude 1 would be the brother of Jesus who becomes head of the church in Jerusalem. Given that this is the Jude intended here, what does that tell us? We have seen an early Christian penchant for putting the names of apostles or famous early Christians on their documents as authors. Is this letter really written by a brother of Jesus or is an unnamed author employing this name pseudonymously?

Most readers find it hard to maintain a brother of Jesus is the author of this text, although a few do so. In either case, we learn remarkably little that helps us read. We know next nothing about Jude, the brother of Jesus, apart from his name. According to Mark 3:21, 32, he initially resisted Jesus' ministry. But the letter of Jude, whether by Jude or someone else, testifies to his eventual support. But we do not know anything about his theology or his history that provides any controlling background to this text. We would certainly guess a Palestinian provenance based on later suggestions that the family of Jesus remained, for the most part, in the Jerusalem/Palestine area. Yet this is not certain and provides little guidance in any case. Thus, the name by itself does not really help us read. In fact, the twenty-five verses before us are all we really know about Jude.

More promising is a reconstruction of the situation in the community of the recipients. Jude gives no location for the recipients, but there seem to be direct descriptions of the opponents and an indirect description of the recipients. These descriptions might give us some sense of the proper context for reading this text.

The bulk of Jude consists of a complicated attack on "certain people who have stolen in among you" (4). The driving purpose of the letter appears to be an attempt to meet the danger posed by these intruders. As Jude 3 asserts, the author originally wanted to write "about the salvation we share," but felt compelled instead to write this combined attack on these intruders and plea for the readers to "contend for the faith." Thus, according to the rhetoric of Jude itself, its argument is forged in polemic. If this is true, then Jude becomes strongly embedded in a particular historical moment. Jude is not offering a calm, universal, friendly account of the gospel. It is formulating theology couched for argument, for a particular disagreement with particular persons. We, the modern readers, must then reconstruct the context if we are to comprehend the argument. While this need to reconstruct context is true for any text any reader might read, a historical text imbedded in polemic, such as is Jude, increases this obligation.

However, it is not clear how to construe the various references to these opponents. With a couple of exceptions, the descriptions are quite stylized, taken either from Old Testament examples, ancient Jewish legends, or standard Greco-Roman polemic. The opening description of the opponents in verse 4 is typical. First, "they have stolen in among you." This may well be an accurate, if unfriendly, description. They are outsiders. Second, they have been long ago designated, perhaps by various ancient writings, as "ungodly." We can find an account of them in the ancient texts. Jude will call on many of these texts in the verses that follow. Third, they "pervert the grace of God into licentiousness and deny our only Master and Lord, Jesus Christ." It is hard to know what to do with this last bit. It may have some kernel of truth in it somewhere, but the accusation is typical of early Christian polemic. Nearly all opponents can be and were so traduced. Thus, many readers think there is no real descriptive data here; this is just the standard rhetoric of early Christian polemic. However, other readers think the suggestions of immorality and denial of the Lordship of Jesus must have some basis in historical fact. Stylized and inaccurate name-calling would hardly be an effective rebuttal.

The rest of the polemic in Jude follows a similar pattern. The pattern entails a citation or loose allusion to a text or story, followed by a direct comment about the current opponents. In fact, this pattern of citation and application is typically seen as the theological heart of this letter. The key theological move of Jude lies in an attempt to connect the present to the past by way of these citations, which we shall explore later.

At this point, we note how difficult this pattern makes any attempt to determine the character of these opponents. The imagery comes mostly from Old Testament texts. It is as though the language of the ancient texts has priority over any precise description of current behavior. Thus, the account of

the opponents in Jude is difficult to use for a reconstruction of their actual behavior or beliefs.

In verses 5–7, Jude appeals to several stories—the disobedience in Egypt,
the rebellion of the angels (the version from *1 Enoch*), and Sodom and
Gomorrah. The author then adds that "in the same way these dreamers also
defile the flesh, reject authority, and slander the glorious ones" (8). Again, it
is not clear what should be gleaned from these references. Some readers see
evidence in the term "dreamers" of exceptional and authorizing visions that
these people were having or had had. Defiling the flesh and rejecting authority are so prevalent in ancient polemic that little can be done with them. But
an accusation of "slandering the glorious ones" is more idiosyncratic. Perhaps
we have an account here of people having visions and slandering part of the
heavenly court.

Verses 9–16 show this same pattern of citation and application. The author
mentions an apocryphal story of Michael fighting with the devil for the body
of Moses. He also alludes to Cain, Balaam, and Korah's rebellion. These citations alternate with language that sounds more direct. These people "slander
what they do not understand" (10) and are "destroyed" by the things "they
know by instinct" (10). They are "blemishes (or "reefs") on your love feasts"
(12), "waterless clouds" (12), trees both dead to themselves and without fruit
for others (12), "wild waves of the sea" (13), and "wandering stars" (13). The
images prove awkward data for any specific historical reconstruction of these
people.

These accusations lead to a declaration of judgment upon them by a direct
quote from *1 Enoch*. This quote calls judgment down upon them for "all the
deeds of ungodliness" and "the harsh things that ungodly sinners have spoken
against him [the Lord]" (15). This quote inspires another specific accusation.
"These are grumblers and malcontents; they indulge in their own lusts; they
are bombastic in speech, flattering people to their own advantage" (16).
Finally, the beloved are reminded of the prediction of the apostles. These
apostles are quoted and then the author adds another final direct note: "It is
these worldly people, devoid of the Spirit, who are causing divisions" (19).

All of this makes for a formidable attack. The combination of ancient texts
and contemporary images produces a rhetorically compelling critique. The
range of imagery alone is impressive. The text evokes classic Old Testament
types. The text also puts forward the wonderful metaphors of "waterless
clouds," "wandering stars," and so forth. The text includes what sounds like
direct address: these people do this and that. But in the end, it is not clear what
we might have in the way of a historically accurate description of these people
that we might use to reconstruct the context of this letter.

Two immediate conclusions are warranted. First of all, there is no single
image or accusation that cannot be read as standard polemic. Every image
here has either a literary function or literary origin that can explain its presence in this text. Thus, there is nothing here that we can use with complete
confidence as straightforward description. Second, there must be some con-

tact between these images and the actual behavior of the opponents. We must assume that the author of Jude thinks these attacks are true, that the images fit the persons. Certainly this fit might vary in the mind of the author. But Jude does not read as a textual game with no reference to the real world.

There is a real historical problem at the root of this text. Jude is written in the context of serious conflict. However, the precise nature of the conflict is very unclear. Most readers suggest that it is with outsiders empowered by visions. These visions may give warrant to denial of the normal authorities in the church and the cosmos. The specifics of all of this are not, however, spelled out in Jude. In any case, as a controlling context for our reading, a reconstruction of the opponents is not much help.

A few readers have suggested that the rhetorical heart of Jude is not the attack in verses 3–19 but the plea to the readers in 20–23. There is some warrant for this, given the tone of the attack. The attack does not seem designed to refute the opponents in a face-to-face confrontation. The attack is unlikely to change the beliefs or behavior of these opponents. In fact, Jude does not seem to be designed to do that. Rather, the attack provides an arsenal for "those who are called" (v. 1). Jude is an appeal to the readers to fight for the faith (v. 3); it is not an attempt to change enemies into friends.

This is important for deciphering the theological method of the letter, but it provides minimal historical data. We can place the text in its proper historical moment only in a most general way. Whatever historical grounding we might put in place for Jude cannot, in the end, control the slippery rhetoric of the letter.

A Theology of Time and Texts

Many readers of Jude complain that Jude lacks any real creative theology. It is simply an arbitrary application of diverse texts to a contemporary problem. Jude, they say, is a series of haphazard proof texts. Both the situation and the ancient texts suffer abuse by these proof texts. When texts are applied in this way, both the original meaning of the text and the originality of the contemporary moment are lost. Our inability to reconstruct the historical situation is but one indication of the theological woodenness of Jude. It does not unpack the real situation; it simply confuses past and present with a series of citations.

This complaint, in my opinion, touches upon the real theological creativity of Jude. Christian theology is funded in part by two curious and intentional confusions. The first confusion is a muddling of time. Past, present, and future are not distinct moments. Past, present, and future touch one another and define one another. The second confusion is an insistence that an ancient text, not written by us or to us, is actually about us. The words of the Bible belong not just to the past but to every present and every future. These two confusions supply the theology of Jude.

Nearly every reader classifies its theology as apocalyptic, although it is not always clear what is meant by that designation. In one sense the theology is apocalyptic because Jude anticipates the final judgment. Specifically, Jude 14–25 contains a series of invocations about that final judgment, which includes both threats and promises, punishments and rewards. Jude is apocalyptic at least in the sense that readers are expected to orient their present lives toward this future. In fact, the truth about the future defines the present. It is as though a truth is a truth always and no matter what. Truths are not bound by time, at least according to the theology of Jude.

But the classic apocalyptic looking-to-the-future in Jude is compromised by the power of the past. According to Jude, the present seems more governed by the past than by the future. In fact, the future is governed by this same past. The past is the primary source of sacred revelations, of sacred texts. The syntax and images from this past are applied without alteration or adjustment to the present. The past names the present. In fact, it is the power of ancient texts to define and order the present that is the fundamental theological force in Jude. Jude does theology by reading the present in terms of the texts of the past.

Most of the citations in Jude are from the canonical Old Testament. But we also have references to later Jewish expansions of Old Testament stories and to *1 Enoch*, texts that are not part of the traditional canon. This apparent carelessness about the proper borders of the canon has troubled Christian readers. If the single most important power in this theology is the voice of ancient texts, then the proper identification of which texts have this power should be crucial. However, we find in Jude a surprising looseness about this classic question of the canon. Jude gives equal weight to the canon, late legends, apocryphal texts, and the predictions of the Christian apostles. Whatever the reasons for this, it is clear that Jude does not share later Christian skittishness about the canon.

Perhaps Jude thinks that truth is not bordered this way. Truth is truth wherever it is found. Perhaps presence in a precise list of texts is not what makes something true. Maybe the direction is the opposite. Instead, the presence of truth is what places a text in the right list. If this is the case, then it is not correct to say that Jude simply surrenders the originality of the present to the syntax of the past. It is not simply that the past names the present. Instead, it may be that Jude perceives a truth about these opponents and these Christian readers. And it is this contemporary truth that drives the argument. Admittedly, this perceived truth may come in part from reading these texts; it may be in part derivative. But the present truth, thus grasped, also opens up the ancient texts. The texts square with this perceived truth. The texts are read through the lens of this truth, through the lens of the contemporary experience. The past and the present belong to each other in such a way that neither surrenders to the other. There is a third term, the revealed truth, that connects them.

The New Testament and early Christianity devoted much thought to the relationship between the ancient texts and the ongoing Christian experience. Christianity even develops accepted patterns for how this past and present can be properly connected. Modern readers of Jude have devoted much attention to defining how Jude connects these ancient texts to the contemporary situation. And we have found connections to several of these common patterns for how Christianity and Judaism read ancient texts. Jude's reading of texts contains aspects of later rabbinic midrash (a rather creative and diverse style of interpretation seen in rabbinic commentaries), of Qumran-style pesher readings (in which ancient texts are read as speaking directly about contemporary persons or events), of Christian typology (in which an Old Testament person is seen as a "type" of a contemporary person), and even of allegory (in which the Old Testament texts are read as riddles). However, it is more adequate to admit that there is a certain disorder, an arbitrariness, in how Jude connects texts to the present. Furthermore, the connection Jude establishes between the textual past and the Christian present is more complicated than these "accepted patterns" of citation suggest.

Readers have often read these citations only for the explicit theological moral that Jude draws from them. The purpose of naming the rebellion in the wilderness, disobedient angels, Sodom, Gomorrah, Cain, Balaam, and Korah is only to show, over and over again, that sinners will be punished. All these citations collapse into one neat theological point. And it is certainly true that Jude insists on the punishment of sinners, both old and new. However, these citations in Jude are more formidable than such a collapse into one theological point suggests.

Jude creates (or witnesses to) an opening between the past and the present by way of these citations. The named examples are not simply those of sinners who were punished. Each name, each citation, can teach something about the varieties of sin and about the diversities of divine punishment. Each citation, each name, has its own integrity and individuality. The points of commonality with the present cannot overwhelm the individuality of the past.

Thus, the force of these citations is not confined to the syntax of Jude. We cannot learn all Jude wants us to learn simply by reading Jude. We need also to read the stories of Cain, Sodom, Balaam, and Korah. We need to read those stories while thinking about ourselves. Jude is not simply citing in order to reinforce a theological point. Jude is inviting a reading not just of itself but of other texts. Jude is creating a permanent connection between past and present.

On the one hand, this coming together of past and present creates difficulties for the modern reader. We want to read each text in its own voice. We have argued several times in this book that an attempt to hear the singular voice of a text is crucial to the ethics of reading. Thus, we want each text to have its own integrity. We want to treat the site of each text as somewhat sacred. But Jude does not permit this. The text of Jude is occupied by other

texts. The place of Jude is unstable. We cannot read Jude well by only reading the words of Jude. Jude gives up its place to other texts. To read Jude well,
we need to read other words not cited here. If you do not know the story of
Cain, then you need to read it, all of it. Jude invites a wandering among these
ancient stories. This wandering is unprogrammed. There is no single pattern
for how we are to connect these texts to our present. It takes the creativity and
freedom of the reader.

On the other hand, this coming together of past and present by way of ancient texts points to something fundamental to Christian theology. Christian
theology is animated, in large part, by a temporal and textual displacement accomplished by the authority and voice of the biblical text. Christians do theology in the context of the canon. Attempts to describe and even prescribe the
proper force of this canonical influence are important—and perhaps even essential. We cannot detail all those options here. Instead, we should note again
the resistance of Jude to any one of the classic categories. Jude connects the
textual past to the present in a disordered way. This disorder seems to reflect
the actual function of the biblical text in Christian thought. The Bible speaks
in many ways. The Bible speaks because readers wander its text. In that wandering they perceive connections to their own lives, their own time.

Some modern readers complain about a lack of theological sophistication
in Jude. This running together of past, present, and future, of ancient text and
modern event, without prescribing the proper principles for such connections, strikes these readers as a bit too simple. We need to be nervous, they
say, about combining past and present in this way. If we read the ancient text
as though it is fully ours, we can abuse both the text and ourselves. Jude is certainly open to this complaint. However, it is not clear who has the better case
here. Jude is indeed remarkably unnervous about combining times and texts.
Sometimes an attempt to prescribe and proscribe how a text might speak effectively silences the texts. If a text can only speak to us along prescribed patterns, then we and the text become effectively divided. Any such division con-
tradicts the basic theological outlook of Jude.

Admittedly, Jude's capacity to trust the reader to perceive connections in
an unconfined way will become the minority viewpoint in early Christianity.
Early Christians would be extremely troubled by unprogrammed reading of
the Bible. Such loose readings are the starting place of heresies. However, it
can also be argued that apart from unprogrammed reading there is no reading
at all.

Furthermore, the dislocations of time and texts that are put in place in Jude
are fundamental moments in the theology of Jude. The dislocations of past,
present, and future that create and order the Christian life are mirrored in the
dislocations of the text. It is as though the author of Jude creates in the site of
the text itself the ordering and disordering forces of Christian experience.
Christians live in the same temporal and spacial dislocations that a reader of
Jude endures.

Safekeeping

In the midst of the powerful series of citations and applications, Jude weaves in the fundamental biblical notion of "keeping." God has the power to keep—to keep "us" for salvation and to keep "sinners" for punishment. The Lord has "kept [the disobedient angels] in eternal chains in deepest darkness for the judgment of the great day" (6). This keeping of ancient figures for punishment parallels the keeping of contemporary ones. The creative name-calling in 12–13 (reefs at your love feasts, waterless clouds, twice-dead trees, wild waves, and wandering stars) ends with the assurance "for whom the deepest darkness has been reserved forever." Here the Lord keeps the darkness rather than the persons, but the point is similar. The Lord not only will punish sinners someday in the future; the Lord is actively preparing this punishment by keeping the sinners and the darkness.

The Lord, of course, also keeps "you" safe (1, 24). This keeping of those who are called is not, however, an absolute keeping. As the citation in verse 5 points out, "the Lord, who once for all saved a people out of Egypt, afterward destroyed those who did not believe." Even though God is keeping "you," the believer, safe now, this is a conditional keeping. If you cease to be a believer, God no longer keeps you for salvation but keeps you instead for punishment.

In this warning we can see how the apocalyptic future, which is fundamental to the theology of Jude, is not confined in its force to the future. The keeping for the future exists in the present. God's keeping acts on the readers of Jude now, even if the final manifestation of that keeping must wait. Moreover, there is in the ancient texts an initial and partial manifestation of this keeping. Past, future, and present are combined in such a way as to intensify the impact of God's power to keep. Thus, even though Jude lacks any real apocalyptic urgency (there is no sense that the end is all that soon), this theology of keeping connects the present to this future.

Jude places us in a present that is haunted by both the past and the future. The past names the present by way of the voices of the ancient text. The wonderful promises and terrifying threats of the future exist in the present by the power of God's keeping. And we the readers are placed on the edge of rewards and punishments. Are we the "beloved" (v. 3)? Or are we the "ungodly" (v. 4)? Jude's opening to the ancient texts invites us to learn the difference between the beloved and the ungodly. These texts, read well, will place the reader in God's keeping.

Thus, it is fitting that Jude ends with an invocation of God's power to keep us safe. In the context of Jude, this invocation is a prayer.

> Now to him who is able to keep you from falling, and to make you stand without blemish in the presence of his glory with rejoicing, to the only God our Savior, through Jesus Christ our Lord, be glory, majesty, power, and authority, before all time and now and forever. Amen. (vv. 24–25)

2 Peter as a Reading of Jude

Second Peter and Jude have a literary relationship of some kind. Approximately nineteen of Jude's twenty-five verses are either cited or echoed in 2 Peter. These connections occur in the polemic against false teachers (especially 2:1–18 and 3:1–3). It is occasionally argued that Jude is reading 2 Peter. But that has proved hard to maintain. It is simpler and more successful to see the central portion of 2 Peter as a reading of Jude.

Given this extensive overlap, it is surprising how different their theological outlooks are. Some of these differences can be perceived in the various changes 2 Peter effects in what is taken over from Jude. But the more significant differences lie in the overall argument of the letter. Second Peter occupies a theological position unique to the New Testament. At first glance, however, Jude and 2 Peter appear much alike. Both maintain an apocalyptic horizon in which final judgment will occur. Both seek to connect that future to our behavior in the present. Both are caught up in controversy and use similar language to describe and attack their opponents. Both are written in the name of a famous and authoritative person. Both weave together biblical quotes and allusions with pronouncements from the apostles. Both combine these authoritative statements from the past with contemporary pronouncements. Thus, many of the same pieces are shared in both letters. However, the results in each case are quite different. Second Peter configures its theology in a remarkably different way from what we find in Jude.

In fact, it is probably not helpful to think of 2 Peter as a reading of Jude. Second Peter is not so much interpreting or even correcting Jude as using it. There is no hint in the text of 2 Peter that it is drawing on a source for its polemic. In fact, if we did not possess Jude, we would probably not, on the basis of the syntax of 2 Peter, suspect its existence. Second Peter obliterates Jude in its taking over.

In some ways, this makes 2 Peter an easier text to read. It is more successful as a single text. There is certainly no sense that one needs to read Jude in order to understand 2 Peter. There is not even the sense we found in Jude that we need to read the Old Testament texts that are employed in 2 Peter. There is more the sense that all we need to know about each Old Testament example is already inscribed in 2 Peter. Thus, the curious temporal and textual displacements we felt in Jude are not present. What we need to know can be learned by reading this text here before us. The work of wandering in texts and time has already been done.

Outline of 2 Peter

1:1–2   Opening salutation
1:3–15   God's gifts of promises and virtues
1:16–21   The transfiguration and prophecy

Simeon Peter, a Servant and Apostle

Of all the books in the New Testament, 2 Peter had the least support and the most problems in terms of canonicity in the early church. As late as the beginning of the fourth century, it still had questionable canonical status. It is not even mentioned until the third century. While the story of how it enters the canon is beyond our needs at this point, the early church's skepticism about Peter as author is not. For instance, Jerome in the fourth century, after comparing 1 Peter and 2 Peter, concluded that the same author could not have composed both. Since 1 Peter was, by this time, acknowledged as being from the hand of Peter, this meant that 2 Peter had to be pseudepigraphical. Apart from the issue of who wrote 1 Peter, Jerome's general conclusion is difficult to refute. In fact, almost all modern historians doubt that the apostle Peter was the author of 2 Peter.

Although we have encountered the awkwardness of pseudonymity already in this volume, 2 Peter employs the image and authority of Peter in such a way as to increase this awkwardness. Second Peter inscribes the face and authority of the apostle Peter into the overall force of its theology. It is not simply that the name Peter lends weight to a theology; it is that the person and authority of Peter is fundamental to the coherence of the theology.

As readers have long noted, 2 Peter is couched as Peter's testimony, an at-the-point-of-death farewell to one's family or followers. Such testimonies carried unusual weight in antiquity. Thus, 2 Peter wants to be more than just a letter from Peter; it wants to be an authoritative and final account of Peter's belief and intentions. This literary and theological move is expressed clearly in 1:12–15. "I think it is right, as long as I am in this body, to refresh your memory, since I know that my death will come soon, as indeed our Lord Jesus Christ has made clear to me." The testimony setting means that the words of 2 Peter stand in the place of the person of Peter. When the person is gone, as he will be soon, his words will remain. Second Peter is not just a letter; it is a substitute, an authorized substitute, for the person. As 1:15 says, "I will make every effort so that after my departure you may be able at any time to recall these things." We can recall these things simply by reading this letter. Because it is couched as a testimony, the words of 2 Peter accrue a unique voice and status.

Of course, this status is derivative. What makes the words of Peter authoritative and potent is not the virtue or power of Peter himself. It is Peter's status as an apostle of Jesus Christ that gives him credence. Peter's status as apostle, as someone sent by Jesus, connects the readers to Jesus himself. Thus

3:1–2, "This is now, beloved, the second letter I am writing to you; in them I am trying to arouse your sincere intention by reminding you that you should remember the words spoken in the past by the holy prophets, and the commandment of the Lord and Savior spoken through your apostles." The commands of Jesus do not come to us directly. The apostles speak these commands to us. Thus, 2 Peter, as the testimony of Peter the apostle, is as close as one can get to the direct commands of Jesus. A saying of Jesus directly quoted in a Gospel has no more authority than the commands of 2 Peter. Both come from Jesus.

We see the beginnings here of a Christology. Jesus is first of all the teacher. However, it does not sound as though Jesus enters the community as teacher through a collection of Jesus sayings. "The commandment of the Lord and Savior" is spoken "through your apostles." Thus, Jesus is present through the teachings of the apostles. This relationship between Jesus and the apostles is further explored in 1:16–18, one of the most controversial passages in the New Testament.

The passage begins (1:16) with the assertion that "we did not follow cleverly devised myths" when we made Jesus Christ known. Instead, "we had been eyewitnesses of his majesty." Does this mean that the opponents, who will be attacked in the following verses, are being accused of following such myths, in contrast to the apostles, who really know the facts? Or is the whole apostolic tradition itself being attacked as no more than "cleverly devised myths"?

This opening assertion is followed by a brief account of the transfiguration (1:17–18), which adheres pretty much to the version found in Matthew. This brief account leads to a further assertion that "we" both heard the voice and were actually there with him on the mountain (1:18). A series of questions emerges from this. First, it is not clear whether it is Jesus or Peter who is being authenticated. The focus of this passage could be to insist that the apostolic teaching about Jesus is true because "we" were actually there and heard what God said. We readers should trust the traditions about Jesus because the apostles are trustworthy witnesses. Or the point of this passage could be to insist on the reliability of the apostles and the text of 2 Peter, because these apostles have this special connection to Jesus. In this case, the trustworthiness of the apostles is derivative of the trustworthiness of Jesus.

Second, it is puzzling that 2 Peter refers to the transfiguration when early Christians typically refer to the resurrection appearances for such authentications. Two explanations have been offered. Perhaps the transfiguration is evoked because it suggests an earthly, human, transfiguration into divine form. This connects to the notion in 1:4 that we "may become participants of the divine nature." The astonishing suggestion that we, through the virtues God gives us, become in some way divine ourselves receives Christological warrant in the transfiguration. Jesus, while still human, before the resurrection, received "majesty." Jesus becomes the prototype of our own transfigurations. The second explanation is that the direct voice of God heard during the transfiguration gives unique authentication to the majesty of Jesus. The transfiguration then reinforces the arguments about the second coming in chapter 3. Jesus' unique majesty, displayed at the transfiguration, authenticated by the very voice of God, will be fully and finally displayed on the "day of the Lord" (3:10). Thus, we need not worry about the delay in his return.

All of this indicates that any attempt to separate the authority of Jesus from the authority of the apostles is misleading. As readers have long noted, 2 Peter builds its theology upon the combined credibility of both Peter and Jesus. And both depend on the other. The promises attached to Jesus, in terms of both the present and the future, seem to be in doubt. The traditions about Jesus need the support of the real voice of Peter. But the credibility of Peter in turn depends on the majesty of Jesus. Peter has authority because Peter has unique access to Jesus and the unique status of apostle. Thus, it seems more correct to suggest that 2 Peter builds a theology on the majesty of Jesus and the apostleship of Peter, which work together with a unique authority and force.

Finally, we can see again how difficult it is to decide what someone was thinking in the moment of writing. Texts, especially complex texts such as this one, create multiple readings. And it is difficult to foreclose the multiplicity of those readings by appealing to the mind of the author.

Piling Up the Virtues

Puzzlement and uncertainty over the mind of an author at the moment of inscription leads many modern readers to focus on the structure of the text itself. We look for orders inside the text and do not try to ground the text in an order outside it. This does not mean that we do not think about the meaning of the text for us, or that the text does not inspire us to think about things other than the text itself. It means that our reading of the text begins with the actual syntax before us. This attention to the rhetoric of the text leads readers to 1:3–11. Many ancient letters, including early Christian ones, begin with a thesis statement of the letter. Furthermore, readers of 2 Peter have long been drawn to these verses as a kind of summary or condensation of the theology of the letter. Like all summaries it does not capture the full implications or complexities of the letter, but it does provide an adequate framework and an effective starting point for what follows.

The passage begins with an affirmation of the present powers and gifts of God. God has already "given us everything needed for life and godliness" (1:3). The focus on the second coming in chapter 3 has led many readers to categorize 2 Peter as apocalyptic. But this categorization is misleading if we mean by this that 2 Peter confines the blessings of God to the day of the Lord. There is indeed in 2 Peter a longing, a waiting. As 3:13 declares, "But, in accordance with his promise, we wait for new heavens and a new earth, where righteousness is at home." However, the waiting for this new reality does not mean that there is no righteousness now. The key affirmation of 1:3–11 is that Christians can live righteous lives now.

The piling up of virtues in 1:5–7 is an expression, a manifestation, an achievement of this divine righteousness. The list of goodness, knowledge, self-control, endurance, godliness, mutual affection, and love is typical of early Christian virtue lists. On the one hand, all of these virtues frequent Greek and Jewish lists. There is nothing peculiarly Christian about any one of them. On the other hand, the overall weight and mood of the list reflects the peculiar early Christian attraction to the "gentle" virtues and, especially, to love as the central virtue. Christians, in their depiction of righteousness, did not discover new qualities as being righteous. They did not say, "Here is something you never thought of as good or righteous, but it actually is." Instead, they selected from the stock of good and righteous qualities a peculiarly Christian set and ordered them under the chief virtue of love.

Perhaps more striking than the list itself is 2 Peter's proposal for how such virtue is acquired and for locating the true roots and destiny of these virtues. God's "divine power has given everything needed for life and godliness." God supplies these virtues. It is not stated precisely how Second Peter connects this funding of virtues with "knowledge of him who called us" (1:3) with "his precious and very great promises" (1:4). Part of this funding must include knowledge of theological truth, but there is also here a sense of divine power that does not collapse fully into words. This interaction of power and words is indispensable to most early Christian accounts of the gospel. First of all, these virtues emerge from God's act of giving.

However, we must also exert ourselves to acquire these virtues. "You must make every effort to support your faith with goodness, and goodness with knowledge" (1:5). In fact, 1:8–10 is a series of exhortations to strive for these virtues. Second Peter articulates here the typical early Christian account of godliness: the virtues of godliness are both a gift of God and the fruit of human effort. The force of God's gift does not cancel the need for human effort. The power of human effort does not efface the force of God's gift. Righteousness, a life of godliness, the living of virtues, all require the full powers of both God and people.

Thus, there is a powerful "already" in 2 Peter. Righteousness already exists in the lives of Christian people. The possibility of becoming "participants in the divine nature" (1:4) is not confined to the day of the Lord. These virtues are of the divine nature. God is virtuous too. The majesty of Jesus is not just his rank but his righteousness. Jesus has glory because he is righteous.

The details of the transfiguration become important here. Indeed, at the transfiguration Jesus receives "honor and glory" from God (2 Peter 1:17). But this God also announces, "This is my Son, my Beloved, with whom I am well pleased" (1:17). If we read 1:3–11 as a theological summary, then God's pleasure with Jesus may be in Jesus' righteousness. Jesus then attains glory because he first attains righteousness. This fits with the order for us in 1:3–11, where the conditions and sequence are clear. If we confirm our call with lives of righteousness, we shall gain "entry into the eternal kingdom" (1:11).

In this theological sequence we encounter again the peculiar temporal dislocations in early Christian thought. If there is an already, a right now, this now does not belong to itself. The present belongs to, is structured by, the past and the future. The past acts of Jesus and the apostles supply the truths of this theology. But it is the future that seems to have the most force over the present. All the truths and values of this Christian life of virtue depend on the forces of the future day of the Lord. Chapter 3, which defends the second coming and final judgment, is not a separate theological concern from the acquisition of virtues in chapter 1. Righteousness in the present depends on this day of the Lord.

Hastening the Coming of the Lord

Second Peter 3:1–13 is the most extensive and explicit defense in the New Testament of the "coming" of the Lord. The defense focuses on "scoffers" who say, "Where is the promise of his coming?" (3:3–4), for they point out that the world has always been exactly as it is now (3:4). All the evidence points to a conclusion that the world will never end and that Jesus will never return. It is not perfectly clear from the syntax of 2 Peter whether "his coming" (3:4) is that of Jesus or of God. God's arrival on the final day, via emissaries, of course, is a classic notion in Jewish and Christian theology. However, most readers of 2 Peter think the author is referring to the coming of Jesus simply because that is the normal way early Christians conceived of the coming of the kingdom. The coming of the kingdom would be the second coming of Jesus. Thus, these scoffers appear to deny the second coming, the return of Jesus, the parousia. This attack on the second coming, as we shall see, is understood primarily by the author as an attack on the life of righteousness itself.

The author gives several responses. First, he points to the power of the word of God (3:5–7). This word formed the earth out of water (3:5), deluged the earth with water at the flood (3:6), and now reserves the present heaven and earth for fire (3:7). The word of God has absolute power over creation. And we know from the flood that this word is willing to destroy. In naming "fire" as the agent of final destruction (3:7), there may be a memory of God's promise to Noah not to destroy the world again by "water." In any case, the opening argument is that God can destroy the world if God wants.

Second, the author points out that divine time is beyond human calculation: "with the Lord one day is like a thousand years" (3:8). There is in this argument a striking version of the early Christian refusal to calculate the end. Second Peter gives the standard Christian response. God's mathematics of the end are beyond the calculations of mere humans. God's timing is beyond our grasp. But ignorance of divine secrets says nothing about the truth of the promise of the day of the Lord. The promise is still there, no matter how impatient we get or no matter how often we miscalculate the end.

Third, the author makes a very controversial comment about God's patience—"The Lord is not slow about his promise, as some think of slowness, but is patient with you, not wanting any to perish, but all to come to repentance" (3:9). It sounds innocent enough. God is not slow, but patient. God does not want anyone to perish, but wants all to repent and be saved. Second Peter touches here on a classic theological problem. We cannot imagine the final shape of God's justice and thus we cannot imagine that it will ever exist in human history. If God ever executes justice, then many (many!) will perish. But God is also merciful. If God is merciful, then God cannot be sufficiently ruthless for establishing justice. God appears to be caught in a conflict between the two characteristics of God's behavior toward humans. God is absolutely just and absolutely merciful. But these are not in harmony. There is an inherent conflict between justice and mercy. Thus, God waits. The end has not come because God hesitates. God cannot stand the violence that divine justice would produce. God does not want to do what God must do at the end.

This depiction of divine hesitation leads to another controversial remark (3:11–13). If God is hesitating, "what sort of persons ought you to be … ?" (3:11). These verses seem to entertain the possibility that God's hesitation could be permanent. Humans must do something to undo God's hesitation. Second Peter's proposal is that we ourselves must reduce the violence that would result from the arrival of God's justice. We reduce the violence by increasing the righteousness. If there is more righteousness, then there will be less need for punishment. Thus, we come to the astonishing conclusion that humans can hasten the end. We should lead "lives of holiness and godliness, waiting for and hastening the coming day of God" (3:11b–12a). Our righteousness not only prepares us for the end, it evokes the end.

There is some warrant here for the nineteenth-century liberal notion of building the kingdom one step at a time. Christians have long puzzled over the problem of how God's kingdom, which celebrates the freedom of humans, can come by force. This kingdom, if it is really one of freedom and peace, needs to be welcomed. Humans must seek righteousness in the same moment that God offers it. We must move, hand-in-hand with God, one step at a time toward the kingdom. Second Peter hardly qualifies as a full progenitor of this liberalism. It certainly envisions a violent end. But it also puzzles over the conflict between justice and mercy that inspires such liberalism.

Second Peter offers a final image in this section that has also provoked controversy. In 3:10 and 3:12, the author declares that the present earth and heavens will be "dissolved with fire." And in 3:13, we wait not for redemption and re-creation of this earth, as in Paul, but for "new heavens and a new earth," as in Revelation. This dissolving of the present heaven and earth underscores the violence and the otherness of the coming of righteousness. The new age is so radically discontinuous with the old age that the old earth and heavens must perish. We need a whole new order, not a redeemed order.

Christian theology about the coming kingdom of God has long debated the nature of the continuity and discontinuity between the old age and the new. It is not clear what is present now that survives the violence of the day of the Lord. Typically we do not say either that nothing survives or that everything survives. Some things last and some things perish. The debate has centered on what and how much of each. Certainly, the cosmic imagery in 2 Peter emphasizes the disruption and terror of the arrival. However, many Christians today balk at such radical disruption and hesitate to surrender the present earth to the newness of the kingdom. The kingdom, they say, must redeem the earth, as it appears to do in the Synoptic Gospels and in Paul. This redemption of the earth mirrors a redemption of human history. Both this time and this space must find place in the new time and place. Such a scenario may be more adequate to the overall biblical vision of God, history, and the cosmos. But 2 Peter does not appear to hold this.

Yet 2 Peter does not envision total destruction of the old. Present righteousness and present righteous people endure the day of the Lord. In fact, present righteousness finally finds its proper place. Whatever righteousness is realized now, before the end, is righteousness out of place and in the wrong time. In the new heavens and new earth, "righteousness is at home" (3:13).

What is victorious in all of this is the idea and possibility of righteousness. In some ways, we can think of 2 Peter as a complex and sophisticated attempt to defend the possibility, reality, and power of righteousness. The attack on the second coming is serious not because the second coming proves that Jesus is indeed the Messiah. It is serious because it throws in doubt the viability of a life of righteousness. Righteousness, in this earth and this heaven, cannot survive. It is not strong enough. Righteousness needs God's power to maintain it. Righteousness needs the vindication and empowerment of the day of the Lord. Thus, the new heaven and new earth are less a home for us but more a home for righteousness. The second coming certainly vindicates Christians, and they certainly find salvation and glory therein. But they do so only as they partake of righteousness. It is righteousness itself which seems to be at stake.

The Prophetic Message

In the midst of the diverse arguments about righteousness, the second coming, and the destruction of false prophets, 2 Peter makes in passing two fascinating comments about "scripture." These comments touch on the ongoing Christian debate about the origin of our canonical texts and the proper way to read them. We can see in 2 Peter how much this community is one of the sacred texts. It is not that these texts are the only theological warrants in the letter; the commands of Jesus and the pronouncements of Peter have unqualified authority. These texts also have authority. However, texts are dangerous, as we know.

The first comment about scripture follows on the heels of the brief reference to the transfiguration: "So we have the prophetic message more fully
confirmed" (1:19). The transfiguration somehow confirms the prophetic message. Readers have long puzzled over the exact nature of the relationship between the transfiguration and the truth of prophecy. One uncertainty concerns the phrases "the prophetic message" in 1:19 and "prophecy of scripture"
in 1:20. Readers have long debated whether a specific prophecy is being
evoked here or whether the reference is to prophecy in general. For the most
part, readers have given up trying to identify a specific prophecy behind this
reference. Thus, we typically read this passage as declaring that the transfiguration confirms the general validity of all prophecy. The second problem is
that prophecy is typically evoked to confirm or reinforce Gospel events and
not vice versa. But the confirmation never flows fully in one direction; there
is always a sense of mutual support. Here the syntax points to the Gospel event
confirming prophecy.

The direction is important. The Jesus story does not replace or correct the
truths of prophecy. The Jesus story reinforces, confirms, and authorizes the
authority of prophecy. Thus, the diverse citations in chapter 2, pulled in large
part from Jude, exemplify the power of "prophecy" to name and direct the
community. Furthermore, the loose combining of scripture with contemporary namings is not really an exegetical process wherein scripture is applied.
Instead, scriptural voices and apostolic voices fold together into one voice.
There is no difference between the truths of scripture and the truths of apostolic preaching. The sense of one true apostolic tradition is emerging here.

Even more controversial is the second part of this first passage. Here we are
told that "no prophecy of scripture is a matter of one's own interpretation, because no prophecy ever came by human will, but people moved by the Holy
Spirit spoke from God" (1:20–21). This brief sentence has become a
formidable force in Christian understanding of scripture. But the argument is
a bit curious. We are first told that no prophecy is a matter of one's own interpretation. This sounds like the warning we encounter in 3:16 that ignorant
people misread scripture. Scriptural interpretation is not a private affair or,
perhaps, even a human affair. The second half of the argument discusses the
origin of prophecy. Prophecy does not emerge from human ideas but is the
mediated voice of God. This seems to mean that a given prophet is not in control of his or her own prophecy. Thus, some readers have suggested that 1:20
is declaring that it is the prophet's interpretation of his or her own prophecy
that is being bracketed. The speaker of a prophecy does not always understand
what is being spoken.

The basic point is clear. Prophecy occurs at the divine level. It originates
from God. And its proper interpretation depends on the Spirit. Second Peter
articulates in its own way the old theological dictum of the authority of scripture: it is spirit speaking to spirit. It is not human to human. It is inspired human to inspired human.

This comment needs to be coupled with the warnings about the letters of Paul in 3:15–16. The author of 2 Peter calls upon the support of Paul for his rendition of the final victory of righteousness. This naming of Paul leads to the famous warning: "There are some things in them [his letters] hard to understand, which the ignorant and unstable twist to their own destruction, as they do the other scriptures" (3:16). Whatever the precise problem with the reading of Paul's letters might be, the general problem of the misreading of scripture is a familiar one.

Good and Bad Reading

Second Peter blames bad reading of texts on the character of the readers. Good people make good readers. Bad people make bad readers. Given the exhortation in 3:17–18 and the larger theology of the letter, 2 Peter seems to place righteousness itself as the ultimate judge of the act of reading. If reading produces righteous behavior, then the reading is proper. If the reading produces ignorance and instability, then the reading is twisted.

It is certainly the case that the different character of different people produces different readings of the same text. We are all bound by some ideology that directs and confines what a text says to us. But it is also true that the texts themselves force multiple readings on even the good readers. Texts are unstable warrants. Second Peter controls the terror of texts by an appeal to the Spirit. Persons properly inspired can read correctly. The Spirit knows what the text really says. Thus, 2 Peter can claim for itself the proper reading. It stands in the apostolic tradition of Peter. It speaks the truths of this apostolic tradition. It speaks the truths of scripture.

The response of 2 Peter to the problem of texts will become a classic one in Christianity. Of course, it does not solve in any final way the problem of reading. Texts to this very day drift from our control, saying things we do not want them to say. And we still cannot decide if that is a good thing or bad.

5

The Letters of John

In the midst of the brokenness of life, the most common and comforting Christian response has been to speak of love. When we face the enormous hatreds and violence of the world around us, we both exhort and comfort ourselves by imagining the possibilities of love. When we become lost in our own brokenness, in our own hatreds, we remind ourselves that God does indeed love us. If God loves us, then hatred, brokenness, and violence cannot be victorious. God's love, we say, is more powerful than human hate. It can make broken humans whole. It can heal the violence of human history. In fact, it is only God's love that heals us. We even like to say, in a stunning simplification, that God is love.

God is love. The enormous impact of this sentence derives not only from its power to speak to so many people in so many situations, but also from the peculiar syntax of the sentence. It does not say, "God loves ... ," with the object being supplied as necessary. God loves us. God loves you, me, all people. God loves good deeds, peace, and so on. If the sentence said "God loves ... ," then love could be one of the many behaviors of God. God loves; God judges; God punishes; God saves. The sentence is also not "God is loving," thus supplying one of many attributes to God. God is loving and righteous and holy and so on. Love is not used as an adjective or noun to evoke one part of the character of the God.

The sentence is an equation; "love" is a predicate nominative. God and love become attached in a necessary and unique way. Through this sentence, for many Christians, and in fact for many non-Christians, love has become the single dominant attribute of God. Our primary sense of God is that God loves us. God can do many things, but all of them must be aspects of love. Thus, even if we can say that God judges or punishes, we can only say those things if judging and punishing belong to love.

Furthermore, the sentence could be reversed: Love is God. If God is love, then love is God. In this form, the sentence suggests that love in any form is God. In fact, we can find God by loving each other. God exists in the loving deeds that pass from one human to another. If love is God, love becomes the central force in life. Love becomes the defining power between persons, whether one of the "persons" is God or not. Love, thought of this way, need not have its immediate origin in God. Love can emerge from the human heart. This human love is, furthermore, not just human love. Love between any two "persons" is God. God is love. God is found wherever love occurs. In fact, love is God.

This reading, wherein "God is love" is equated with "Love is God," has occasioned considerable debate. The reasons are obvious. First of all, human love is, at its very best, a pale imitation of God's love. To equate our flawed human love with divine love is to misunderstand them both. We need to be much more wary of human love than this equation suggests. And we need to be much more in awe of divine love if our faith is to remain intact. To reduce God to our level is to undermine the ground of our faith. Second, believers typically experience human love as derivative of divine love. God loves us first. Receiving divine love occasions our capacity to love in return. God loves, then we love. The order should not be reversed. Third, no predicate nominative should be assigned to God. God is not equal to any thing. It is more theologically correct to say "God loves…" or "God is loving." But the only predicate nominative worthy of God is "God." We can properly say "God is God" or even, as Christians, "God is Jesus," but that is all. "God is love" is perceived as a flawed sentence.

However, the awkwardness of this sentence is not so easily dismissed. Not only is the sentence an important part of the Christian lexicon; the sentence, in this awkward form, comes from scripture. In fact, it occurs twice in 1 John. First John 4:8 reads, "Whoever does not love does not know God, for God is love." First John 4:16b reads, "God is love, and those who abide in love abide in God, and God abides in them." While these are the only two instances of the sentence "God is love" in the Bible, these sentences belong to a wonderful complex of images in 1 John concerning God, Jesus, love, hate, and us. The powerful theology of 1 John, which we shall explore below, demonstrates the undeniable force of this sentence. According to 1 John, if God is love, this implies many things about us and our relationships to one another and to God.

The initial occurrence of the sentence indicates the complex relationship 1 John creates around the image of love. "Beloved, let us love one another, because love is from God; everyone who loves is born of God and knows God. Whoever does not love does not know God, for God is love" (4:7–8). Our relationship to other people and our relationship to God are folded together in these verses. We cannot, according to 1 John, separate God and the other person. Loving God and loving the other person occur in the same act.

The concern for the proper order, wherein God loves first and we love second, seems to be largely ignored here (although in 4:19 the traditional order is affirmed). First John does not say "everyone who is born of God loves," but "everyone who loves is born of God." If we read the syntax of these verses as straightforwardly as we can, it seems that we know God when we love another person. Or as 4:16b declares, "those who abide in love abide in God." To love another is to live in God.

This entanglement of our love "of" and "from" God with our love "of" and "from" other persons becomes a fundamental conviction of most Christian thought. The face of God mirrors the faces of people, and the faces of people, all people, mirror the face of God. Christian thought is haunted, and sometimes even energized, by this confusion of identity. In fact, this confusion of God and others is perceived as not really being a confusion. We are people who belong to God. God is a God who belongs to us. Each is always in the place of the other.

The letters of John explore this place of love, where the face of God and the face of people come together. It is a place that only exists in an actual moment of love. The existence and exploration of this place is the program of these letters.

Metaphorical Theology

We shall find herein a unique way of doing theology. Probably everyone who has ever read these three letters has thought immediately of the Gospel of John. And one of the great puzzles for readers of the New Testament is the relationship among the Gospel of John, 1 John, 2 John, and 3 John. We shall touch a bit on aspects of that puzzle in what follows. At this point, we need only take note of the common theological rhetoric that unites these four documents.

The theological rhetoric of this Johannine corpus is often described as dualistic. Whether the theology is fundamentally dualistic is the subject of much debate, but the rhetoric of these texts often works by the gathering and combining of opposing terms. The letters do not employ the full range of the dualisms we find in the Gospel, but crucial to the argument of 1 John are dualisms of light and darkness, love and hate, truth and falsehood, and being a child of God or a child of the devil. Furthermore, the larger arguments typically run along dualistic lines in the sense that absolute oppositions and clear choices are put in place. We either love or hate. We either obey the commandments or we do not. We either confess or we deny. Clear choices between this and that are put in place. Crucial to any reading of these letters is how these dualisms are perceived.

The theology of the Johannine corpus is also often described as metaphorical. Johannine theology avoids the formulation of simple and unequivocal theological sentences. Instead, it works with the provocations and instabilities of metaphors. This seems especially true of the gospel wherein we find such images as "I am the bread of life" (John 6:35), "I am the gate for the sheep" (John 10:7), and "I am the true vine" (John 15:1). Jesus is not literally bread or a gate or a vine. Although the letters lack the range of metaphors we find in the gospel, it may be that 1 John is built around two such metaphorical assertions.

Many readers of 1 John divide the body of the letter into two sections, each governed by a single theological image. 1:5–3:10 is an exposition of the assertion that "God is light" (1:5). 3:11–5:12 is an exposition of "God is love" (4:8, 16). Again, it is often said, God is not literally light. This must be read as metaphor. Metaphors work, in part, by way of an unstated combination of likeness and unlikeness. God is like light in that both provide knowledge and truth. God is not like light in that light is just one of the forces of the world and is, in fact, created by God. We typically read metaphors by thinking through (often unconsciously) this likeness and unlikeness.

However, the question of how to read such theological metaphors is hotly debated. Again, as readers have often pointed out, in John 6 Jesus comes very close to actually being bread. And in 1 John God comes very close to being light and may actually be love. The literalness of a metaphor cannot be replaced by a derived theological truth. It is not the same thing to say "God is the only source of truth and knowledge" as is it to say "God is light." The cognitive content of "God is light" can only be expressed by "God is light."

Of all the texts in the Bible, the Johannine writings take us the furthest into the question of how to frame a theological truth. These writings explore an impasse at the very heart of theology. On the one hand, God is the ultimate other. God is beyond our knowledge and beyond any words. God exceeds the grasp of all human language and thought. On the other hand, God is not sheer mystery, absolute otherness. God enters language and life and thought. In fact, God seems to fund such language. Faith is not purely blind. There is knowledge of some kind that is necessary to faith. Theology is impelled to speak, but it must speak what ultimately cannot be spoken.

The letters of John are written on this border between the knowledge of God and the mystery of God. In these letters there are things we know. There is knowledge that comes with faith. These letters speak this knowledge. However, in speaking this knowledge, these letters witness to the ineffability of God. For instance, you cannot speak love. Love is not a content of knowledge. Love is an event.

Finally, what we know in these letters is God. And God must escape any language, any thought, and any feeling. This is, of course, true for any person. We may know our loved ones. We can even say things about them that are true. But we always know that they themselves escape our knowledge of them. They are more than our words about them. This unsolvable mystery of the person, which belongs to every human, is intensified when we speak of God. We can say true things about God. But after all our words are spoken, God's mystery remains intact. In fact, the purpose of our words is to witness to this mystery. We speak not in order to destroy the otherness of God; we speak in order to voice this otherness.

The letters of John (and 1 John in particular) draw for us a powerful map of what it is like to "abide in God" (4:15). The central conviction of these letters is that our knowledge exists only in the doing. We only know God, "abide in God," when we love our brothers and sisters. Knowledge comes into being in the deed. Just as God and the other become entangled in the theology of 1 John, so do knowing and doing. It is only in loving that we know God. In fact, it is only in loving that we know that we know.

Outline of the Letters of John

1 John
1:1–4   Opening witness to word of life
1:5–3:10   God is light
    1:6–10   God is light; call to confession
    2:1–2   Jesus the atoning sacrifice
    2:3–11   The new commandment
    2:12–14   Reasons for writing
    2:15–17   Do not love the world
    2:18–27   Warning against antichrists who deny the Son
    2:28–3:10   The sinlessness of the children of God
3:11–5:12   God is love
    3:11–17   Love and hate
    3:18–24   Love and abiding in God
    4:1–6   Testing the spirits
    4:7–21   Love and abiding in God
    5:1–5   Being born of God
    5:6–12   Testimony of the Spirit, water, and blood
5:13–21   Concluding call not to sin

2 John
1–3   Opening salutation
4–6   The love commandment
7–11   Warning against deceivers
12–13   Greetings

3 John
1   Opening salutation
5–8   Praise of Gaius for his love and hospitality
9–12   Attack on Diotrephes; praise of Demetrius
13–15   Greetings

The Prologue

Determining the literary structure of 1 John is not easy. As we noted above, some readers divide the body of the letter into two sections. The first section, which is governed by the heading "God is light," extends from 1:5 to 3:10. The second section, which is governed by the heading "God is love," extends from 3:11 to 5:12. Even though this basic structure is employed in the preceding outline, such an outline greatly oversimplifies the content of these sections. Each section deals with much more than light or love. In fact, these two sections have much more in common than they do in distinction.

The letter does move cleanly from topic to topic. And whatever shifts from topic to topic there might be do not follow clear argumentative logic. Furthermore, the various subsections of the letter overlap and repeat what occurs in the other sections. Thus, some readers have suggested a different kind of outline, arguing that 1 John follows a pattern of proclamation and parenesis:

1:1–4   Proclamation

1:5–2:17   Parenesis

2:18–27   Proclamation

2:28–3:24   Parenesis

4:1–6   Proclamation

4:7–5:5   Parenesis

5:6–12   Proclamation

However, most readers find such a pattern a bit forced. A glance at these sections shows how much the letter constantly moves from "proclamation" to "parenesis." It certainly does not occur simply in these large blocks. In fact, the inseparability of proclamation and parenesis is an essential part of the theological rhetoric of the letter. One can never do one without the other.

Thus, most readers find a gentle shifting of topics as the letter progresses. It should, therefore, not be read under the control of a firm outline or explicit argumentative order. The letter builds its theology by adding images, piece by piece, to this account of the Christian life. The rhetoric supports the theology. We should never focus on one force in Christian reality without connecting it to the other forces. All the terms need to be everywhere at once. Thus, as new terms emerge in the letter, the author always connects them to all the others.

The clearest self-contained rhetorical piece in the letter is the so-called prologue. Readers of 1 John have long noted the formative role of the first four verses in the overall program of the letter. They are sometimes read as a summary of its theology. But it is more helpful to see them as a programmatic piece providing a framework for the theology of God as light and love. Or perhaps it is even better to think of them as a nice theological summary when and only when they are coupled with the images of God as light and love.

In particular, these opening verses introduce the categories of witness, life, and fellowship, all three of which are crucial to the theological program of the letter. Equally important is how carefully these verses track the difficulty of speaking what cannot be spoken.

> We declare to you what was from the beginning, what we have heard,
> what we have seen with our eyes, what we have looked at and touched
> with our hands, concerning the word of life.
>
> (1:1)

The first letter of John announces itself as a declaration, a witness, to "what was from the beginning" (1:1). The letter is an articulation of the tradition. Throughout the letter there is a sense that what is being said has already been said before, that the readers already know "what was from the beginning" (see, for example, 2:7; 2:12–14; 2:20–21; 2:27; 3:11). There is a witness to something objective. This "what" can be heard, seen, touched, and then declared to others. There is a hint here of real content and the possibility of knowledge. Of course, the precise referent of this "what" is not made perfectly clear.

At the end of the verse this "what" is connected to "the word of life." The "what" is not equated with the word of life; the "what" is "concerning" the word of life. A sense of the ineffability of life is implied in this connection. We can say things concerning the real content of tradition; but we cannot fully speak it. The content of tradition is life or, as 1:2 makes clear, eternal life. This eternal life has been revealed. And "we" can speak about this life even if life itself cannot fully submit to words.

At the heart of this letter is this sense of a new life, a new way of living. This living can be characterized by many images: light, righteousness, obedience, faith, and love. These words give shape and even direction to this new life. But life exists as real life, in real moments. Words are part of life; words can even accurately describe life, even this new life; but words and life are not fully the same. For 1 John, the "what" of tradition can be heard, seen, and touched because life, love, obedience can all be heard, seen, and touched. Life gives birth to words. Eternal life, which has been revealed, creates tradition. First John will chart a wonderful path through the complex relationship between words about life and life itself.

Abiding in God

This prologue leads to what many readers think is the governing image of all of Johannine theology—that of abiding in, living in, God. In fact, 1:3 declares that the purpose of the witnessing is "that you also may have fellowship with us; and truly our fellowship is with the Father and with his son Jesus Christ." Although the vocabulary of "fellowship" occurs only here and in 1:6, 7, the basic idea occurs throughout the letters. The most common language is that of "abiding" or "being in." We have seen this imagery already in 4:16b: "God is love, and those who abide in love abide in God, and God abides in them." Throughout the letters of John, this notion of living in, abiding in, and being in occurs repeatedly. We cannot, therefore, read these letters without coming to some understanding of this notion of "abiding."

The Greek word typically translated as "abide" occurs twenty-four times in 1 John and three times in 2 John. The usual syntax is that someone or something abides in someone or something. The variety here is quite striking.

Believers abide in God   1 John 2:6; 3:24; 4:13, 15, 16

Believers abide in Jesus   1 John 2:27, 28; 3:6

Believers abide in Jesus and the Father   1 John 2:24

Believers abide in light   1 John 2:10

Believers abide in love   1 John 4:16

Believers abide in the teaching   2 John 9

A person without love abides in death   1 John 3:14

God abides in believers   1 John 3:24; 4:12, 13, 15, 16

The word of God abides in believers   1 John 2:14

Truth abides in believers   2 John 2

What was heard abides in believers   1 John 2:24

The anointing abides in believers   1 John 2:27

God's seed abides in believers   1 John 3:9

Eternal life does not abide in nonbelievers   1 John 3:15

Love of God does not abide in nonbelievers   1 John 3:17

To this diverse list must be added a range of other terms and constructions that evoke a similar sense of presence. The second most common construction that evokes this sense of being "in" comes from some form of the verb "to be" coupled with the preposition "in." Again, we have a diverse set.

Believers in God   1 John 2:5

Believers in the Father and Jesus   1 John 5:20

The spirit of truth in believers   1 John 4:4

Nonbelievers in darkness   1 John 2:9, 11

Love of the Father not in nonbelievers   1 John 2:15

Truth not in nonbelievers   1 John 1:8; 2:4

Word of God not in nonbelievers   1 John 1:10

Sin not in believers   1 John 3:5

Stumbling block not in believers   1 John 2:10

There is also the image of "fellowship." Fellowship occurs with "one another" and with the "Father" and "Jesus" in 1 John 1:3, with "God" in 1:6, and again with "one another" in 1:7. Finally, there is the image of walking in darkness in 1 John 1:6 and 2:11. These lists could be easily expanded with other instances of "in" and other constructions suggesting presence and fellowship. It is clear that this sense of "being in" is crucial to the theology of these letters.

Through all these images of presence, the letters of John create a geography of the Christian place. The Christian place exists where God, Jesus, love, truth, light, obedience, and faith also exist. The Christian place exists only when all these faces and forces are present. In this place, questions of sequence and separation become confused. Each face and force exists in this place only in interconnectedness and dependence on the other faces and forces. This place is life, even eternal life. This place is where we abide in God and God in us. This place is where we love and are loved. It is to this place that 1 John is giving its witness.

The Elder and the Opponents

The letter of 1 John lacks the name of both sender and recipients. It also lacks the normal salutations and final greetings of a letter. This absence of the typical signs of a letter suggests that it should be considered a general epistle, an essay, composed for broad circulation in a community. The letter itself gives no hints as to the identity of the author apart from the rhetoric of "we" who witness to "what was from the beginning" (1:1), which suggests only some kind of connection to eyewitness tradition.

This lack of data leads most readers to look to 2 and 3 John for assistance. Second John is written by "the elder to the elect lady." Third John is written by apparently this same "elder to the beloved Gaius." Thus, this elder is typically posited as the author of all three letters. But turning to 2 and 3 John can be justified only if we can determine the relationship among these three letters and the relationship of the letters to the Gospel of John. As we might expect, this has proven to be difficult.

In general, readers perceive the letters as coming from a later moment in the history of early Christianity than the time of the writing of the Gospel. The political problems that are hinted at in 2 and 3 John do not seem to be present at the writing of the Gospel. And the difficult problems of Judaism and the place of Christianity in the synagogues, which surface so frequently in the Gospel, seem to be a thing of the past. The letters are typically dated later than the gospel.

Furthermore, shifts in theological perspective, especially the focus on theology rather than Christology, the changing role of the spirit, and a more emphatic eschatology, suggest that the letters and the Gospel have different authors. Typically scholars identify at least four separate individuals behind the formation of the Johannine corpus: John the apostle, who gave the initial shape to the rhetoric and theology of the corpus; the initial and primary composer of the Gospel; the subsequent editor of the Gospel and author of John 21; and the author of 1, 2, and 3 John. Some readers would add considerably to this number. Many see the Gospel more as the product of a community than of one or two or three individuals. And many others suggest a separate author for 1 John from that of 2 and 3 John.

All of this means that readers tend to read the letters of John while holding the Gospel at some distance. It must be admitted that the Gospel and the letters have a certain claim on each other and that it is nearly impossible to read one without drifting toward the other. But it must also be admitted that an assumption of common authorship and unified theology will lead to a misreading of both. Thus, it is best to read the letters as part of a complex of Johannine documents each of which has a distinctive voice in these interrelated texts.

In fact, it is common to read the letters of John as though written to combat a misreading of the Gospel. By pulling together the negative descriptions of the opponents of the elder in 2 and 3 John and of the children of the devil in 1 John, scholars have constructed a portrait of this misreading. This misreading entailed a slightly "docetic" reading of the Gospel. The docetists of the second century were known for denying the true humanity of Jesus. Spirit and flesh cannot be combined. Whatever flesh the son of God wore was a covering and not an essential part of who he was. Scholars point to the language in 1 John 4:2 and 2 John 7, where these opponents are described as denying that "Jesus Christ has come in the flesh."

This docetic reading leads to other errors. These Christian docetists naturally deny the importance of the death of Jesus and the efficacy of his blood. This leads the elder to reinforce the power of Jesus' blood (1 John 1:7; 2:2; 4:10; 5:6). They become more individualistic, denying the importance of love within the community. So the elder insists that the love of God for us is necessarily linked to our love for others (e.g., 1 John 2:2–11). And finally their docetic reading leads to a vaguely privatized understanding of the spirit wherein any experience of the spirit is self-justifying and beyond questioning. The elder thus insists that the spirit must issue in the proper confession and proper loving behavior. "Beloved, do not believe every spirit, but test the spirits to see whether they are from God" (4:1).

However, there are considerable problems with this scenario. The evidence for a docetic reading is not completely convincing. The expression "Jesus Christ has come in the flesh" may simply mean "Jesus Christ has come here among us." The center of the phrase may not be the word "flesh." In fact, when the elder describes the correct confession, he often does not mention the flesh at all. Thus, 1 John 2:22 reads, "Who is the liar but the one who denies that Jesus is the Christ? This is the antichrist, the one who denies the Father and the Son." There is no hint here of docetism. First John 4:15 uses different terms but also lacks any mention of the flesh: "God abides in those who confess that Jesus is the Son of God, and they abide in God." So also 1 John 5:5: "Who is it that conquers the world but the one who believes that Jesus is the Son of God?" Elsewhere we are described as believing "in the Son of God" or "in God" (5:10). If docetism is an issue, if flesh is the key concern, then the elder does a remarkably poor job of highlighting it.

There is controversy here; but it is not over docetism or flesh or the humanity of Jesus. The Christological problem seems to be much more basic than this. The question is whether Jesus is the Christ or not. The question is still the question which drives the Gospel of John: Does Jesus come from the Father or not? This question is not of course a self-contained one. If Jesus is not the Christ, is not the Son of God, then the entire Christian life unravels. If Jesus is not the Christ, then love and light are not the center of life.

The frequent negatives, the depictions of liars and sinners, of persons who deny the truth and make false confessions, may be less an attempt to describe an actual group of heretics in the Johannine communities and more an attempt to map the logic of faith. It is the readers who are the potential liars (1 John 2:4). It is perhaps even the readers who are the potential antichrists (2:18), although others have clearly preceded them here. The elder is charting the "no" that lies at the heart of the "yes" of faith. Faith is not just a turning to God, an obedience to the commandments of God; it is not just a willingness to love your brothers and sisters. Faith is also a turning away, a denial of the world, a turning from hate. Good faith is carved out in the presence, danger, and temptation of bad faith.

The identity and authority of the elder must remain a guess. The controversies in 2 and 3 John indicate, on the one hand, a person with authority and responsibility, and, on the other hand, a person whose authority is circumscribed by that of others. He writes as though he has voice but a voice with a limited range. It is clear he has adversaries.

The term "elder" remains one of our best clues. It is striking that the author can identify himself with just this title and without a name. It is also important that he assumes, in these letters, considerable (albeit limited) authority over his recipients. The term "elder" itself, of course, was used in early Christian communities to designate a particular office that had ruling authority over a community. The elder of 2 and 3 John does not seem to function as part of a presbytery nor does he assume a comparable authority. This suggests that the word is being employed in its more common usage as a word of respect and dignity. Used this way, it gives little hint as to the formal role of the elder who wrote these letters. He assumes for himself respect and authority. He assumes that the church in 2 John (the so-called "elect lady") and Gaius in 3 John will recognize this authority.

The specifics of his argument give further clues. The elder assumes in 1 John 1:1–4 that he is an authoritative witness. In 3 John 12, he assumes that Gaius, at least, knows his testimony is true. It is not necessary to assume that the elder himself was an eyewitness to Jesus' earthly ministry; we need only assume that he believes that the tradition of which he is a witness is an eyewitness tradition.

The details of the conflicts in 2 and 3 John are also interesting. In 2 John the elder writes to a church (assuming "the elect lady" refers to a single congregation). He first states the love commandment as a reminder for them to walk in the truth (2 John 4–6), then warns them not to receive the "many deceivers" who "have gone out into the world" (2 John 7). The tone of the letter suggests that he expects his instructions to be heeded.

Third John has a different feel. Here the elder writes to Gaius pleading with him to give hospitality to the "brothers" who are coming to see him (3 John 5–8). This appeal flies in the face of a certain Diotrephes who refuses to welcome these "brothers" and expels from the church anyone else who tries to do so (3 John 9–10). Further details into this conflict are beyond us, although many guesses have been made. We do not know anything about Diotrephes. We cannot reconstruct what his authority might have been and how his authority compared with that of the elder. As usual, there are too many plausible possibilities.

It is in any case ironic that the elder, who builds his theology around love of the brother and sister, should find himself in such a conflict. His insistence in 2 John that the "deceivers" should not be received into the community and not even be greeted (10–11) has struck many readers as contrary to this theology of love. In addition, his attacks on his adversaries in 1 John and his condemnations of Diotrephes in 3 John strike many readers as not being particularly loving. It does not make much sense to espouse love as the center of the Christian life when love becomes so circumscribed. For love to be love it must reach not only into our relationships with our friends but also, perhaps especially, into our relationships with our enemies. Some readers have commented that the elder's vision of love limps; it falls short, for instance, of the kind of love Jesus commands in the Sermon on the Mount.

It becomes then a question of how we understand love.

God Is Light

Love cannot be separated from truth, from light. Crucial to the elder's understanding of love is this connection between love and light, between the act of love and knowledge of truth. The body of 1 John opens with the affirmation that God is light (1:5). This notion of light will give space to notions of knowledge and truth, without which there is no love.

But not only does the letter affirm that God is light; it adds "in him there is no darkness at all" (1 John 1:5). That is not to say that there is no darkness anywhere but that there is no darkness in God. In fact, for the elder there is indeed darkness, and life and light exist in the midst of darkness (cf. John 1:5). This dualism is crucial to the theology and rhetoric that follows. Every "yes" of the believer to the light is also a "no" to the darkness.

Perhaps the most stunning aspect of the rhetoric of 1 John is the persistence with which every theological notion is placed in the full context of the letter's theology. The various combinations of light and love, knowledge and obedience, being loved and loving, shape each theological image in the letter. The notion of light and darkness is immediately taken up into the complex theological geography of the letter.

> If we say that we have fellowship with him while walking in darkness, we lie and do not do what is true; but if we walk in the light as he himself is in the light, we have fellowship with one another, and the blood of Jesus his Son cleanses us from all sin.
>
> (1:6–7).

If God is light, then we can walk in light. But this walking in light is not something we do on our own. We do not find a truth and then simply hold firmly to it. We find a light that is the "person" God. To walk in this light is to have fellowship with this God who is this light. The Christian place is always animated by this face-to-face with God. To be a Christian is to be in fellowship, to live in God and have God live in us. Light is not objective knowledge; it is personal; it is the face-to-face of persons. Light is fellowship.

However, this Christian place is never simply an experience; we are never in a purely passive role; there is always an act by the Christian. The language in 1 John 1:6–7 reflects this. We are not in light or in darkness; we walk in light and walk in darkness. Being in light and being in darkness involves our behavior. In fact, one of the most revealing expressions in the entire letter may be the syntax of 1:6 wherein we "do not do what is true." We must do the truth. The strangeness of this image points to the uniqueness of the elder's thought. We do not first know the truth and then do the good. We simply do the truth. Knowing and doing become fused in the same deed. Truth and love become bound together. As the elder will insist over and over again, the way we treat our brother and sister tells us whether or not we abide in God and God in us.

At the same time that this sense of face, of persons, of relationships complicates any notion of objective knowledge, the images of light and truth indicate that objective knowledge is not simply being dismissed here. We can indeed speak the truth of this light; in fact, we must, as witnesses, speak. God, as light, funds this speech. Thus, the intervention of doing into the realm of knowing does not silence the knowing. Doing supplies knowing. Our words emerge from our deeds. We do the truth. This doing gives force to our words. But we should be careful in these letters whenever we think we have found a secure theological sequence among these Christian forces. First John places them in a necessary relationship and seems to resist any attempt to make one force completely derivative of another.

We can see in the complexity of this theology why the letter seems so metaphorical. The metaphorical force is not confined to an attempt to come up with just the right single metaphor for God. The metaphorical force occurs more at the level of syntax. Normal ways of putting things are not adequate. To speak of Christian faith we must force our syntax into strange disruptions and contradictions. We must devise phrases such as "doing the truth." Only in the awkwardness of such syntax can the true character of Christian faith be expressed.

Jesus as Atoning Sacrifice

Readers have long noted that in 1 John it is God who is the light, while in the Gospel of John it is Jesus who is the light. First John redeploys the language used for Jesus in the Gospel and uses it to describe God. For instance, 1 John focuses on fellowship with God the Father, while our fellowship with Jesus is derivative of that fellowship. In the Gospel it is the opposite. There, fellowship with Jesus leads to fellowship with the Father. In both cases, it is probably just a question of syntax rather than real theological sequence. In both the Gospel and the letters, fellowship with Father and Son is always simultaneous. It is theologically impossible to have one without the other. Nevertheless, the syntactical sequence indicates a curious shift. Readers have often suggested that 1 John is more theological than Christological. But it is probably better to think of a *different* Christological focus in 1 John than of a diminished one. In any case, in 1 John, Jesus takes on a much more traditional early Christian role than he has in the Gospel.

Classic images of atonement are outlined in 1 John 1:7b–2:2. "The blood of Jesus his Son cleanses us from all sin" (1:7). "He who is faithful and just will forgive us our sins and cleanse us from all unrighteousness" (1:9). "We have an advocate with the Father, Jesus Christ the righteous; and he is the atoning sacrifice for our sins, and not for ours only but also for the whole world" (2:1b–2). It is impossible to decide, from these brief images, which of the various theories of atonement might be in play here. Furthermore, the ancient world, including Christians, simply assumed that sacrifice and reconciliation with God or gods were necessarily connected. There was little need to detail the theological logic of sacrifice and forgiveness.

It is striking, nevertheless, that Jesus' blood can be assigned a propitiatory role without any explanation. The elder can simply assert that Jesus' blood cleanses sins. He seems to feel no need to verify that claim. Perhaps even more striking is the peculiar syntax of these verses. Again, the sequence is instructive. It is not said that Jesus' blood cleanses us, that we receive this gift in faith, that we then live the Christian life. Rather, the elder declares, "If we walk in the light, … the blood of Jesus his Son cleanses us from all sin" (1:7). I do not think we should read this as establishing an order in which we first must live righteousness and love in order to receive forgiveness; rather, these things all occur in the same place and moment. It is as we walk that we receive forgiveness. It is as we love that we are loved.

This sense of expiation surfaces later in the letter in two other ways, both of which are curious and the occasion for controversy. The letter of 1 John, like many ancient letters, returns at the conclusion of the letter to themes from the beginning of the letter. The sense of "witness" that we observed in 1:1–4 receives a quite different treatment in 5:6–12. The main emphasis of these latter verses is that the "what" of 1:1 has both human and divine testimony. While the elder and his letter may function as human witness, this human witness is joined by divine voices: "If we receive human testimony, the testimony of God is greater" (5:9a).

There is nothing surprising at this point in this overlap of divine and human witness. After all, this seems to be one of the main theological axioms of the letter. The "what" of tradition, the geography of Christian faith, the place of love, is a place where human and divine live together. It is the mutual abiding of human and divine faces and forces that make the place the Christian place. Thus, it is to be expected that the elder would account for witnesses to this place as being both divine and human. In fact, if there is not both divine and human testimony, then it is not the place of faith.

What is surprising is the *way* the elder depicts the divine witness.

> This is the one who came by water and blood, Jesus Christ, not with water only but with the water and the blood. And the Spirit is the one that testifies, for the Spirit is the truth. There are three that testify: the Spirit and the water and the blood, and these three agree.
>
> (5:6–8)

The problem here is obvious: it is not clear how we are to understand "water" and "blood" as witnesses; nor is it clear precisely in what sense the Spirit testifies. There are several possible explanations. Some readers see "water and blood" as a reference to the fleshly existence of Jesus. Other see this reference as indicating the baptism and crucifixion of the historical Jesus. This view works better since it explains the added phrase "not with water only but with the water and the blood." That is to say, not only does the anointment of Jesus at baptism witness to him, his death on the cross does also. The Spirit then becomes not so much a separate witness as one that gives voice to both by testifying to these events through the words of tradition.

However, these three witnesses are more often read as references to ongoing forces in the Christian tradition. Water refers to Christian baptism; blood refers to the Lord's Supper; and Spirit refers to the words of tradition. And, of course, many readers think we should not confine these words too much. Water can refer to both the baptism of Jesus and the baptism of Christians. Blood can refer to the blood spilled on the cross and the blood of the Eucharist. And the Spirit can testify in innumerable ways.

In any case, all of these readings connect atonement, forgiveness of sins, and the blood of Jesus. If we are to love and be loved, this must include and require the presence of forgiveness of sins. We cannot live the Christian moment without grace at the heart of it. The past must be cleaned of its sinful weight in order for this new moment, in which we can love and be loved, to exist. The present must be unencumbered by the sins of the past. To love we must be loved. To love others we must partake of God's forgiveness. Again, the elder does not, at this point, articulate a set order. He does not say that we are first forgiven and then we love. They come into being in the same moment.

Perhaps this freedom from sin in the moment of love explains the curious language in 1 John that "those who have been born of God do not sin, because God's seed abides in them; they cannot sin, because they have been born of God" (3:9). Readers have long wondered what it means that people born of God do not sin. The two obvious readings of this seem too unorthodox. It could mean that if you are born of God then your sins are forgiven ahead of time. Thus, even if you sin, it is not counted as sin. It could also mean that once you become a child of God, because of the power of God's seed in you, you never commit a sin again. So either you do not sin at all or your sins no longer count. Both of these possibilities are troubling. If either were true, it makes little sense for the elder to also say that he is "writing these things to you so that you may not sin" (2:1a). Nor does it make much sense for the elder to declare, "But if anyone does sin, we have an advocate with the Father" (2:1b).

Furthermore, both of these scenarios undo the larger theology of the letter. The elder describes life and love as carved out under the very real possibilities of darkness, sin, and hate. Unless these possibilities are in place, the theology of choice, of deed, makes no sense. Being God's child is not a status; it is an event, an ongoing event. Only if sin is a real possibility for believers can the event character of faith be maintained.

Thus, this awkward sentence must mean something else. In 1 John, we are God's children when we love. But if we sin, we are children of the devil. "Everyone who commits a sin is a child of the devil" (3:8). We only know if we are a child of God or a child of the devil by our deeds. We do not become a child of God and then later and separately learn to love and obey. We are only a child of God in the very act of love. Thus, a child of God cannot sin. It is an impossible contradiction. To be a child of God is to be in the very act of loving and being loved.

The language of blood and the account of atonement emphasize a sense of dependence on God in the act of being God's child. God creates the possibilities of being God's child through the force of blood and its atoning power. It is blood that separates us from the moments before the event. It is blood that enables us to love anew. It is blood that enables us to escape past hate and accomplish new love. Blood breaks the power of the past with its hold on both us and God, and thus opens the present to us. Because of blood, God is not required to remember our sins. Because of blood, we can escape the power of our sins upon us.

Christians cannot become Christians on their own. It is not done by a sheer act of human will. It takes God and humans together to create the place of love.

Obedience

At times 1 John sounds almost rabbinic in its language. The atonement language is, of course, extremely Jewish. Moreover, the connection of atonement to the classic notion of obedience to his commandments gives a very traditional Jewish feel to much of the letter. Furthermore, the account of God's righteousness in 2:29–3:24, especially when it is coupled with the idea that "sin is lawlessness" (3:4), shows how deeply Jewish this letter is. The elder also includes in the Christian place numerous other Old Testament concepts.

As we noted above, atonement is connected in a quite traditional way to obedience. To seek forgiveness apart from obedience is an act of impiety. The very petition of sacrifice assumes an intention of faithful obedience. Thus, it is natural for the account of expiation in 1:7–2:2 to blend into an account of obedience in 2:3–11. But as often seems to be the case in this letter, a traditional image receives a curious twist.

"Now by this we may be sure that we know him, if we obey his commandments" (1 John 2:3). Perhaps the folding together of knowledge and deeds which animates so much of this letter comes out of traditional Jewish theology. One knows God only through the experience of obedience to the law.

Knowledge of God does not come from thinking a certain thing or feeling a certain way. Knowledge of God comes in the attempt to live righteousness. Only in the very acts of disobedience and obedience do we learn the true nature of God. In the success of following the law, of really and truly obeying a commandment, we begin to understand who God is.

The elder evokes this connection in the following verses through a series of positive and negative examples.

> Whoever says, "I have come to know him," but does not obey his commandments, is a liar, and in such a person the truth does not exist; but whoever obeys his word, truly in this person the love of God has reached perfection.
>
> (2:4–5)

We see again how the image of obedience is taken up into the theological rhetoric of the letter. Every theological concept must submit to this interplay of light and love, of knowledge and deeds. Nevertheless, deeds have a public character that gives them a certain priority. We only know the truth of a person by what he or she does. In fact, people only know the truth about themselves by their deeds. Words and thoughts have a power to deceive and mislead that deeds do not have. We can even fool ourselves by what we say to ourselves. For 1 John, we only know what we know by seeing what we do.

The image of obedience is a necessary balance to a possible misreading wherein our deeds are perceived to have absolute force on their own. Such a reading is, of course, contrary to the whole theology of 1 John. It is not that we carve out love and righteousness by doing love and righteousness out of our own private powers. We carve out love and righteousness by doing love and righteousness in obedience to God. Our deeds emerge from and depend on God's presence, power, and words. There is in every act of love a sense of dependence on God. Love is obedience. By linking love to obedience in this way, 1 John keeps in place the sense of divine and human cooperation that creates love. Only when humans obey God is love possible.

These images fit with the provocative account of God's righteousness in 2:29–3:10. "If you know that he [God] is righteous, you may be sure that everyone who does right has been born of him" (2:29). The account of righteousness and sin, which leads in 3:11–17 to an account of love and hate, builds on the notion of whose child you are. A sense of dependence on God also animates this argument.

It is, first of all, God who is righteous. If we do a righteous deed, it can only be because we are God's children. Righteousness cannot come out of ourselves. If we perform righteousness, it is a sign in itself that we are not alone. If a human does a righteous deed, God must be present. All righteousness belongs to God. In fact, the human who does righteousness cannot be just a human; this human must somehow belong to God.

No one who abides in him [God] sins; no one who sins has either seen him or know him. (3:6)

Everyone who commits a sin is a child of the devil. (3:8a)

Those who have been born of God do not sin. (3:9a)

The children of God and the children of the devil are revealed in this way: all who do not do what is right are not from God, nor are those who do not love their brothers and sisters. (3:10)

For all the subtlety of this argument the basic geography is clear: if you sin, you are a child of the devil; if you do what is right, you are a child of God. It is not that by doing right you become a child of God or by sinning you become a child of devil. The deeds show who you are. You are who you are in the deed.

It becomes impossible to articulate a final order to all these relationships and events. They simply belong together. There is a pervasive sense in all of this that God is the primary source of these events, but we misunderstand that priority if we make it purely temporal. God funds all moments of righteousness in the very occurrence.

The images of these verses push toward the most fundamental argument of 1 John. Theology is not a set of ideas; theology is a set of relationships. Faith is not belief in a sequence of words; faith is a decision about persons, about humans and about God. How we behave shows not simply who we think we are but to whom we belong. We belong to God or to the devil. "No one who abides in him sins." To do or not do righteousness is a decision for God or for the devil. God is righteous. To decide to belong to God is do righteousness. We cannot decide to belong to God apart from an actual righteous deed. To do the deed is to decide to belong.

In fact, to decide to belong to God is to decide to love a brother or a sister. To belong to God is to belong to others. We have returned to where we started. For the elder, love is the best and fundamental image of the Christian life.

Love

There is no single definition of love in these letters that can account for all the elder wants to say about it. Although the image of love occurs throughout 1 John, the main accounts of love are concentrated in three passages: 2:7–11; 3:11–24; and 4:7–21. Although these passages clearly overlap, each of them articulates slightly different aspects of love. It is only by reading all three that we can get a proper sense of what love is for the elder.

First John 2:7–11 begins with the famous distinction, which plays off the Gospel of John (John 13:34), between love as an old commandment and love as a new commandment. The love commandment is old, of course, because "you have heard [it] from the beginning" (2:7). It is not clear whether "from the beginning" means from the Old Testament, from the ministry of Jesus, or from the beginning of the Christian tradition. In any case, the readers have heard this commandment before; it is, in this sense, an old commandment. But it is also new. "I am writing you a new commandment that is true in him and in you; because the darkness is passing away and the true light is already shining" (2:8).

There are two crucial insights that come from this sense of the newness of the love commandment. First, the commandment is always new because it is new in the new moment. The commandment exists as command only when it comes to us now. It is command only in the moment it is speaking to us. Although we have heard the words before, in this moment, with this brother or sister before us, the command to love is a new command. The peculiarities of the moment, the unique needs of the person before us, and our own idiosyncratic capacities and limitations make every act of love a unique and unparalleled event. Love is always a new act. There is never a mechanistic way to apply the love command. Only a creative individual who can perceive the powers of the moment and understand the needs of the other can love. The love commandment must be new in every moment.

Second, the ongoing reiteration of the command to love in each moment is, according to 1 John, a testimony to the victory of the light over the darkness. Love is only possible if the light is winning. For us to love is a witness to God's victory over evil. If we love, then we are in the light. If we are in the light, then darkness has not won. As many have commented, we can only have the courage to love if we believe that the light is victorious. Love is a testimony to our ongoing faith in God's victory. It is no surprise that the elder's account of the victory that is evinced in our acts of love leads to a celebratory "hymn" to the victories of the "children," the "fathers," and the "young people" (2:12–14). Love is an act of faith, faith that God can take a meager act of love and empower it against the darkness. Love is, then, a celebration of our faith in God's victory.

A quite different account of the geography of love is explored in 3:11–24. Here Cain is placed as a necessary temptation to the possibility of love. Love must be carved out in the presence of hate. After a brief reference to the fact that we have heard the command to love each other "from the beginning," the passage introduces a surprising imperative: "We must not be like Cain who was from the evil one and murdered his brother" (3:12). The initial and defining problem of Cain is the possibility that we might be Cain ourselves.

We can see in this warning against the Cain in us how much 1 John insists on the event character of love. Love is not something we have; it is not our possession; God does not give it to us in such a way that it becomes an automatic part of who we are. Love is an event. Love is always accomplished in the midst of the temptation to hate. This possibility of hate on our part is then woven into the larger themes of knowledge, truth, life, death, and the ongoing question of who abides in whom. This rhetorical pattern is, of course, crucial to the theological force of the letter. Bad theology results from forgetting one of the key forces or faces that make up the geography of faith. The elder never makes this mistake. Here the terror of Cain, of ourselves being Cain, is immediately connected to the other forces of faith. Cain is a wonderful negative example because Cain kills his brother and because he demonstrates how hate becomes and even is murder. For a Christian to hate a brother is to become Cain, which is to belong to the evil one and to become a murderer. The first terror of Cain is that we may become Cain ourselves.

The terror of Cain is also external. There are Cains in the world who will and do hate us. Hate accompanies love not only in the sense that we must overcome our own capacity for hate in order to love, but also in the sense that love often receives hate in return. In fact, according to 1 John 3:12, the cause of hate is that the unrighteous person will always hate the righteous deed. Thus, since there are always going to be people of darkness, people of the evil one, people whose deeds are evil, any and all righteous deeds will draw hate to them. Thus, not only must we overcome our own capacity for hate if we want to love our brothers and sisters, we must also be willing to attract hate and its terrors to us. We must be willing to attract the various terrors of the evil one if we want to love. We could only do this, of course, if we truly believe that light conquers darkness.

This passage also gives us our first hints about the shape of love itself. It is not surprising that the primary image of love comes from Christology. "We know love by this, that he laid down his life for us" (3:16). The Christological basis of love is detailed more extensively in 4:7–21. In both of these passages, we learn two things above all from what God has done in Jesus Christ. First, we learn that God loves us. God loves because God sent his son. "God's love is revealed to us in this way: God sent his only Son into the world" (4:9). In Jesus, the core character of God is revealed in a unique way. It is not that God never loved before; it is that in Jesus this love "is revealed to us." The first thing we learn from Jesus is that God is love.

The second thing we learn is what love is itself. It is not that we already know what love is and have been waiting to see if God matches the proper standards of love. It is rather that in Jesus Christ God shows us what love is. "We know love by this, that he laid down his life for us—and we ought to lay down our lives for one another" (3:16). "Beloved, since God loved us so much, we also ought to love one another" (4:11). "We love because he first loved us" (4:19).

There seems to be almost no sentimentality in the elder's account of love. Even if we pass through the dual terrors of Cain to dare to love our brothers and sisters, that act of love is itself its own terror. To love is to give one's life for another. To love is to love only in the way God loves. Nothing else is love. Only if we love in the love that comes from God do we actually love. We know what God's love is by knowing Jesus Christ. Thus, to love is to be the very opposite of Cain (3:14–16). Cain takes the life of his brother. We "take" or give our own lives for the needs of our brothers and sisters. Love is indeed haunted by death. To love is to call the powers of death onto ourselves. We can only do this if we can believe that love conquers hate, that light shines in the darkness, that God in Jesus Christ is victorious.

The elder's insistence that love is a real act, a real transaction between one human and another, that it is not just a feeling, an attitude, or an intention, surfaces in the plain-sense advice of 3:17. "How does God's love abide in any-one who has the world's goods and sees a brother or sister in need and yet re-fuses help?" Love involves the goods of the world. Love involves meeting the material needs of the other. Love therefore involves justice and politics.

However, love is not something purely external to us; there is a certain mystical quality to love. This passage evokes that mystical quality in two ways. First, the heart is enlisted and confirmed in its power to tell us whether or not we live in love. "If our hearts do not condemn us, we have boldness before God" (1 John 3:21). Our hearts have the power to monitor the truth of our love. Our hearts know whether we truly have acted in love or not.

This power inscribed to the heart raises an obvious problem. It is not clear from this passage whether the heart of each and every human, including the hearts of the children of the devil, has this capacity to know love, or whether only the hearts of believers, sanctified by the experience of being loved, have this capacity. Nearly all readers prefer the latter. It fits better with the con-stant sense in 1 John that our love is somehow, even if not sequentially, de-pendent on God loving us first. "We love because he first loved us" (4:19). But it must be admitted that 3:18–22 is not completely clear on this. It may be that every human heart, by the power of God's creation, has some knowledge of love.

Perhaps we should not divide things too aggressively here. We noted above that we learn what love is by what God reveals in Jesus Christ. But an absolute divide here makes little sense. There must be some sense of recognition that what God is doing in Jesus Christ is love. There must be some prior sense of love to learn that this new way is a new way of thinking about love.

The second way this passage evokes the mystical quality of love is through the sense of God's presence in love. This presence is evoked through the usual Johannine language of abiding (3:17, 24). But it is also evoked by a reference to the Spirit. "By this we know that he abides in us, by the Spirit that he has given us" (3:24b). We have seen that 1 John usually asserts that we know who we are by whether or not we love (2:10; 3:14, 24a; 4:7, 8, 12, 20; 5:2). Here we are told we know that God abides in us by the "Spirit that he has given us."

Unfortunately, the letter does not say what having this Spirit feels like. Instead it gives an account of the external evidence for who has the "Spirit of God" (4:2) and who has the "spirit of the antichrist" (4:3). Of course, the pri-mary evidence of the presence of the Spirit of God is, as 3:24 suggests, the presence of love. If we love, that is a sign of God's presence, a sign of the presence of God's Spirit. However, 4:1–6 adds some other possibilities. First, every spirit that confesses that "Jesus Christ has come in the flesh" is a spirit from God. And, conversely, every spirit that does not "confess Jesus" is not a spirit from God. This sudden shift to proper confession fits with the constant rhetorical rhythm of 1 John. God is light and love. If we focus too much on either what we do or what we know, we misstate the nature of faith. To speak too long of the act of love is to neglect the sense of knowing that pervades these letters. People who love are people who can think and speak the truth.

We also hear that people who have the Spirit of God have conquered those who have the spirit of the antichrist (4:4). The elder points to a sense of victory that occupies the Spirit of God. The language here is one of reminder. These verses (4:4–5) have the feel of comfort to them. Yes, there are evil and powerful spirits out there. Yes, your love and your confessions will attract the hatred and violence of those evil spirits. But remember, "Little children, you are from God and have conquered them; for the one who is in you is greater than the one who is in the world" (4:4).

Finally, in an echo of the controversies of 2 and 3 John, the elder insists that "whoever knows God listens to us, and whoever is not from God does not listen to us" (4:6b). This sudden exclusionary move in the midst of this account of love irritates many modern readers. But for the letters of John, to love involves a rejection as much as a reception. To love is to say "no" to hate. To love as God loves is to deny the force of the usual powers of the world. Most modern readers can tolerate this rejection of hate. What bothers us is that the victory of love seems incomplete. There is no sense here that love is going to convert all the hate. Light does not turn darkness into light; in fact, light is what shows darkness to be darkness. Thus, the victory of love is not that hate and evil will become love and good; the victory of love is that hate does not conquer it. This means, in the letters of John, that people who are children of the devil may well remain eternally children of the devil. The devil, the evil one, darkness, hate, and falsehood will have their victims in this theology.

The extensive account of love in 1 John 4:7–21 reiterates in the wonderful and complex rhetoric of this letter most of the themes we have mentioned already. However, one additional image from these verses warrants comment. Love is connected in 4:17–18 with the notion of perfection. And this notion of perfection is in turn connected to final judgment. The initial image is a startling one: "Love has been perfected among us in this: that we may have boldness on the day of judgment, because as he is, so are we in the world" (4:17). This reads as though we are already perfect or at least that we are perfect when we love. However, such a reading is difficult to square with 3:2: "Beloved, we are God's children now; what we will be has not yet been revealed. What we know is this: when he is revealed, we will be like him, for we will see him as he is." The syntax of 3:2 implies that we are not yet what we shall be, that our true future remains hidden from us. So if we are to be perfect as Christ is perfect, that perfection can only occur on the last day.

The tension between these readings is as close as the letters of John get to classic early Christian eschatological tensions. So much of early Christian theology is driven by the tensions between the already and the not yet, between what is already present of the kingdom and what is still in the future. In a move typical of the theological rhetoric of 1 John, this tension is not defined by identifying what is or is not present now. Instead the tension is evoked by the articulation of seemingly contradictory sentences. We are perfect now; we are not yet what we shall be. To understand the true conditions of faith we must say both. In love, we are already perfect. At the same time, there is much about love and truth that we do not yet know and live. Love defines the moment now. It exists in the moment now. It exceeds all that we do and think. It belongs to both the revelation and the mystery of God. It belongs to both the presence and the transcendence of God.

Celebration

Our account thus far has underplayed the sense of celebration that animates 1 John (and to some extent 2 John). As many readers have pointed out, the entire Johannine corpus has less need for final judgment than do any other writings in the New Testament. The miracle of love itself is self-contained in its power, purpose, and justification. It needs no outside warrants or future confirmation. An act of love is the kingdom in itself in the very moment it occurs.

We can see this focus on the fullness of the present moment in the relationships we have noted between love and hate, light and darkness, truth and falsehood, and even God and the devil. Love does not turn hate into love, nor does light turn darkness into light, or truth turn falsehood into truth. And the devil does not need to become an obedient child of God. The victory of love and light and truth and God is that they exist and persist in the ongoing and terrifying presence of hate and darkness and falsehood and the devil. Love that is not accomplished amid the terrors of Cain, Cain inside and outside, is not really love. Love that is not accomplished under the shadow and power of death is not love. For the letters of John, and end in which everything is love and truth and goodness is almost a contradiction of the truth of God's love. God's love is the giving unto death of his only Son.

Thus, the letters of John seem to turn toward the present to an unusual degree. It is not that the letters of John have no need or place at all for a better future. As we have seen, there is a future aspect to God's victory. There is more of God's mystery yet to be revealed. Rather, the present seems more complete in itself than is the case in most early Christian theologies.

Perhaps it is the elder's sense of God abiding in us that gives such fullness to the present. We have already noted how many different expressions and how frequently the elder evokes this sense of God living in us. The letters of John are inscribed in the midst of a pervasive sense of God being here with us.

In some ways, every sentence in these letters witnesses to this sense of presence. I know of no reader of these letters who does not recognize that peculiar witness to the presence of God now in our midst.

This sense of presence may be what animates the sense of celebration in these letters. There is almost an astonishment that God loves us this way, astonishment that we can actually love each other. That we can love each other is proof itself that God is victorious. Every act of love becomes not only a witness to God's victory but a celebration of it.

Believers of all faiths have long struggled with how to witness to such a strong sense of divine presence. A sense of having God in us makes us talk. Our talk witnesses and evokes such presence. And yet our talk is not the same as God. It may be the case (in fact, I think it is) that any object or person which or whom we inscribe in our words escapes our words. It may be the case (again, I think it is) that language always struggles a bit, that language always limps. However, the fragility of language becomes especially obvious when it wants to speak of God.

I do not mean by this just that we have experiences that are more real than our words about them. I would say that even those experiences limp. It is not that we really do experience God in a direct and absolutely full way and that we then have trouble conveying in words the perfect wholeness of our experiences. Rather, the brokenness of our rhetoric articulates a real brokenness at the heart of the experience of God. Even in 1 John, God remains mystery and there must be a somewhat unknown and better future.

The best theology conveys in its very rhetoric the contradictions at the heart of faith. The letters of John are wonderful theology, in part because they have these syntactical tensions. When we speak of God's presence here, our language must strain. In 1 John we can see the strain in the wonderful twists in the syntax. In our next chapter, on Revelation, we shall see language breaking in a different way. In Revelation, the words themselves seem to collapse under the weight of the task.

6

Revelation

Of all the books in the Bible none has proven more difficult to read than Revelation. It is filled with bizarre images. There are beasts in these pages with multiple heads and horns. The narrative logic of the text is almost impossible to follow. The world seems to end several times. But the most difficult aspect of Revelation for most readers has not been the outrageous imagery and convoluted narrative of the text; it has been the incredible violence that is inscribed here. Revelation is a violent and bloody text.

The great whore of Babylon is described as "drunk with the blood of the saints and the blood of the witnesses to Jesus" (Rev. 17:6). Her end at God's hand is in turn bloody and violent (17:16–18; 18:4–8, 21–24). Her desolation inspired a great multitude in heaven to praise God for God's vengeance:

> Hallelujah! Salvation and glory and power to our God,
>   for his judgments are true and just;
> He has judged the great whore
>   who corrupted the earth with her fornication,
> and he has avenged on her the blood of his servants.
>   (19:1–2)

When one of the angels reaps the vintage of the earth with a sharp sickle and throws the "grapes" into "the great wine press of the wrath of God" (14:17–19), the blood from that winepress flows "as high as a horse's bridle, for a distance of about two hundred miles" (14:20). When Jesus and the armies of heaven make war with the nations in 19:9–21, all the birds that fly are called to attend the "marriage supper of the Lamb" (19:9). "Come," they are told, "gather for the great supper of God, to eat the flesh of kings, the flesh of captains, the flesh of the mighty, the flesh of horses and their riders—flesh of all, both free and slave, both small and great" (19:17–18). At the end of the battle we read that "all the birds were gorged with their flesh" (19:21).

The enemies of Christ are vengeful and violent. The followers of Christ are also vengeful and violent. Even God and Jesus are vengeful and violent. Most modern readers do not want to go into a place of such anger and violence. Our resistance to the violence of this text does not come merely from normal human squeamishness about blood, but primarily from our theological convictions. The violence and implacable anger that drive the theology of Revelation are not seen by most of us as the proper forces upon which to build a theology. A better Christian theology should begin elsewhere, perhaps with Jesus' commandment to love or with Paul's notions of grace. In Revelation, God is a God who judges all persons individually, "according to their works" (20:12). And no slack at all is given. In Revelation, if God still has any attributes of grace and love, these attributes are strangely hidden or even more strangely manifested in God's terrible wrath.

All the books we have read in this volume, with the possible exception of the letters of John, have tried to increase our perception of the dangers of evil. For instance, we noted that part of the force of Hebrews was an attempt to reinforce the absolute nature of human sin. In fact, an attempt to raise the stakes in the choice between evil and good is a normal aspect of most theology. One of the results of faith is the belief that the world, humans, and life itself can be much better than they are. What were once perceived as little, normal, and even inevitable failures become critical assaults on the possibility of good. Each moment in life suddenly gathers enormous weight. Little sins become big sins. And evil is perceived as more powerful and pervasive than we ever dreamed.

Revelation is the most intense account of the absolute conflict between good and evil in the canon. Revelation lifts the mask of evil. It displays the true, terrible, and nearly ubiquitous face of this evil. Revelation is a great warning to its readers of the awful power of evil in their lives and the world. Evil is everywhere and is much more powerful than anyone ever dreamed. Our careless compromises with it will lead to our own destruction. Let any form of this evil into our life and evil puts its mark on us. We are in danger, unbelievable danger, of becoming part of this evil.

Revelation also lifts the mask of good. If anyone here on earth truly loves God's kingdom, truly follows Jesus, then life here on earth will be very hard. The powers of evil will assault anyone who truly follows Jesus. The whore of Babylon is drunk with the blood of the saints. Evil seems to be winning. Its enormous power is part of its seductiveness. In response, Revelation unveils the enormous power of God. The devil will not win in the end. God will win in the end. God's victory has been hidden from us, sealed in sacred books in the heavens. But now God's secret plan is being revealed. This is the real revelation of Revelation. John, the seer, unveils the secrets of the universe. And we, who are tempted by the present power of evil, learn of the coming victory of God. Thus, Revelation is also a comfort—a comfort to the saints of the world who are being crushed every day by the powers of evil. In the end, God will wipe away all our tears (Rev. 21:4).

The conflict between absolute good and evil is a bloody one. There is no possibility of the fight going away. There is evil and there is good. Both insist on absolute victory. There is no space for compromise. Evil and good are in absolute discord. Revelation is the story of the great battle in the heavens and on earth between good and evil, between God and the devil, between the armies of heaven and the evil dragon and the evil beasts, between the evil nations that rule now and the good saints who shall rule in the end.

The true story of this conflict does not collapse readily into normal human language or normal human narratives. If there is an unveiling here, which there is, in the very unveiling the secrecy of this story is maintained. Revelation as a text strains under the impossibility of the task. Its imagery becomes bizarre and impossible to think. The sequence of its story becomes unstable and confusing. The ultimate truth may be revealed here but it comes in forms that remind us that only God can think ultimate truth. When humans speak of the final secrets, our words will become ungainly and awkward.

For example, when Revelation imagines the final battle between Jesus and the devil, Jesus is described as having a sharp sword coming from his mouth (19:15; see also 1:16). Readers struggle with how to imagine this. Some suggest that the sword is a symbol for power. Revelation is just saying that Jesus will come with power. We should not, they say, draw pictures, as many artists have done, of a human Jesus with a real sword in his real mouth. Other readers prefer to maintain the literalness of the image. Revelation, they say, is imagining a real sword. This sword will, of course, have unusual power and reach, but it will still be a real sword made of real metal. They would also say, there are real beasts with real horns. There will be a real battle in the end. And there really is a real lake of fire (Rev. 9:18; 19:20; 20:10, 14, 15). Again, other readers would say these are symbols of theological truths. There is not really a real lake of fire to hold the bad people. And the new Jerusalem will not really be made of gold and shaped like a cube (21:16, 18).

Revelation throws its readers into a sea of surrealistic images and impossible narratives. And much of how we configure the theology of this text depends on how we render these images and stories. It seems to me that a clean divide between the literalness of the text and the symbolic nature of the text cannot be maintained. We cannot say simply that there will be a real city made of gold in the shape of a cube that will come down from heaven, as though the simple fact of this is established by the text. We cannot say, to the contrary, that the depictions of the new Jerusalem mean simply that God will make everything OK. Instead, we should affirm both the literalness and the symbolism of this text. We need to read in such a way as to remember both. In this book we have the revelation of the final secret; this revelation includes, for instance, imagery of a new Jerusalem. No simple reading, either literal or symbolic, can master the unveiling that occurs here.

Outline of Revelation

1:1–3   Title and blessing
1:4–3:22   Letters to the seven churches
    1:4–8   Hymns and blessings
    1:9–20   Vision of the Son of Man
    2:1–3:22   The seven letters
4:1–5:14   Vision of the heavenly court
6:1–8:1   The scroll; seven seals
    6:1–17   Breaking of six seals
    7:1–17   Sealing of the 144,000
    8:1   The seventh seal
8:2–11:19   Seven trumpets; the little scroll
    8:2–9:21   Blowing of six trumpets
    10:1–11   The little scroll
    11:1–14   The two witnesses
    11:15–19   The seventh trumpet
12:1–13:18   The woman, the child, the dragon, and the beasts
    12:1–17   The woman, the child, and the dragon
    13:1–10   The first beast
    13:11–18   The second beast
14:1–20   The Lamb and the reaping of the earth
    14:1–5   The Lamb and the 144,000
    14:6–13   Three angels
    14:14–20   The Son of Man reaps the earth
15:1–16:21   The seven bowls
17:1–19:10   The fall of Babylon
    17:1–18   Vision of the great whore and the beast
    18:1–24   Laments for Babylon
    19:1–10   Rejoicing in the heavens
19:11–21   The victory of Christ and the great supper of God
20:1–15   The millennium and the final judgment
21:1–8   Vision of a new heaven and a new earth
21:9–22:5   Vision of the new Jerusalem
22:6–21   Warnings and blessings

A Map of the Future

If Christians have shied away from this text due to its violent and surrealistic images, they have also flocked to it in hopes of learning the true secret to the future. From this text, many Christians have produced many maps of the future. In fact, these persistent attempts to use Revelation in order to calculate the end of the world have clearly been the single major factor in maintaining the voice of Revelation in the church. There have been, and still are, many

Christians who think that a proper reading of the book of Revelation can disclose the timing and the shape of the coming day of the Lord. Time and again, Christians using the book of Revelation have calculated the end of the world.

Other Christians have critiqued and even ridiculed these attempts. So far, it is easy to note, everyone has been incorrect. "All things continue as they were from the beginning of creation" (2 Peter 3:4). The world has not ended. Furthermore, the readers who critique these calculations argue that Revelation is not trying to give a precise map of the future. To read it that way is to misunderstand the nature of ancient "apocalyptic" texts. There is something to this critique, as we shall see.

However, the text itself encourages such readings. Even if it is very difficult to determine what is the exact sequence of events according to Revelation, there is a sequence of some kind detailed here. It is true that the cosmos seems to unravel at least three separate times (6:12–17; 16:17–21; 20:11–21:1). It is true that the sequences seem to overlap and repeat. And it is certainly true that readers who have tried to detail the sequence in Revelation and to calculate the end have come up with astonishingly different results. Nevertheless, there is a sequence of some kind in Revelation in which a series of cosmic and historical events culminate in final judgment and the coming of a new heaven and a new earth. The obscurity of the sequencing does not mean that there is no sequence at all. There is some attempt in Revelation to map the future. Admittedly, the future, for all its disclosure in this text, remains opaque. This sense of sequence coupled with lack of clarity in the proper referent of these sequences funds both the attempts to calculate and the multiplicity of results.

The fantastic nature of the imagery in Revelation also gives space to these modern calculations. When imagery becomes as bizarre as it is in Revelation, it becomes nearly impossible to control its meaning with a single historical referent. Even if most scholars want to refer the strange descriptions of the dragon and the two beasts in chapters 12–13 to real Roman political movements and Roman historical figures, the images resist such taming. A beast that has ten horns and seven heads, and that looks like a combination of a leopard, bear, and lion, cannot simply be Rome. Even if it is an allegory for Rome, the fact that it is a beast indicates that the beast is more than Rome. Perhaps the beast is Russia or the U.S.A. or Nazi Germany or all of them. Fantastic imagery has the wonderful and irritating ability to evoke many different historical possibilities. The many readings of them show how vulnerable they are to such diverse applications.

Revelation itself encourages and permits these many Christian calculations. Two kinds of readings seem to dominate. One reading attempts to identify something in the text with a specific event in history. These readings tend to look for a key. If we can ever absolutely and securely attach one image or one event in the text to one historical event or face, then the rest of the text and the rest of history will fall in place. The beast is Russia or it is the U.S.A, but it is not both. The other reading wants to apply the theological forces in

Revelation to any and all moments in human history. Revelation is unveiling the great theological conflict that undergirds all of human history. At the time it was written, the beast may have been Rome or the Roman Empire. But this beast is also any evil historical face. The beast is Rome, Russia, the U.S.A, Nazi Germany, and many other names. The beast is any evil empire of the past, present, or future. The opaqueness of Revelation, in this reading, does not warrant a single solution. Its opaqueness enables it to speak to all times and places.

The Mystery of Apocalyptic Literature

To most readers there is something disconcerting about the seemingly limit-less range of meanings and applications to which Revelation has been sub-jected. As we have noted before, historical readings find their warrant largely out of an attempt to hear a text on its own terms, to hear the intentions of the original author and to hear with ears of the first readers. This attempt to em-bed the text in its moment of origin becomes, then, an attempt to limit mis-readings of the text. In this volume we have pointed to two typical moves that historical critics employ: the literary and the historical.

In the case of Revelation the literary move has proved to be especially im-portant. As most readers will readily note, there are other books in the Bible that sound a lot like Revelation. Daniel, Ezekiel, and parts of the prophets (es-pecially Isaiah 24–27) share with Revelation a fondness for bizarre imagery and a focus on future judgment. Furthermore, further reading in the literature of ancient Judaism and early Christianity uncovers many other texts that read a lot like Revelation. The existence of this set of similar texts has led many readers to suggest that there was in antiquity a type of literature that can be called "apocalyptic." The word "apocalyptic" itself comes from the book of Revelation, which in Greek is titled the "Apocalypse of John." The Greek word, in its general sense, refers to the uncovering of something that has been covered, or the revealing of a secret. "Revelation" is simply the Latin version of the Greek "apocalypse." Thus, the genre is defined in part by the basic character of the book of Revelation itself. Apocalyptic literature is, in some ways, just literature that is like Revelation.

Nevertheless, literary critics point to certain typical features of apocalyptic literature. As we have already noted, this literature employs fantastic imagery and focuses on future judgment. Typically, there is a vision of some kind in which either an angel or some such figure journeys to earth to "reveal" cos-mic secrets, or the human author of the text takes a journey to the heavens. The revealed secret concerns God's plans for the future of heaven and earth; typically an apocalypse details final judgment, but it may focus on coming his-torical eras. Apocalyptic texts seem to assume, more often than not, times of great suffering or persecution. This leads to a focus on evil and the relationship between present evil and God's coming justice. This conflict between evil and good gives a dualistic cast to much of this literature. The dualism tends to include both cosmic and historical aspects—there are both wars in the heavens and wars on earth. There is, finally, a preference for pseudonymity, in which the author writes in the name of a great figure of the past.

However, this literature is quite difficult to categorize. Every apocalyptic text is different in some important way from every other apocalyptic text. The distinctiveness of each has led many people to suggest that there is no single genre of apocalyptic. What we have instead is a certain way of making arguments, a particular kind of theological imagery, and a concern for a peculiar set of theological questions that are shaping lots of different texts. We have a set of "apocalyptic" questions and a mode of "apocalyptic" rhetoric that Revelation shares with many other ancient texts.

But even this tells us something. The book of Revelation is part of a large movement in ancient Judaism and early Christianity that is exploring historical evil and final judgment by way of heavenly visions and fantastic narratives. The account of the end that we find in Revelation is one of many different accounts penned by Christians and Jews. Thus, if John the seer has a vision that funds his text, its contents do not come out of nowhere. Although we do not have space to detail the constant connections between the images in Revelation and similar images in other texts, it is the case that nearly every single image in Revelation seems to have roots in other apocalyptic texts. If John the seer had a real vision on the Lord's day, as he says he did (Rev. 1:10), it was a literary vision. Revelation reads, in part, like a reading of other texts.

This deep connection to other literature does not vitiate the uniqueness of the visions and narratives in Revelation. If Revelation is a reading of other texts, it is a creative and aggressive reading. The particular sequence of events narrated in Revelation is specific to this text. The combination of letters, seals, trumpets, and bowls is unique to Revelation. In fact, for all the echoes of other texts, Revelation in its final result is quite idiosyncratic. It offers a unique account of God's impending judgment.

All of this means that the text must be read for both its connectedness to other texts and its uniqueness. Revelation is a particular account of the end in a sea of such ancient accounts. Some readers suggest that the multiplicity of these apocalyptic visions coupled with the unique accounts in Revelation means that the visions in Revelation had to compete for acceptance with many other visions. Revelation is trying to replace these other accounts. The warning not to add or subtract from the text in 22:18–19 reflects this competitive setting. Other readers suggest that Revelation wants to add to or clarify these other visions, not replace them. Its account of multi-headed beasts is building on, even playing with, the accounts in Daniel. It is reading Daniel, not correcting it.

How we decide this issue has a tremendous impact on how we understand the theology of this book. For example, if Revelation is saying that Daniel's

account (in Dan. 7:3–7) suffers from certain inaccuracies that are being clarified here, if Revelation is replacing earlier visions and making a claim for
unique and final inspiration, then we probably should read the imagery in
Revelation as literally we can. There is a real beast that looks like the one in
Revelation 13:1–4. And the four beasts in Daniel will not really appear.
However, if Revelation is saying, "At this point in my vision I saw this amaz-
ing image of a beast, which looked, by the way, like a strange combination of
the four beasts in Daniel 7," then we should probably read the imagery in
Revelation as more evocative and symbolic than literal. Evil appeared this day
as a beast with ten horns and seven heads (Rev. 13:1), but no one knows how
evil will appear tomorrow. Our reading of Revelation in this volume leans
somewhat toward the latter view. However, as we noted above, symbols must
maintain both their literal quality and their referential quality in order to
function as symbols. If the author wanted to calmly announce that evil has certain beastly qualities, he could have done so. Instead the author had a vision
of a ghastly cosmic beast. The visceral force of that beast must be remem-
bered.

As we often do in these discussions, we find ourselves haunted once again
by the intentions of the author. And we should note once more how literary
readings and historical readings tend to overlap. Our ongoing attempt to embed these texts in their proper history always includes an attempt to identify
and understand the intentions of the author.

The author identifies himself in 1:9: "I, John, your brother who share with
you in Jesus the persecution and the kingdom and the patient endurance, was
on the island called Patmos because of the word of God and the testimony of
Jesus." Beginning with Justin Martyr in the second century, this John has often been identified as John the apostle. However, in the third century
Dionysius of Alexandria and other Alexandrian scholars, noting the differences in language, style, and theology between Revelation and the Gospel of
John, argued that the same person could not be author of both. Most modern
historians accept these linguistic arguments and think that the John of
Revelation, often called John the seer, was an otherwise unknown early
Christian named John.

The circumstances of writing have met with surprising agreement. The author understands Christianity as a persecuted and abused sect living under the
terror of Roman rule. There is evidence of persecution in 2:10, 13; 3:10.
Under God's altar in heaven are "the souls of those who had been slaughtered
for the word of God and for the testimony they had given" (6:9). These souls
cry out for vengeance (6:10). The hatred for the rich, which surfaces in the
laments over the fall of Babylon (18:3, 11–20), suggests either a community
composed mostly of the poor or one divided in itself by economic disparities
(3:17–18). These communities are threatened by theological disagreements
and by desertions (2:6, 14–15, 20–23). Only the date is seriously debated.
Some readers want to place Revelation during the persecutions of Nero (c. 64

C.E.). But most readers want to date Revelation from the latter part of the reign of Domitian (81–96 C.E.), probably in the 90s. Of course, the general conditions described in Revelation would fit almost any time during the late first century or early second century.

In any case, the book of Revelation is deeply connected to a particular moment in the complex history of early Christianity and the Roman world. This embeddedness of the text in this historical setting places anchors on the ability of the images in the text to travel anywhere for any reader. These images belong first of all to this Christian-Roman history. For instance, the two beasts in chapter 13, the first of which carried the number 666 (or 616 in some texts), refer first of all to Rome and the politics of the empire. The identity of the whore of Babylon in chapters 17–18 is no mystery: she too is Rome. If these images warrant application to modern empires and modern evil, they belong first of all to the Roman world. And we who want to read them into our own times should do so only by bringing Rome with them.

A Vision of the Son of Man

The opening verses of Revelation are fascinating. In eight short verses, we have a classic Greek prologue declaring the basic contents of the book, a typical epistolary salutation, and two blessings, one to the reader and one to Jesus. The composite cast of the beginning seems to convey the composite nature of the text that follows. The text itself is a revelation of Jesus Christ through an angel to John, as 1:1–2 declares. The text is also a letter to seven churches, as the salutation suggests. And the blessings here are the first of many blessings and hymns that follow.

The opening two verses set the agenda not only for the book of Revelation, but in some ways for all apocalyptic texts.

> The revelation of Jesus Christ, which God gave him to show his servants what must soon take place; he made it known by sending his angel to his servant John, who testified to the word of God and to the testimony of Jesus Christ, even to all that he saw.
>
> (Rev. 1:1–2)

The text is a revelation, the making known of a secret. The content of the revelation is "what must soon take place." What is revealed is not simply the future but the future as predetermined by God — "what *must* soon take place." The deterministic character of Revelation is stressed at the very beginning.

The revelation also occurs through an intermediary (4:1); it is not direct. The necessity for an intermediary suggests not only the need for a guide and an interpreter (if we dare to peek into the heavens) but also the bizarre and incomprehensible character of the revelation itself. This secret will not enter readily or unaffected into normal human discourse. The revelation will put a strain on the imagery and narrative sequences of the text. Perhaps language will even put a strain on the content itself. We cannot speak of divine secrets directly. We need angels and fantastic symbols to speak of God's ultimate plans. In fact, it may be that we should not distinguish between real content in the revelation and the imagery of the revelation. The revelation is the bizarre imagery.

We should also note that the seer himself plays a unique role. He is a witness. He will be told by Jesus himself in 1:19 "to write what you have seen, what is, and what is to take place after this." Revelation raises the classic question of the proper role of the seer which haunts all visionary texts and even all prophecy. It is not clear to what extent John creates or shapes the revelation and to what extent he simply passes it on.

Finally, in these opening verses some of the key attributes of God and Jesus are introduced. God is "the Alpha and the Omega" (1:8). God is the one "who is and who was and who is to come" (1:4, 8). Part of what may be at stake in Revelation is the character and even the adequacy of God's power. The question is whether God can or will overcome evil. Thus, Revelation points at the very beginning to God's sovereignty. God is the beginning and the end; God spans all time (see also Rev. 1:17; 2:8; 21:6; 22:13).

The character of Jesus is more complex. Jesus is "the faithful witness, the firstborn of the dead, and the ruler of the kings of the earth" (1:5). He is also the one "who loves us and freed us from our sins" (1:5). And, finally, "He is coming with the clouds; … and on his account all the tribes of the earth will wail" (1:7). Jesus has multiple functions in the theology of Revelation. As faithful witness, he models the witnessing that his followers must do (1:9; 2:13; 6:9; 12:11; 17:6). As firstborn of the dead, Jesus will appear as a "Lamb standing as if it had been slaughtered, having seven horns and seven eyes" (5:6). As the ruler of the kings of earth and as the one who comes with the clouds, he will appear riding a white horse (19:11–16). His eyes are like fire; he has diadems instead of horns; he has a secret name inscribed on a robe that has been dipped in blood. The simple fact that Jesus appears in such strikingly different personas indicates to many readers the symbolic character of these visions. Jesus cannot be a slaughtered lamb and a conquering warrior in the same moment. These manifestations, thus, are not portraits to be taken literally, but symbols.

Nevertheless, the narratives in which the visions occur have such a matter-of-fact feel to them. They read as simple, straightforward narratives filled with surrealistic moments. The opening vision of Jesus as the Son of Man is typical and instructive (1:9–20). John is "in the spirit on the Lord's day" (1:10), when he hears a voice telling him to write to the seven churches. He turns to see seven golden lampstands, which we assume refer to the menorahs in the temple (Ex. 27:20–21). In the midst of the lampstands John said, "I saw one like the Son of Man" (1:13). A remarkably detailed and straightforward description follows of the appearance of this Son of Man. His head and hair are white; his eyes are like fire; his feet are "like burnished bronze"; his voice is "like the sound of many waters." In his hand he holds seven stars; a sword comes from his mouth; and his face shines like the sun.

This is, for most of us, a strange way to do theology. When modern Christians think of the appearance of Jesus, we think of a human like us. We think of Jesus of Nazareth, who lived a real human life with nothing bizarre about him. This human Jesus is strangely disfigured in this text, as he will be in all his manifestations in Revelation.

Such visual disfigurements would have seemed much less bizarre to someone schooled in the imagery of Greco-Roman cults. Although most depictions of gods and goddesses in the Roman world were of a standard anthropomorphic variety, many depictions were bizarrely symbolic. The many strange depictions of Artemis with her many breasts (or bull testicles) and her various holy objects illustrate how powerful and pervasive such images could be in Greco-Roman religions. On the one hand, the statues of Artemis really do depict her with many breasts. On the other hand, these breasts seem to be universally connected to her power over the fertility of both land and humans. Whether her fertility is so potent that it produces multiple breasts on her body or if they evoke for humans this real fertility does not seem to be the question. Both the breasts and the fertility are real. Such may be the case in these visions of Jesus: both the symbols and the things symbolized are real.

The Son of Man interprets his own appearance in Rev. 1:20: "As for the mystery of the seven stars that you saw in my right hand, and the seven golden lampstands: the seven stars are the angels of the seven churches, and the seven lampstands are the seven churches." The stars are angels. What is so complex and unusual about this mode of theology is that we cannot read this vision as being either of stars or of angels. The text insists that the stars are angels. In one place, there are both angels and stars. Thus, the question of whether Jesus really has seven stars in his right hand or is not actually holding stars but simply has authority over seven angels cannot be answered. The vision cannot be dissected this way. Symbols work only if both the literalness of the symbol and the evocative power of the symbol are maintained.

The Seven Churches

Apart from the vision of the New Jerusalem in chapters 21–22, the letters to the seven churches are the most commonly read part of Revelation. These combinations of praise, critique, warning, and promise give us a provocative window into these seven churches, or at least into John's view of these seven churches. Little is known about these churches, except perhaps the church in Ephesus. They cover a fairly small geographical area in what was the ancient Roman province of Asia and now is the western coastal region of Turkey. John has strikingly different views of the faithfulness of these churches. For instance, he has nothing but good to say about the churches in Smyrna and

Philadelphia, although he warns and encourages them both (2:8–11; 3:7–13). He has nothing but bad to say about the churches in Sardis and Laodicea (3:1–6, 14–22). He has both good and bad to say about Ephesus, Pergamum, and Thyatira (2:1–7, 12–17, 18–29). The character of this good and bad gives us interesting insights into the theology of Revelation.

Readers have long noted how similar in structure the seven letters are and how unlike letters they seem to be. They read more like prophetic announcements with eight formal parts: (1) destination, (2) the commandment to write, (3) a formulaic "these are the words of," (4) an attribute of the Son of Man, taken from the description in 1:9–20, usually with some relevance to the exhortation that follows (for instance, in the letter to Smyrna the description of the Son of Man in 2:8 as "the first and the last, who was dead and came to life" anticipates the call to "be faithful unto death" in 2:10), (5) the opening words "I know…," (6) the actual exhortation, (7) the call to "anyone who has an ear," and (8) a closing promise to whoever "conquers."

The form is important because it manifests the authoritative structure of the theology of Revelation. The messages here come with divine warrant; they are reinforced by God's power to reward and punish. In fact, it is the criteria of final judgment that seem to fund the exhortations. These are not messages from one Christian to another. This is a single message from the empowered Son of Man, who will be the final judge. These messages are absolutely true in the sense that they come from the mouth of the Son of Man, the final judge. The truth of the message lies in the authority behind it. Thus, if you care what happens to you on the last day, you had better listen and obey. This is, of course, the mood of the whole book of Revelation.

There seem to be three dangers confronting all seven churches. We have already mentioned the presence of persecution, although its precise nature is not clear. The reference to Antipas in the letter to Pergamum is evidence of at least one Christian being put to death (2:13). Furthermore, when that reference is coupled with the general exhortations to endure in 2:3, 2:10, and 3:8–10, an impression of some kind of general persecution is hard to resist. But it has proved very difficult to be more precise than this. We encountered this same difficulty in our reading of 1 Peter. References to persecution in early Christian literature tend to be so stylized and obscure that the precise nature of the persecution cannot be reconstructed. Most readers think that this persecution would have been sporadic and disorganized. We do not yet have official, organized attacks on Christians in general in this part of the world this early. Nevertheless, we should assume that real violence and some kind of political and social abuse is being inflicted on these communities by Roman authorities. As we have noted, violence and conflict prove to be the ultimate powers in the theology of Revelation. God is victorious because God is finally the most violent and most powerful.

At least three of these communities are also enduring false teaching. The Ephesians are commended for hating "the works of the Nicolaitans" (2:6).

The Nicolaitans are also mentioned along with the teaching of Balaam in the letter to Pergamum (2:14–15). The letter to Thyatira warns against Jezebel and her teachings (2:20–23). It may be that those "who say they are Jews," who are attacked in the letters to Smyrna and Philadelphia (2:9; 3:9), are also false teachers. The only content mentioned in any of this false teaching is the eating of food sacrificed to idols and the practicing of fornication (2:14, 20). These brief allusions give us some good hints about the general critique John has of these communities.

We encounter the problem of eating food sacrificed to idols in 1 Corinthians (8:1–13; 10:6–11:1). The issue seems to be twofold. First of all, food sacrificed to idols maintains its connection to pagan gods and goddesses. Thus, eating it can be seen as idolatry. Secondly, eating this food could be important in one's social and economic life. As Paul's account in 1 Corinthians 10:23–11:1 indicates, the eating of meat was often connected to one's social obligations. If one never ate meat sacrificed to idols, it would be difficult to maintain one's place in society. Thus, even in the remarks in Revelation 2:14 and 20 about meat sacrificed to idols we hear echoes of the major issue of this book. These communities seem to be drifting toward accommodation with the Roman world. Revelation will insist that any accommodation is surrender. This is, in fact, the basic conflict which drives the theology of this text. The ongoing question is whether one can endure the hard Christian road or not.

The reference to fornication is also indicative of this conflict. Although it is possible that in this context fornication may refer to aspects of temple idolatry, it is more likely that the reference is to the stringent early Christian sexual ethic. For the most part, Christians regarded any sex other than between husband and wife as fornication. Paul constantly warns against fornication in this sense (1 Cor. 5:1; 6:13; Gal. 5:19) and even summarizes the whole focus of the Christian ethic as abstaining from fornication (1 Thess. 4:3). Thus, what we have here is not people actively promoting and encouraging fornication, but more likely people who do not hold to the most stringent form of Christian sexual ethics. Again, Revelation regards this accommodation as denial of the faith.

Accommodation to Roman social norms may be what lies behind the accusations against Sardis and Laodicea. The Christians in Sardis are accused of being "dead" (3:1); those in Laodicea are said to be "neither cold nor hot" (3:15).

The conflict between John and these churches may be a conflict between two versions of Christianity. John has a radically sectarian view of the church. The Roman Empire and all the accoutrements of it are evil. Christians must be absolutely separated from the Roman evil that surrounds them. The situation of the church is one of irresolvable conflict, and the resolution of this conflict will be through violence. However, in these churches we see evidence of a more relaxed view of the church. The church and the Roman Empire are not absolute opposites. It is possible for them to live together. John sees these

Christians who are making a home for themselves in the Roman world, who are being Christian and Roman at the same time, as denying the faith. They are not really Christians. The seemingly casual decisions and compromises that people must make when living in the world are, in the theology of Revelation, momentous choices between good and evil. There is no easy middle road.

Thus, when God's punishment falls on Rome, it also falls on everyone attached to her. These Christians who try to remain Romans will feel God's wrath just as much as any non-Christian Roman will. The terrifying narrative of God's wrath that begins in chapter 6 is directed at both Rome and the church. In fact, everyone who does not follow the strict sectarian views of Revelation, whether they understand themselves as Christian or not, will endure the terrors of God's wrath. Only a faithful few within the church will enjoy the new Jerusalem. It may be that most Christians will end up alongside the beasts in the lake of fire.

The Terror That Must Take Place

The theological and literary center of Revelation is the series of visions that detail the coming woes of divine judgment (4:1–20:15). These visions have the feel of a slowly intensifying nightmare. The woes grow in their severity until they culminate in the last battles and final judgment. It is in these visions that Christians have tried to tease out the secrets of the future. As we noted above, this map of the future is and is not a map. On the one hand, a narrative in which event follows event is certainly articulated in these visions. There is a manifestation in these visions of the coming judgment. On the other hand, the manifestation comes in a form that partially hides it from human understanding. The narrative is broken and confused. And the imagery eludes any simple reading.

Attempts to outline these core chapters have proven frustrating. In one sense, there is a narrative engine driving this story of judgment. There are three series of seven woes leading to the events of the final battle and judgment. The seven seals in 6:1–8:1 lead to the seven trumpets in 8:2–11:19, which in turn lead to the seven bowls with their seven plagues in 15:1–16:21. These series of seven seem to be further divided into sets of four and three. The seals are divided into the famous four horses and their riders (6:1–8), followed by three woes of a very different sort. The first four trumpets (8:7–12) are also separated from the last three (8:13–11:19). Unfortunately, for those looking for numerical consistency, the bowls do not seem to be evenly divided. In fact, these series of seven prove to be insufficient as a determinative outline. Too much is left out. In addition, the series themselves create narrative disorder in their repetitions, gaps, and overlaps.

There have been other attempts to outline these visions. Some readers suggest a narrative shift with the great sign in 12:1 and want to divide the visions in 4:1–11:19 and 12:1–22:5. Without a doubt there is a shift in the focus of the narrative in 12:1 where the trumpets end and a "woman clothed with the sun" appears in the heavens. In fact, many readers see chapters 12–14 as the theological heart of the book. However, most readers doubt this shift warrants dividing the visions into these two sections. Others have pursued complicated counting schemes built on the notion of the three series of seven. As any reader will note, there is a lot of counting going on in Revelation. Divine math is at work. Nevertheless, none of the counting schemes has proven conclusive for an outline.

We thus seem to have a series of interlocking visions. They interact with one another in terms of concepts and sequence, but they do not seem to fall out into a neat ideological or narrative system. We have a loose order, with some overlap, in the unfolding of the terrifying divine woes. These woes culminate in the great battle and final judgment in chapters 19 and 20, but they do not lead simply step-by-step to that end.

In the midst of these sequences other visions of different orders intervene. We have the story of the little scroll (10:1–11), the intriguing account of the two witnesses (11:1–13), the portent of the woman, child, and dragon (12:1–17), the emergence of the two beasts (13:1–18), the vision of the 144,000 and the three angels (14:1–13), an initial and very bloody reaping of the earth (14:14–20), the appearance of the great whore (17:1–18), and hymns and laments over the fall of the great whore (18:1–19:8). These diverse visions do not fit into any neat chronological or theological order. They seem to interact like prophetic pronouncements placed next to each other in a single prophetic corpus. Each vision has its own life and integrity, but each gains force by its association with another.

In some ways these intervening visions are the most interesting part of the book, for they take us deep into Revelation's theology of the church and of evil. But in other ways these visions are subsumed beneath the growing violence and terror of the divine woes that are falling upon the earth and its inhabitants. The theological engine of Revelation is this account of the terror that must come. This account is driven by these three series of seven divine woes. At any moment, another seal can be broken, another trumpet blown, or another plague poured from a bowl. The woes are brutal in their thoroughness. God has many terrifying ways to torment the earth: from sword, famine, and pestilence (6:7) to the destruction of a third of earth and all the water on it (8:7–11), from locusts with scorpion tails that sting only humans (9:10) to demonic frogs that gather an army to fight "on the great day of God the Almighty" (16:14). Every moment is a fearful one. The inhabitants of the earth will and should hide in caves and pray for mountains to fall upon them (6:15–16). "In those days people will seek death but will not find it; they will long to die, but death will flee from them" (9:6). Revelation is a terrifying account of the pouring out of God's inescapable wrath. Every vision and every promise has its proper place only in the context of that righteous terror.

The Scroll and the Lamb

In the midst of this terror a door is opened to salvation. In fact, the prelude to the coming terror is a harmonious vision of the throne of God. This opening vision creates the possibility of peace and happiness in God's presence. It also sets the proper order for being in God's presence. The four living creatures with six wings, "day and night without ceasing," sing, "Holy, holy, holy, the Lord God the Almighty, who was and is and is to come" (Rev. 4:8). The twenty-four elders who sit on thrones around God's throne, "cast their crowns before the throne," and sing, "You are worthy, our Lord and God, to receive glory and honor and power, for you created all things, and by your will they existed and were created" (4:10–11). These brief hymns are the first of many such hymns in Revelation. In the midst of the terror, the heavenly court and faithful Christians sing praises to God. This scene draws the proper destiny of heaven and earth, which is to gather around God's throne and sing praises. Thus, there are two possible destinies opened to humans—to endure God's wrath or to praise God's holiness.

This idyllic scene is compromised by the presence of a scroll in God's right hand. The breaking of the seven seals of this scroll will occasion the opening terrors of these visions. But first the scroll itself presents a problem, because a scroll with seven seals is not a normal scroll. A scroll with that many seals cannot be opened by just anyone. Thus, the questions arises, "Who is worthy to open the scroll and break its seals?" (5:2). Someone with unique authority must be found.

That it is Jesus who is worthy to open the scroll is no surprise, but the nature of his authority is surprising. He is introduced at the beginning with full messianic authority: "The Lion of the tribe of Judah, the Root of David, has conquered, so that he can open the scroll and its seven seals" (5:5). There is nothing surprising here. The traditional messiah is the perfect one to open such an august scroll. However, the form in which this messiah appears changes the overall character of the heavenly court. Suddenly all is not peace and praise. "I saw ... a Lamb standing as if it had been slaughtered" (5:6). This image of Jesus as a slaughtered lamb introduces the violence that drives the rest of the book. Jesus is worthy because he has been slaughtered. In fact, the four living creatures "sing a new song" to that effect.

> You are worthy to take the scroll and to open its seals, for you were slaughtered and by your blood you ransomed for God saints from every tribe and language and people and nation.
>
> (5:9)

It is the fact that Jesus has been slaughtered that makes him worthy to open the scroll. Unless you endure the violence of Rome you cannot be worthy of the heavenly court.

The key to so much of this book is blood, violence, and power. In the options laid out in Revelation for humanity, there is no way for humans to avoid violence and blood. If they choose to appease the power of Rome, and if they thereby escape the violence of the dragon, the beasts, and the whore, it only means they will fall under God's wrath. And that wrath and its violence is much worse than any Roman violence. If they choose to be faithful Christians and to separate themselves from the evil around them, the Roman beasts will shed their blood. The choice is only between which violence one prefers, that of Rome or that of God. Part of the rhetorical force of Revelation is to make the violence of God as terrifying as possible.

The conflicted character of Jesus himself illustrates the core conflict in the theology of Revelation. Jesus is both a slaughtered lamb and a conquering warrior. This is the key Christological move of the book. If Jesus is one without the other, then the real tension in the theology of Revelation is effaced. God is not simply a God of wrath and violence. God is a God who submits to the violence of Rome, at least for a time. There may be weakness in God's historical force right now, but this weakness will evolve into power. To see God as permanently weak or strong is to misunderstand the secret of the cosmos. There is a time in which the power of the dragon has its place. But there will be a new time, in which God's wrath and God's victory unfold. Jesus is both slaughtered lamb and conquering warrior. Christians too must be both.

> Worthy is the Lamb that was slaughtered to receive power and wealth
> and wisdom and might and honor and glory and blessing.
>
> (5:12)

It is only because the lamb is slaughtered that he receives power. The peaceful scene of the heavenly court in chapter 4 must have blood stains on it somewhere.

The 144,000

The time of God's wrath is also the time in which faithful Christians are separated from everyone else. God's wrath on Rome and her followers includes protection and promise for faithful Christians. Thus, the new time, the time in which God's victory begins and the power of Rome crumbles, is also the beginning of salvation for Christians.

Nevertheless, the woes of the first six seals seem to fall on everyone. It is always difficult to know how literally to read narrative sequences in Revelation. The explicit sequence is that the famous sealing of the 144,000 occurs "after this" (7:1), in which "this" refers to the first six seals. This sequence is, nevertheless, a bit awkward when taken literally, since the plea not to damage the earth or sea or trees is difficult to square with what happens at the breaking of the sixth seal. In spite of this awkwardness, most readers perceive a sequence here. This would mean that Christians are not spared the terrors of the first six seals. Christians must endure violence from both Rome and God, at least for a time. God's wrath against the evils of human history falls on everyone, both bad and good, at the beginning. This fact is a small break in the absolute sectarian cast of Revelation. The initial blows on the earth by God hurt everyone on the earth. Even Christians who hate the evil of the earth are part of the earth. The separation between Christians and the world around them is not absolute.

After this opening violence, "the servants of God" are protected from the ensuing woes by "a seal on their foreheads" (7:3). The counting system of this sealing—in which 12,000 from each of the twelve tribes for a total of 144,000 (7:4–8)—has occasioned much debate. Some readers conclude the symbolism of the twelve tribes indicates that it is only Jewish Christians who receive this initial protection. The "great multitude that no one could count, from every nation, from all tribes and peoples and languages," who appear after the sealing of the 144,000 and who are before the throne of God, are the Gentile Christians. However, such a divide between Jews and Gentiles has no support elsewhere in Revelation and it seems to contradict their introduction as "servants of God" in 7:3. Thus, other readers suggest that the 144,000 are those who happen to be alive at the breaking of the sixth seal. The multitude would be every Christian not alive at that precise moment. Still others see disparate images that cannot be combined into a coherent relationship. But most readers see a combination of special sealing of the church as a symbolic new Israel and an account of the universality of Christianity.

In any case, the sealing of the 144,000 occasions celebrations in the heavens that anticipate the final victories of the last battles and the new Jerusalem. In the midst of the woes, those gathered in heaven not only praise God for God's victories but speak of the final denouement, in which "they [the great multitude] will worship him [God] day and night within his temple ... [and] they will hunger no more, and thirst no more; the sun will not strike them, nor any scorching heat; ... and God will wipe away every tear from their eyes" (7:15–17). The echoes of chapter 21 and the time of the new Jerusalem are unmistakable. At the heart of much apocalyptic thought is a compromising of the normal sequences of time. The future exists, to some degree at least, in the present. This means that Christians who live in the time of the woes, and who must endure both the violence of Rome and God, will also enjoy God's blessings. The time of the woes is not purely a time of wrath for Christians, because the end-time victory and the final peace is present, in some mysterious way, now.

Visions of Rome and the Church

This sealing of the 144,000 anticipates a series of visions that intervene on the growing terror of God's wrath. Between the final seal in 8:1 and the final battle in 19:9ff. a complex of visions exploring the character and story of Rome and the church interrupt the unfolding sequence of woes.

At the center of these visions is the appearance of a second scroll. Since the angel who holds this scroll in his hand comes down from heaven and sets his right foot on the sea and his left foot on the land, the "little scroll" in his hand is usually read as giving the historical counterpart to the cosmic contents of the first scroll (10:1–2). The debate really centers on how extensive the contents of the scroll might be. Some readers understand this little scroll to contain only the vision of measuring the temple and the story of the two witnesses in 11:1–13. Others see this scroll as opening the whole series of visions about Rome and the church. This debate shows how difficult it is to control the narrative sequences in Revelation. It is not clear how extensive the contents of the first scroll might be, much less the little scroll. Some readers confine the first scroll to the events of seven seals in 6:1–8:1. Others see this scroll as containing the whole story of Revelation.

In my opinion, it is impossible to connect all the visions in Revelation into any one coherent sequence of visions. These visions overlap and attach to each other without simply repeating each other. The seer travels from heaven to earth and sees and hears many things. There is a sequence in these visions and in the narrative of judgment that these visions display. But the sequence is a broken and confused sequence. My own sense of both scrolls is that their content in some ways never ends. They symbolically open the revelations about cosmic and human history. Thus, they do not end until the very end. Their force is still in place in the last word of the book.

In whatever manner we read the force of the scrolls, the focus of Revelation from 10:1 until the final battle is on the dynamics of the historical, cosmic church and the historical, cosmic Rome. Each of the visions in these chapters tells us more about this awful conflict between the powers of Rome and the church.

Perhaps the most puzzling of these visions is that of the two witnesses in 11:1–13. The vision opens with a classic symbol of protection, reminiscent of the scaling of the 144,000 (Rev. 7:4). John is given a measuring rod and told to measure the temple and the altar. He is forbidden to measure the court of the Gentiles, "for it is given over to the nations, and they will trample over the holy city for forty-two months" (11:1–2). This measuring, of course, is a familiar image of setting something apart as not to be profaned. To this image of protection is appended a fascinating account of two witnesses.

The identity of these two witnesses remains a puzzle. Few readers try to connect them to past, present, or future known historical figures. Typically, they are seen as Christian parallels to the frequent pairing of prophetic figures in Jewish literature. Thus, they are Christian versions of Moses and Elijah. On the other hand, their story, in which they are first victorious and then are killed in the streets of the great city, closely parallels certain later Jewish messianic traditions. In some Jewish literature, the victorious messiah, the son of David, must be preceded by another messiah, the son of Joseph, who must die in battle. These two witnesses can be seen as two dying messiahs who must precede the conquering messiah.

In any case, their story contains classic elements of the theology of Revelation. The two witnesses are given incredible power. If anyone tries to harm them, "fire pours from their mouth and consumes their foes" (11:5). They can shut up the sky so that no rain may fall and can turn water to blood (11:6). They have authority "to strike the earth with every kind of plague, as often as they desire" (11:6). This is more than a story of protection from evil. These witnesses will have power over the earth, at least for a while. When they finish their testimony, "the beast that comes up from the bottomless pit will make war on them and conquer them and kill them" (11:7). Their bodies will lie in the streets. The nations will rejoice at their destruction (11:8–10). Then, after three and a half days, God will raise them up and call them into heaven. An earthquake will strike the earth and seven thousand people will be killed (11:11–13).

The implacable violence of the story of the church and Rome is effectively displayed here. This story is not one of dialogue or reconciliation, it is simply a story of who has power when. Whoever has power uses it against the other. Rome typically has the historical power in these stories. It kills Jesus and Christians. God's power is slightly withheld until the breaking of the seals, where it unfolds in increasing force. In this story, however, at least two Christians have historical power over Rome for a short period of time. This vision imagines a future when, even in the course of history, Christians will, at least for a time, have power against the usually more powerful Rome. Perhaps this vision of the two witnesses prefigures the coming millennium in which the martyrs come to life and reign on earth with Christ for a thousand years (20:4). Victory in the heavens, victory in the new Jerusalem, is not enough. There will be a time on earth when Christians will have power over Rome.

Many readers think the heart of Revelation is the vision of the woman, the dragon, and the two beasts in chapters 12–13. This vision, they say, gives us the best description of how Revelation really understands the relationship between Rome and the church. In this vision, we see the powers of human history configured by this cosmic and symbolic account. While this may be true, we must not forget that all these visions occur in the context of the unfolding wrath of God. Thus, even if this vision gives the best articulation of the present time, it is not the last time. And the configurations of power that hold now are already doomed. Power finally ends up in God's hands alone. Thus, the terror of the dragon and the beast, which is effectively displayed in these chapters, is restrained by the more powerful wrath of God which is pouring forth.

Nevertheless, this vision unmasks the horrifying character of the Roman world. It begins with the appearance in heaven of a woman clothed with the sun (Rev. 12:1). This woman is pregnant; in fact, she is already in the pains of childbirth (12:2). A great red dragon also appears in the heavens, awaiting the birth of the child so that he can devour it. As the vision unfolds, the identity of these figures becomes clear. The cosmic woman is the mother of Jesus and of the church. Whether she is conceived as Israel herself or as a more symbolic, behind-the-scenes cosmic power is debated, although the latter is more likely. The child is Jesus. The woman will have other progeny, who are identified as the church (12:17). The dragon is "that ancient serpent, who is called the Devil and Satan, the deceiver of the whole world" (12:9). Therefore, this vision looks behind the historical faces and configurations of both Rome and the church into their true cosmic nature. The battle between Rome and Christians is actually a cosmic battle between good and evil, between God's intentions for the church and the evil designs of the devil.

As the vision continues, both the child and the woman escape the attacks of the dragon (12:5, 13–16). The dragon and his angels are thrown out of heaven by Michael and his angels. This occasions a loud voice in heaven to declare, "Rejoice then, you heavens and those who dwell in them! But woe to the earth and the sea, for the devil has come down to you with great wrath, because he knows his time is short" (12:12). The dragon is now loose on earth. He is angry and has set his sights on Christians (12:17). This is the real truth of history: the devil is devoted to destroying each and every faithful Christian. If you are a Christian, you are at war. All the violence, power, and evil of the devil is directed at you. Furthermore, this devil is a cosmic figure with powers far beyond you. You are helpless against its violence. Only God has power to resist the power of the devil. All you, the Christian, can do is be faithful. If you are faithful, God's powers will come—as wrath upon Rome but as salvation upon the faithful.

The dragon gets some cosmic help. The infamous two beasts rise up, one from the sea and one from the earth (Rev. 13:1, 11), in order to serve the evil designs of the dragon. The identity of these beasts has occasioned much discussion. Most readers connect the first beast to Roman imperial power and the second to the imperial cult. But we probably should not confine these images too narrowly. Both clearly embody Roman power, and their character displays both the awesome power and horrible evil that is Rome.

The power of the first beast is carefully described. It blasphemes God and all God's company (13:6). "It was allowed to make war on the saints and to conquer them. It was given authority over every tribe and people and language and nation" (13:7). It is not clear whether God or the dragon gives this beast absolute power over the earth, but it is clear that it has it. And also, clearly, it enjoys the worship of all the inhabitants of the earth—except the faithful Christians (13:8). In fact, furthering this worship of the first beast seems to be the primary task of the second beast. The second beast performs miraculous signs on behalf of the first beast (13:13–14). It even enables the image of the first beast, which has been constructed by its worshipers, to speak (13:15).

The basic choice of human life is articulated here. Rome has the primary historical power. She is able to perform miraculous tasks. If you worship her, she can and will reward you. If you do not, she can and will punish you. God's power remains hidden. However, God's power is the ultimate and final power. If you worship God and are a faithful follower of the Lamb, God will protect you now (somehow) and will reward you in the new Jerusalem. If you do not worship God now, God's wrath will strike with unbelievable and eternal violence.

Added to this scenario is a brief comment about the mark of the beast (Rev. 13:16–18). What has most attracted readers through the centuries about this account is the curious note that the number of the beast is 666 (13:18). Speculation about this number seems to be endless. Historians tend to make two proposals. Ancient people were fascinated with counting. The endless counting in Revelation is a classic example. One way of counting involved totaling the numerical value of the letters of a name. For example, the name "Nero Caesar" when transliterated from Greek to Hebrew totals 666. But if the name is taken from its Latin form into Hebrew, the number comes to 616. (Interestingly, several early Greek texts read "616" instead of "666.") Thus, 666 is a reference to Nero. Other readers think such a reference to Nero is too specific. It is more likely, they say, that 666 is formed in analogy to the sevens and twelves, which are holy numbers. Thus, the holy numbers (e.g., 777) are parodied by this 666 of the beast. In the end, I think, we cannot be certain about the implications of 666. As in most of Revelation, the symbols remain, as symbols must, a bit obscure and unsolvable.

What is probably more important for the theology of Revelation is the connection of this mark of the beast, which is found on either the right hand or forehead, to economics. You cannot buy or sell without this mark (13:17). The beast rules, in part, through economics. And part of how one worships the beast is by participating in Roman economic life.

The economic force of Rome is even more prominent in the vision of the great whore (17:1–18:24). This great whore, Babylon (which is Rome), is "drunk with the blood of the saints and the blood of the witnesses to Jesus" (17:6). In the account of her destruction it is particularly those who "have grown rich from the power of her luxury" (18:3) who lament her fall. "The kings of the earth, who committed fornication and lived in luxury with her, will weep and wail over her" (18:9). "The merchants of the earth weep and mourn for her, since no one buys their cargo anymore, cargo of gold, silver, jewels, pearls, fine linen, purple, silk, and scarlet, all kinds of scented wood, all articles of ivory, all articles of costly wood, bronze, iron, and marble, cinnamon, spice, incense, myrrh, frankincense, wine, olive oil, choice flour and wheat, cattle and sheep, horses and chariots, slaves—and human lives" (18:11–13). The terror of luxury has rarely been so effectively penned. This cargo list builds through an extensive and repugnant account of classic Roman luxury items to the stunning conclusion "and human lives." In this scenario, the rich collect both gold and people. And the acquisition of luxury is always a bloody affair.

This connection between wealth and violence is apparent in the two basic characteristics of the whore: she is covered with wealth and with blood. "Alas, alas, the great city, clothed in fine linen, in purple and scarlet, adorned with gold, with jewels, with pearls" (Rev. 18:16). "And in you was found the blood of prophets and of saints, and of all who have been slaughtered on earth" (18:24).

Many readers think that in this condemnation of wealth we have come to the real heart of Revelation. At the core of this theology is a radical rejection of ancient society. The only real choice in life is either to opt out of Roman culture in its entirety and to join this outsider, persecuted sect of Christians or to make a cozy and meaningful place for oneself in the Roman world. The primary way to worship the beast is not by going to a temple but by simply going along with the world around you. To buy, sell, and acquire any nonessential-to-life items is to partake of the violence of the beast. You either have the stamp of the beast on you or the "seal of the living God" (7:2).

The question of how Christianity relates to culture was controversial in the early church and remains so today. Christians do not agree about this. In fact, the New Testament is not of one viewpoint about it either. For John the seer, the very existence of this debate in Christian circles shows the awesome seductive power of evil. For John, there is only one possible choice. The fact that many Christians equivocate about this, that many want to be good Christian citizens of whatever state they live in; that many buy, sell, and acquire many, many things; and that many shed the blood of others rather than shed their own, shows that they are not Christians at all, but members of the legion of the beast.

The Final Battle

The final battle is really no battle at all. Although the beast and the kings of the earth gather "to make war against the rider on the horse and against his army" (Rev. 19:19), there is no real resistance to the overwhelming power of God. God, through the hands of Jesus and various angels, simply asserts final punishment and judgment. There is no real strain or effort on the part of the divine armies. There is no heroism in this battle. It is a totally one-sided slaughter. In the theology of Revelation, once God's power is unleashed, no other power has any real force. The power of Rome, which is so dominant and real now, becomes impotent and even nonexistent in the end.

As we have noted before, the Jesus that appears in 19:1–21 is a terrifying and violent figure. He displays no sympathy or tenderness. He comes as a warrior only to kill and conquer. The interweaving of his slaughter of the kings of the earth with the image of "the marriage supper of the Lamb" (19:9) produces a particularly horrifying effect. The supposedly comforting image of the messianic banquet is bizarrely transformed into a nightmare. Instead of the messianic meal, the marriage supper of the Lamb, being a peaceful and joyful gathering of diverse peoples around the wonderful abundance of the messianic era, the meal becomes a gorging by flesh-eating birds on the abundance of slaughtered human flesh. The future coming of the messiah and the celebration of the messianic meal will be a terrifying and nauseating event.

With the victory of the armies of heaven, the final judgments are put in place. Judgment occurs in a series of events. First, the dragon is locked in the pit for a thousand years and "the souls of those who had been beheaded for their testimony to Jesus" come to life and reign with Christ for a thousand years (20:1–6). Although the timing and character of this millennium has occasioned much debate among Christians, its placement in Revelation reflects a crucial aspect of the theology of the book. Part of what the visions in Revelation establish is the necessary and eternal connection between conditions in heaven and conditions on earth. Heaven and earth share a story. Thus, God's victory over the powers of evil cannot occur either outside of time or outside of the history of the earth. God's victory must come here in real time. Thus, there must be an actual sequence of time in which the powers of the dragon are broken here on earth and the saints really rule right here. This is the millennium. The dragon is in the pit. The saints rule the earth.

After this period of historical vindication, a rather perfunctory battle between God and Magog leads to the final judgment (20:7–15). This final of the final battles reads like a non-event. All the suspense is gone. God's ultimate power has already been proven; it only needs to be enforced in a final way. The famous scene of the last judgment also reads as a non-event. The dead are raised. The book of life is opened. Names are read. And you are assigned to the lake of fire if your name is not in the book of life. Judgment does not really occur here. Your name is either in the book or it is not. God is not at this point still mulling your fate. There is no place given for the slightest possibility of mercy in all of this. Everyone's destiny is already written down. The judgment is not a judgment in the sense that any decision is being made; it is judgment in the sense that prior decisions are announced and enforced.

Death and Hades and all humans whose names are not in the book are thrown into the lake of fire, where the dragon and the beasts await them. The confining of Death itself to the lake of fire is a final bit of horror. The worshipers of the beast do not have the option of nothingness. They might wish for death, but death is locked away. Instead they have life, a horrible life, life in the lake of fire.

The New Jerusalem

Exhausted perhaps by the endless violence, we finally come to the part of the book we like to read in worship. With the vision of a new heaven and a new earth, the entire mood of the narrative shifts. Even if we have enjoyed a few

moments of anticipation of this final peace along the way, those moments occurred under the cloud of the growing wrath of God. But now the past and the
present are truly past. There is only the time of peace and comfort and
blessedness. The visions of the new heaven and new earth and of the new
Jerusalem, where the faithful live, luxuriate in the wonder of God's blessings.
These final visions of the book of Revelation contain the most untainted
imaginings of perfect peace that we have in the canon. It has been a hard journey, through terrible nightmares, but we finally arrive at a conclusion as perfect as one could speak.

The gathering of images from earlier visions in this book and from elsewhere in the canon gives these final visions a wonderful sense of completion.
So many earlier themes, places, and forces are gathered and transformed in
this new place. It is a new place built on the ruins and recreation of the old.
Thus, the new that breaks in is not wholly new; it belongs to and coheres with
the old. It may be that Revelation asks Christians to wait for what is not yet
here, for what may not even yet exist, but Christians are not asked to wait for
a perfect mystery, a perfect unknown. This future can be imagined and spoken through the language of the polluted earth around us. In this new place,
there will be water (21:6; 22:1) and a wonderful fruit-bearing tree (22:2). The
new city will be both like and unlike the old Jerusalem. It will have walls
(21:15–20) and gates (21:21) so wonderful as to defy the words walls and gates.

Most of all, in this new place the separation between God and humans,
which has shaped all of life heretofore, will have collapsed. The painful distance between God and people will be gone. There will be no temple, because
God is the temple (21:22). There will be no sun or moon, for God will be the
light (21:22; 22:5).

> See, the home of God is among mortals. He will dwell with them as
> their God; they will be his peoples, and God himself will be with
> them.
>
>   (21:3)

We may in this final vision encounter the perfect ending of an apocalyptic
narrative—all the distance between God and humans will finally be overcome.

The Perfect Ending

The real genius of the book of Revelation may be that it faces directly the terror of God's absence. If human history is a place where the most powerful
force is an evil dragon and its beasts which spill my blood, the problem of
God's absence becomes intensified. If things are kind of OK here on earth,
then God's distance and weakness are tolerable. But Revelation intensifies our
sense of the evil around us and thus intensifies our sense of distance from God.

Revelation increases the pain and terror of life. Both Rome and God become more and more terrifying as the narrative unfolds. The nightmare

becomes darker and light more elusive with each successive vision. We are meant, I think, to come close to despair. Just the act of reading Revelation is a test of faith. The book wants to repay the reader for the terror it has created with the wonders of the new Jerusalem. The final vision of this marvelous communion between God and us at the very, very end fills the places of despair that the terror has carved in us. The end wants to pay off all theological, historical, and spiritual debts.

The problem, of course, is getting to and staying in this perfect ending. Readers have long complained that after such unrelenting violence no ending can suffice. If peace is bought at the cost of so much blood, then it is not peace. This ending reads more like the deathless quiet of desolation than the fullness of real peace. These same readers point to a strange sense of failure on God's part that pervades the book. Although Revelation gives no numbers, the overwhelming impression is that a lot more people end up in the lake of fire than in the new Jerusalem. The dragon seems to have more people on his side than God does. The dragon, thus, in some ironic way really wins.

John the seer would respond that such readers misunderstand the nature of evil. Evil is not some curious absence, some momentary misstep on the way to righteousness; evil is an eternal, bloody, clever, and endlessly violent cosmic force. John would say that such readers underestimate the power of evil and the consequent need for righteous violence—not for violence in itself, but for righteous violence. The violence in John is a peculiar combination of historical and theological violence. It is not advocating the taking up of arms. Christians themselves are not permitted violence. Violence belongs only to Rome and her armies and to God and the armies of heaven. Righteous violence is that of the Psalms, wherein we ask God to smite our enemies but do not plot to smite them ourselves. This is the violence of the Sermon on the Mount, wherein we submit to evil now and love our enemies, knowing that God is and will be the final judge. Violence and revenge belong not to us but to God.

Whatever our judgments about the ending of the book, Revelation raises for us the disconcerting problem of the ubiquity and necessity of violence. Even in the perfection of the final vision, memories of violence persist. Amidst wonderful promises from the "one seated on the throne" to those who conquer, God also promises, "But as for the cowardly, the faithless, the polluted, the murderers, the fornicators, the sorcerers, the idolaters, and all liars, their place will be in the lake that burns with fire and sulfur, which is the second death" (21:8). All peace remembers the violence and force that gives it its place. Thus, the claim that the past is truly past does not hold. The final peace must slip back into the violence that gave birth to it.

Blood has already been spilled. Violence has had and is having its day. It is already too late for a perfect ending. Any peace, now or tomorrow, will have blood on it.

Suggestions for Further Reading

The readings suggested here focus on introductory works that are deemed appropriate for nonspecialists. Usually one or two more advanced works are also mentioned. There are many standard introductions to the New Testament which provide helpful orientations to the classic historical and literary questions. In particular, Raymond Brown's extensive volume is recommended. Brown also provides more detailed bibliographies.

Abbreviations

BNTC	Black's New Testament Commentaries
HNTC	Harper's New Testament Commentaries
MNTC	Moffatt New Testament Commentary
NCBC	New Century Bible Commentary
NICC	New International Critical Commentary
NICNT	New International Commentary on the New Testament
WBC	Word Biblical Commentary

Brown, R. E. *An Introduction to the New Testament*. Anchor Bible Reference Library. Garden City, N.Y.: Doubleday, 1997.

Hebrews

Attridge, H. W. *Hebrews*. Hermeneia. Philadelphia: Fortress, 1989.
Bruce, F. F. *The Epistle to the Hebrews: The English Text with Introduction, Exposition and Notes*. NICC. Grand Rapids: Eerdmans, 1964.
Käsemann, E. *The Wandering People of God: An Investigation of the Letter to the Hebrews*. Translated by R. A. Harrisville and I. L. Sandberg. Minneapolis: Augsburg, 1984.
Lane, W. L. *Hebrews: A Call to Commitment*. Peabody, Mass.: Hendrickson, 1988.
Lindars, B. *The Theology of the Letter to the Hebrews*. New Testament Theology. Cambridge: Cambridge University Press, 1991.
Westcott, B. F. *The Epistle to the Hebrews*. 3rd ed. London: Macmillan, 1909.
Wilson, R. McL. *Hebrews*. NCBC. Grand Rapids: Eerdmans, 1987.

James

Adamson, J. B. *The Epistle of James*. NICNT; Grand Rapids: Eerdmans, 1976.
Adamson, J. B. *James: The Man and His Message*. Grand Rapids: Eerdmans, 1989.
Chester, A. "The Theology of James," in A. Chester and R. P. Martin, eds., *The Theology of the Letters of James, Peter, and Jude*. New Testament Theology. Cambridge: Cambridge University Press, 1994.
Dibelius, M. *James: A Commentary on the Epistle of James*. Edited by H. Greeven. Translated by M. A. Williams. Hermeneia. Philadelphia: Fortress, 1976.
Martin, R. P. *James*. WBC. Waco, Tex.: Word Books, 1988.
Maynard-Reid, P. U. *Poverty and Wealth in James*. Maryknoll, N.Y.: Orbis Books, 1987.

1 Peter

Achtemeier, P. J. *1 Peter: A Commentary on First Peter*. Hermeneia. Minneapolis: Fortress, 1996.
Beare, F. W. *The First Epistle of Peter*. 3rd ed. Oxford: Oxford University Press, 1970.
Elliott, J. H. *A Home for the Homeless: A Social-Scientific Criticism of 1 Peter*. New ed. Minneapolis: Augsburg Fortress, 1990.
Goppelt, L. *A Commentary on 1 Peter*. Edited by F. Hahn. Translated by J. E. Alsup. Grand Rapids: Eerdmans, 1993.
Kelly, J. N. D. *A Commentary on the Epistles of Peter and Jude*. BNTC. London: Black, 1969.
Martin, R. P. "The Theology of Jude, 1 Peter, 2 Peter," in A. Chester and R. P. Martin, eds., *The Theology of the Letters of James, Peter, and Jude*. New Testament Theology. Cambridge: Cambridge University Press, 1994.
Selwyn, E. G. *The First Epistle of Peter*. 2nd ed. London: Macmillan, 1947.

2 Peter

Bauckham, R. J. *Jude, 2 Peter*. WBC. Waco, Tex.: Word Books, 1983.
Kelly, J. N. D. *A Commentary on the Epistles of Peter and Jude*. BNTC. London: Black, 1969.
Martin, R. P. "The Theology of Jude, 1 Peter, 2 Peter," in A. Chester and R. P. Martin, eds., *The Theology of the Letters of James, Peter, and Jude*. New Testament Theology. Cambridge: Cambridge University Press, 1994.
Mayor, J. B. *The Epistle of St. Jude and the Second Epistle of St. Peter*. New York: Macmillan, 1907.

Jude

Bauckham, R. J. *Jude, 2 Peter*. WBC. Waco, Tex.: Word Books, 1983.
Kelly, J. N. D. *A Commentary on the Epistles of Peter and Jude*. BNTC. London: Black, 1969.

Martin, R. P. "The Theology of Jude, 1 Peter, 2 Peter," in A. Chester and R. P. Martin eds., *The Theology of the Letters of James, Peter, and Jude.* New Testament Theology. Cambridge: Cambridge University Press, 1994.

Mayor, J. B. *The Epistle of St. Jude and the Second Epistle of St. Peter.* New York: Macmillan, 1907.

The Letters of John

Brown, R. E. *The Epistles of John.* Anchor Bible. Garden City, N.Y.: Doubleday, 1982.

Dodd, C. H. *The Johannine Epistles.* MNTC. London: Hodder & Stoughton, 1946.

Houlden, J. L. *A Commentary on the Johannine Epistles.* HNTC. New York: Harper & Row, 1973.

Lieu, J. M. *The Theology of the Johannine Epistles.* New Testament Theology. Cambridge: Cambridge University Press, 1991.

Smalley, S. *1, 2, 3 John.* WBC. Waco, Tex.: Word Books, 1984.

Revelation

Beasley-Murray, G. R. *The Book of Revelation.* NCBC. Grand Rapids: Eerdmans, 1974.

Caird, G. B. *A Commentary on the Revelation of St. John the Divine.* 2nd ed. BNTC. London: A. & C. Black, 1984.

Ellul, J. *Apocalypse: The Book of Revelation.* New York: Seabury, 1977.

Roloff, J. *The Revelation of John.* Minneapolis: Augsburg Fortress, 1993.

Schüssler Fiorenza, E. *The Book of Revelation: Justice and Judgment.* Philadelphia: Fortress, 1985.

Yarbro Collins, A. *Crisis and Catharsis: The Power of the Apocalypse.* Philadelphia: Westminster, 1984.

CPSIA information can be obtained
at www.ICGtesting.com
Printed in the USA
LVHW031226050821
694540LV00004B/593